Unequal Achievement is a series of
articles describing the Irish experience
of government⸱⸱⸱⸱⸱ ⸱⸱⸱⸱ ⸱957. It was
ori⸱⸱⸱⸱⸱⸱⸱ ⸱⸱⸱⸱⸱⸱⸱⸱ ⸱⸱ ⸱⸱⸱ ne 30/2,3
⸱⸱⸱⸱⸱⸱ ⸱⸱⸱ ⸱⸱ ⸱urnal of
⸱⸱⸱⸱⸱⸱⸱ ⸱⸱ ⸱ stration,
⸱ ⸱ of the
⸱ ago on
⸱ November 1957

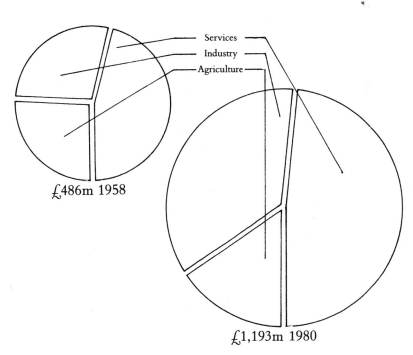

Services
Industry
Agriculture

£486m 1958

£1,193m 1980

Gross Domestic Product 1958 and 1980
(at 1958 prices) with sectoral shares.

UNEQUAL

ACHIEVEMENT

The Irish Experience 1957–1982

Editor: Frank Litton

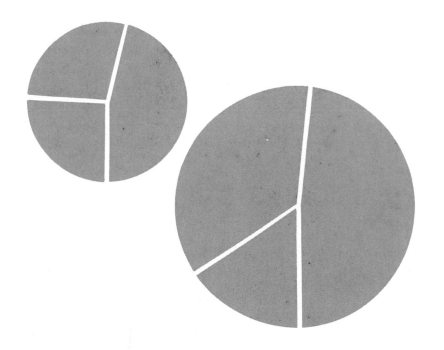

Institute of Public Administration

Contents

Page 1 **Society and Culture**

Page 21 **Change and the Political System**

Page 43 **Government, Economy and Society**

Page 63 **The Changing Social Structure of Ireland**

Page 89 **Whatever happened to Irish Government?**

Page 115 **The Central Administration**

Page 133 **Local Government**

Contributors

Joseph Lee
Professor of Modern History and Vice-President at University College, Cork, his latest book 'Government and Politics in Ireland' will be published during 1983.

Tom Garvin
Lecturer in Politics, University College Dublin, his study 'The Evolution of Irish Nationalist Politics' was published in 1982.

John Blackwell
Formerly an economist with the National Economic and Social Council, he now works at the Resource and Environment Policy Centre, University College, Dublin.

David Rottman
Research Officer with the Economic and Social Research Institute, his report on Class and Income in Ireland was published in 1982.

Philip O'Connell
is a research assistant at the Economic and Social Research Institute. He has published an Income Distribution in Ireland.

Thomas J. Barrington
First Director of the Institute of Public Administration, a paper-back version of his 'The Irish Administrative System' was published in 1982.

Peter Gaffey
Deputy Secretary in the Department of the Public Service, he was secretary to the Public Service Organisation Review Group.

Desmond Roche
Former head of research at the Institute of Public Administration, his book 'Local Government in Ireland' was published in 1982.

Page 147 **The Health Services and their Administration**

Page 165 **State-Sponsored Bodies**

Page 183 **A Generation of Public Expenditure Growth: Leviathan Unchained**

Page 203 **Social Policy: 1957–82**

Page 225 **Ireland and the World 1957–82**

Page 243 **The Physical Environment**

Page 267 **Law and the Legal System 1957–82**

Page 281 **Politics and the Arts: The Dáil Debates**

Brendan Hensey
Former secretary of the Department of Health, a third edition of his 'The Health Services of Ireland' was published in 1979.

John Bristow
Associate Professor of Economics and Fellow of Trinity College, Dublin. He has published numerous articles on Public Sector Economics.

Moore McDowell
Lecturer in Economics at University College, Dublin. His history of the ESB (written in collaboration with Maurice Manning) awaits publication.

Anthony McCashin
Lecturer in Social Administration, University College, Cork. The report on 'Poverty and Social Policy' he compiled together with Laraine Joyce for submission to the EEC Commission was published in 1982.

Patrick Keatinge
Associate Professor of Political Science, Trinity College, Dublin and chairman of the national committee for the study of International Affairs (Royal Irish Academy) his book 'A Place Among the Nations' was published in 1978.

Frank Convery
Heritage Trust Professor of Environmental Studies, University College, Dublin. His study on Energy Policy in Ireland will be published shortly by the Economic and Social Research Institute.

James Casey
Dean of the Faculty of Law, University College, Dublin and part time member of the Law Reform Commission, his study on 'The Office of the Attorney General in Ireland' was published in 1980.

Bruce Arnold
Parliamentary Correspondent for the Irish Independent, art critic and novelist. His latest book, 'William Orpen: Mirror to an age' was published in 1981.

Published by
Institute of Public Administration
Vergemount Hall, Clonskeagh,
Dublin 6, Ireland

First published as
Administration Volume 30/2,3 1982
First published as
Unequal Achievement 1982

Set in 11/12 Bembo by Design & Art Facilities
Printed and Bound by Iona Print Ltd.

Preface

FRANK LITTON

The Irish economy is in recession. Unemployment is rising and the social problems which follow from economic stagnation are growing. Despondency seems to be on the increase, as though the intractability of our problems had at last sapped our will to solve them. It is difficult to avoid recalling the grim fifties, the last severe economic depression. Of course, the memory should be encouraging. We survived the fifties to enjoy the boom of the sixties. What was accomplished once can presumably be accomplished again. External circumstances undoubtedly played an important part in our recovery then; equally conditions in the world economy set limits to the chances of success to-day. But the important lesson of the fifties is not about our dependence on the world economy. Things improved then because the administrative and political leadership searched out and responded to the opportunities which the improving world conditions brought. This responsiveness reflected not only a will to win: joined with it was a clear perception of reality and an understanding of the means required to transform it.

Our society, its culture, politics and economy, has changed in many ways over the last twenty-five years. The reality confronting to-day's politicians and administrators is very different from that which their predecessors took on in the late fifties.

The years since 1957 have seen a considerable increase in the resources devoted to understanding the dynamics of our society. The universities have played their role. Substantial contributions have been made by new organisations like the Economic and Social Research Institute, An Foras Talúntais, An Foras Forbartha, the National Economic and Social Council, the Irish Management Institute and the Institute of Public Administration. These organisations which had their

ix

origin in the fifties and early sixties are state-sponsored or aided. Their existence is a recognition of the fact that national development requires continued efforts to develop and apply understandings in strategic areas. The Institute of Public Administration is typical. The public sector has a significant role in our society. Its effectiveness in executing this role is conditioned in large measure by the competence and dedication of the people who staff and control its various organisations. The Institute, founded twenty-five years ago this year by public servants themselves, has sought to increase and communicate understandings of public administration and of the skills which make it work. In the last twenty-five years the Institute has developed an organisation with over 120 employees busy in training, education, publishing and research.

To mark the Silver Jubilee, the Institute's quarterly journal *Administration* commissioned the articles published here. Our purpose was to draw on the knowledge which has been accumulating of our society to present a picture of how Ireland has changed in the last twenty five years. We believe that understanding our present circumstances and the role of the public sector in shaping them is crucial to any sustained effort to overcome our difficulties. It is especially important that students of public administration and related subjects should have a stimulating account of contemporary history. So we asked experts in particular areas for an account of how they saw developments. Their articles add up to a sobering picture of problems and delineate the challenges for politicians and administrators.

Society and Culture

JOSEPH LEE

If Lonergan's definition of culture as 'the set of meanings and values that informs a way of life' be adopted, then T. K. Whitaker's *Economic Development* must loom as a landmark in the mid-twentieth century cultural landscape. Ireland had not enjoyed the instructive experience of wartime occupation. There was little post-war feeling of a new era inspired by the spirit of the Resistance. It took the frightening emigration figures of the 1950s to generate an Irish substitute for the shame of Sedan. Responses varied. There were those like Whitaker whose sense of honour, outraged at the humiliation, drove them to embrace an Irish version of the Resistance mentality. Whitaker belonged to a Department of Finance long suspicious of what it deemed the reckless initiatives emanating from the Industry and Commerce of Sean Lemass. In 1957, in the major revolution in Irish administrative history, Whitaker adopted something of the Lemass approach. Though no instinctive gambler, Whitaker found himself cast in the role of the conservative revolutionary from above, launched on a struggle to restore the vanishing self-respect of his country.

The economic growth of the 1960s, bringing a dramatic decline in emigration and a corresponding rise in national morale, silenced the sceptics, at least temporarily. But there remained many who had been quietly accommodating their interests to the stagnation of the 1950s. They were the collaborators in the wasting away of Irish society. The collaborationist mind with which the Resistance mentality had to wrestle, considered emigration 'a useful safety valve', on the grounds that 'when all that can be done has been done to absorb the supply of labour locally, it is better to allow the unemployed surplus to move to areas of rising demand than to condemn it to chronic unemployment'. By definition, 'all that can be done' had, of course, always been done.

1

Emigration was due to the unreasonable expectations of the natives. 'If Irish people could be induced to refrain from measuring economic progress by British standards, they might take a much more cheerful view of their condition'. Once they abandoned presumptuous Anglo-American criteria, 'they might be content to pursue their own way of life that would conform closer to the patterns and the standards of other European countries.[1]

The maturity of a culture, no less than of an individual, is reflected in the urge to search for, and the capacity to confront, the truth about itself. Behind its sober prose, *Economic Development* extended an invitation to Irish society to embark on a search for self-knowledge, and not to flinch from the findings. There was much territory to be explored. A 'Hidden Ireland' – hidden by the Irish from themselves – awaited investigation. 'We are only beginning to produce good native studies of our formal decisionmaking institutions like the Oireachtas, and of the state sponsored bodies . . . we have not a single study of the informal decision making bodies, like pressure groups, and virtually none of the community 'elites', a vital subject in the analysis of power. We have no large scale study of class structure in Ireland . . . we have not as yet any professional study of the Catholic Church in Ireland as a social and political influence. . . ' wrote David Thornley in 1957.[2] The list might have been expanded almost indefinitely. There was scarcely a solitary standard general work on subjects or topics like anthropology, constitutional law, contemporary history, economics, education, management, politics, public administration, social policy, social psychology, sociology, trade unionism. The standard works had yet to appear. Many still remain to be written. Nevertheless, intellectual activity in most of these areas has increased significantly. Ritualistic invocation of emotively elastic terms like 'spiritual', 'tradition', 'family', 'materialism', have now begun to be subjected to scholarly scrutiny, as research probes, however hesitantly, the realities shrouded in the comfortable drapery of ignorance or hypocrisy.

That it is now difficult to recapture the bleakness of the intellectual terrain of twenty five years ago itself testifies to the change that has occurred. Promising inter-war initiatives, usually by foreigners, like Kohn on constitutional law, Moss on political parties, Arensberg and Kimball on social anthropology, remained isolated, sad reminders of the harvest the natives failed to reap. There were some hopeful, if still sporadic, signs of the coming Spring. *Christus Rex* began in 1947, *The Furrow* in 1950, *Administration* in 1953, *Irish Banking Review* in 1957.

2

No Irish weekly has reached the level of sustained intellectual power to be found in the *Leader* in the early 1950s under the editorship of Desmond Williams. But there was still in 1957 no ESRI, with its impressive publication list, no NIEC or NESC, no Foras Forbartha, no NBST. There was no *Crane Bag*, no *Irish Economic and Social History,* no *Irish Educational Studies,* no *Irish Journal of Education,* no *Irish Jurist,* no *Scríobh,* no *Studia Hibernica,* to name only a few of the more stimulating subsequent arrivals.

Though the world of scholarly publication has been transformed since 1957, fundamental gaps remain, above all at the level of general comprehension. Of the relevant intellectual disciplines, as conventionally organised, it is history, anthropology and sociology that most aspire to a holistic perspective, however much individual practitioners may remain content to burrow in their own holes. Unfortunately, if understandably, the most institutionally advanced discipline, history, tended to shirk the challenge of the contemporary until the 1970s. The flight of the historians imposed a burden on sociology and anthropology which they were institutionally too under-developed to bear. Indeed fifty years after Arensberg and Kimball began their researches in Clare, there is still no chair of anthropology in a southern Irish university. Subsequent sectoral advances, particularly in economics and more recently in politics, have not yet been fully incorporated into total perspectives.

Sustained scholarly activity in the social sciences in the 1950s would have found itself quickly frustrated by glaring gaps in the official supply of information, itself a revealing index of the complacency of the collaborationist mentality. Nevertheless, it would be unhistorical to indict civil servants exclusively for this. When scholars subjected so little of the available information to systematic analysis, they could hardly complain about shortage of information. The supply, however many specific gaps continue to be identified as research frontiers pushed forward, has increased rapidly in the past twenty five years. Unfortunately, the civil service has managed to provoke widespread suspicion that it fails to disseminate information that may provoke expert criticism of its policies.[3] Tussing's sources generously attributed the shortage of useful information on the Irish educational system to conspiracy rather than incompetence. 'We have been told, again and again, by people within the educational system, and even by people within the civil service, that the State will resist publication of the kinds of information called for here, not because of any administrative costs or difficulties, but because they fear that public knowledge will limit their own freedom of action'.[4] That would be a reassuring tribute to the intelligence, if not necessarily the benevolence, of the state. More disturbing reservations arise where crucial information is not even collected, as appears to be the case in the field of social policy where the lack of adequate information 'about the distribution of income and wealth . . . prevents any evaluation of trends in inequality and therefore any overall assessment of the impact of social policy'.[5]

In its great years, Finance actually felt sufficiently self-confident to invite a scholar to examine its archives and write a detailed history down to the fairly recent past.[6] Other departments, most unhappily Foreign Affairs which has done so much to achieve a respected voice for Ireland internationally, have shown an unfortunate reluctance to open their archives in the manner now accepted as normal in western cultures.[7] The very publication of *Economic Development* indicated a reappraisal of the role of the civil servant. That an official should put his name to a virtual manifesto dismayed those whose power lay partly in their ability to stifle dissent behind the amiable facade of 'ministerial responsibility'. By venturing to publish, Whitaker showed he had come to accept the view of Patrick Lynch that public confidence in the quality of the official mind was itself an important prerequisite for national progress.[8] That this attitude has failed to permeate the civil service may contribute to what seems to be a growing lack of public confidence in the calibre of the official mind.

The civil service attitude, however, merely reflects instincts common to the wider culture. 'We markedly lag behind other industrial countries', for instance, 'in disclosure of information on company profitability'.[9] A leading liquidator, echoing the words of a bishop,[10] asks 'Why are people so chary of the workers and investors knowing the financial facts?'. He suggests a cultural rather than a technical explanation: 'There is involved here a whole morass of status seeking and pursuit of self-interest'.[11] The peasant residue in the Irish psyche confuses the distinction between necessary confidentiality and furtive concealment. This confusion is reinforced by suspicions grounded in the face to face nature of society and the petty scale of activity.

Lack of adequate evidence often makes it difficult to advance confident generalisations about cultural trends over the past twenty five years. The impact of television, especially since 1962, is a perennially controversial subject, and 'if the sociologists had been on

4

the ball, a survey of attitudes and behaviour then would have provided us with valuable information against which a comparison could be made now. . . '[12] as Colm O Briain observed. But they were not, partly because there were so few sociologists, partly perhaps because the urge for self-knowledge was still underdeveloped. Claims to the effect that 'our latter day affluent society' is 'incomparably richer, also incomparably more selfish and greedy' than the Ireland of forty years ago,[13] or that 'economics has quietly but inevitably replaced religion as the dominant value in Irish society',[14] however plausible on impressionistic evidence, must remain unproven. So must the hypothesis that circumstances have changed much more than attitudes.[15]

Comparative perspective is required to make the most effective use of the growing corpus of information. In 1957 comparative perspective meant comparison with Britain. The ignorance of continental languages produced by the school syllabus made systematic comparison with continental countries virtually impossible and left Ireland, in many respects, a European country only in a geographical sense. Exposure to the EEC and the OECD came as a culture shock to Irish officials and directly stimulated the seminal enquiry, *Investment in Education.*[16] But the later cultural impact of the EEC has been muted. The prediction that 'within the EEC, we shall continue to have a derived or provincial British culture with a diminishing Roman Catholic tinge and diminishing relics of a Gaelic past'[17] has proved broadly correct. The Brussels connection has been largely domesticated to reinforce the powerful sponger syndrome in the Irish value system while leisure patterns have become, if anything, even more responsive to Anglo-Saxon influence in the age of television. However stimulating the potential western European cultural impact in the broader or narrower sense of Ireland, the harnessing of that potential demanded political vision and leadership on a grand scale. If there was a historic opportunity it was scarcely perceived, much less seized.

Ireland entered a period of rapid economic change with little grasp of the criteria by which it might assess and guide its own performance. This poverty of perspective was peculiarly unfortunate at a time when the cult of technological determinism became increasingly fashionable. The technology lobby succeeded in blurring central issues about the nature of future society by skilful propaganda which convinced credulous observers that technology was not only an indispensable tool for enhancing the potential national welfare, but that it held the secret of all socio-economic progress, that there was a crock of gold buried at the end of the technological rainbow, and that if one looked after the technology the society would look after itself. There seems to be a danger that even the Department of Education may be succumbing to the cult. The chapter on third level education in the latest White Paper fails to contain a solitary mention of the significance of the quality of social thought, or indeed of any thought, for the well-being of society. Yet the Department of Education has deserved well of public opinion in the past two decades. It has suffered much abuse, often selfish, often ignorant, in a period when it has itself changed from a centre of stagnation to a centre of activity. Nor has there been much sustained outside reflection on higher education on which it could draw. Nevertheless, the Department may be in danger of slithering from one set of axioms concerning the nature of higher education to another set of directly contrary axioms, without offering a sustained defence of either set.

The cult of technology has discouraged serious thought about its own social consequences. The technologists were, qua technologists, unqualified to provide that thought, lacking training in the relevant areas of social and political analysis. The 'something for nothing' syndrome attached to the cult appealed to the instincts of some of the consumers. It served as an alternative to serious social analysis, offering yet another alibi to avoid grappling with enduring problems of social structure, social justice, and public morality.

If 'the true locus of the problem' in post-industrial society 'is not in the technology *per se* but in the social system in which that technology is embedded',[18] more Irish thought has to be devoted to that problem. If Patrick Lynch's fundamental contribution, 'Whither science policy?'[19] does not appear to have yet exerted the full influence it deserves, at least the introduction of technology assessment under the aegis of the National Board for Science and Technology (NBST)[20] suggests an encouraging, though belated, recognition of the problem. The success of this programme may determine whether the NBST will play a central role as the umbrella organisation for reconciling 'the two cultures'. The first futurist enquiry conducted under the auspices of An Foras Forbartha and the NBST concluded that 'as Irish society will become more pluralistic, heterogenous and socially fragmented than in the past, the major problems will hinge on political and social issues rather than on the technological concerns themselves'.[21] The contents,

6

however, generally revealed the distance still to be travelled in technology assessment. As a perceptive reviewer commented, the enquiry conveyed the impression that 'technology ordains that a happy future is our destiny . . . but 'social factors' could cheat us of this happiness . . . the prevailing belief appeared to be that individuals were not up to the technology which would guide their affairs; recalcitrant civil servants blocked the reforms required if the public sector is to effectively plan us; selfish workers demand ruinously high wages and distort the labour market; people everywhere are individualistic, given to sectional interests and altogether unplannable'.[22] This attitude was eloquently expressed in the observation that 'people often go berserk for no good reason at all'.[23] 'No good reason at all' simply means, of course, a reason that cannot be comprehended within the thought processes of technological determinism!

Research might appear to be urgently required into those alien creatures, 'people'. The futurist enquiries have refrained from this suggestion, unlike the major OECD investigation which, identifying the main 'trouble spots' as 'values and the organisation of society', logically concluded that 'thorough and comparative studies on the evolution of values in the advanced industrial societies'[24] was likely to prove a rewarding investment, even by the most mercenary criteria.

Values deeply influence that key variable in any society, the relationship between individuals and institutions. It is encouraging that so much analytical work has been devoted to the study of institutions in the past fifteen years, at least in connection with the public sector, especially through the stimulus of the Devlin Report and the work of the Public Service Advisory Council. But it is apparent too that the forces of inertia remain powerfully entrenched. If a small open society must largely live on its wits, if its main weapon in improving the quality of its life is the calibre of its own mind, then sustained analysis of the quality of decision-making, and action based on that analysis, are crucial to the overall performance of the society. This becomes even more the case if 'the alleviation of our problems will, in large measure, be dependent on the ingenuity, enterprise and development capacity of the policy formulators within our public service',[25] for a glaring characteristic of Irish decision-making elites is an extraordinarily uneven range of ability among individuals who have reached posts of similar level. If, in the French public service, 'one is struck again and again by the gulf between the small elite at the top, vigorous and efficient, and the junior employees whose muddle or lethargy simply sabotages the technocratic',[26] in Ireland one is struck again and again by the gulf *within* the elite. If the gap between the best and the second best can be so wide in Irish institutions, this increasess the urgency of making the most effective use of scarce talent and of removing obstructionists.

The constraints of the domestic intellectual market have already driven some outstanding minds abroad. A striking proportion of research in the social sciences has relied on imported investment, whether in the form of private scholarly enterprise or of consultancies. There is, however, no conclusive evidence that imported talent is generally superior to the domestic product. Dangers as well as advantages arise from the heavy intellectual dependency on imported thought, whether in the form of persons or of models. It can be argued that Ireland, no more than Italy, 'cannot be interpreted by using the same models as are currently applied to western societies'.[27]

Obsession with personal animosity ranks high among the diseconomies of small scale. Many derive as much satisfaction from dragging others down to their own level as from getting things done themselves. Nor does the prevailing culture decisively discourage such attitudes. It is not only trade union resistance, but inherited values, that still preclude the measures necessary to burn, or at least chop off, dead wood or poisoned limbs. The indulgence displayed towards leeches remains a cultural phenomenon. A vigorous chairman of the RTE authority, having asserted that 'RTE has more than its share of excellent, creative and dedicated people . . . its fair share of people who, though dedicated, will never set the world alight, and . . . a number who would cause trouble wherever they were', concluded resignedly that 'it will always be so, because RTE, like all organisations, has to settle for what is available'.[28] The culture does not yet demand that 'troublemakers' should be rendered unavailable. An attempt by the Irish public service to emulate the American approach towards 'a rigorous weeding out of those who do not measure up to requirements'[29] would create culture shock. But until that happens, one cannot confidently assert that 'there is an overall culture which seeks to attain excellence'.[30]

A strange hesitancy appears to afflict normally decisive minds on the crucial question of the quality of the public service. The National Economic and Social Council (NESC) has sponsored much valuable research. Yet, when confronted with the verdict of its own

subcommittee on enterprise in the public sector that 'the central theme
of this report is that within the public sector in this country there are
many talented, able and willing people, who would contribute much
more effectively to economic and social developments in Ireland', if
given the opportunity, the NESC simply evaded the question with the
plea that 'it is difficult to take a view on this issue, since
entrepreneurship is a most elusive factor'.[31] 'Entrepreneurship', in the
heroic Schumpeterian sense, may be an elusive factor. Talent, ability
and willingness are not. The small scale of Irish organisations makes it
a simple matter to identify the thrusters, and the sleepers, as well as the
not inconsiderable class of dozers. Identification is not the difficulty.
Stimulation is. It is puzzling that the NESC should shy away from this
problem, which is central not only to the public service, but to the
entire culture. If it gets the answer right, many of its reports would be
unnecessary. If it doesn't get it right, many of the reports, however
worthy their individual merits, may be doomed to remain monuments
of futile endeavour.

This attitude also appears to influence the approach of the Review
Body on Higher Remuneration in the Public Service. Its
recommendations reinforce the view that it is status, not merit, that
should be remunerated. Where Lemass stated bluntly that 'the
performance of a state corporation depends, in our experience, on the
capacities of the individual holding the chief executive post . . .'[32] the
Review Body would only concede that 'the scope of a job can be
influenced by the personal qualities of the person filling it'. But it
went on to insist that 'we evaluate the demands of the job',[33] not
the merits of the man. Whatever the practical difficulties involved in
matching merit and reward in the civil service, and that too may be
more a question of cultural attitude, as the Americans demonstrate,
than of technical difficulty, this approach seems strange where the
calibre of the decision making can have a major influence on the
performance of the whole enterprise. If the Reports of the Review
Body are not necessarily monuments of mindless diligence, the
culture-bound nature of their assumptions nevertheless deserves
sceptical scrutiny.[34]

The view that status rather than merit should be rewarded also
affects the response of the comfortable classes to the demands of the
less privileged. It is characteristic of a society where objective equality
of opportunity appears to be somewhat limited by western standards[35]
to disproportionately blame the poor for their poverty.[36] Equality of

opportunity does not hold irresistible appeal for those who have a shrewd suspicion of just where they themselves would be if objective merit were the criterion for material success. The view that women suffer disproportionately from lack of opportunity makes little impact on those whose own pockets are lined with the rewards of inheritance, seniority, contacts, influence, and luck. The less a culture emphasises merit, the more resistant to equality of opportunity for women are the males likely to be (and perhaps many females also, clinging to their own 'successful' males), if only because the supremacy of the dominant males does not depend on superior merit. They are therefore likely to feel vulnerable to what they perceive as a threat posed not so much by women, as by ability in women.

A cluster of historically conditioned reflexes continues to influence the work ethic. From the Land Acts to Common Agricultural Policy, many farmers have reaped a higher return from investment in politics than investment in agriculture. Livestock farmers felt themselves heavily dependent on 'luck' when it came to the fortunes of the fair, where the market price might bear no obvious relation to productive efforts. The assumption that return on investment was a function more of bargaining skill than of objective merit etched itself deeply on Irish consciousness. The influence of professional norms reinforced this assumption. The view remains widespread that the fees charged by professional people bear 'little or no relationship to the value of what they actually do'.[37] Further along the social scale, entry to the craft unions was historically as closed as was entry to university professional faculties. The main industry in which the Irish flourished at home and abroad, construction, was even more heavily dependent on contacts, politics, and luck, than was much of manufacturing industry. It was claimed sixty years ago that 'success in Dublin . . . is not the prize of ceaseless toil. It is the fruit of influence widely used'.[38] The morality of the 'just price' had difficulty taking deep root in the Irish psyche in those circumstances. When Alec Wrafter expressed himself 'struck by the apparent lack of any qualitative set of criteria by which results can be judged . . . we are not a nation of managers – we are a nation of fixers',[39] he identified one conspicuous element in Irish attitudes. His conclusion that 'we would have to change our attitudes because we are not living in the real world' may underrate the resilience of the sponger syndrome. While Lemass asserted in 1957 that 'the world does not owe us a livelihood on our terms'[40] much effort, though less than in the 1950s, continued to be devoted to the proposition that it did.

10

Controversy about work ethics revolves essentially around concepts of public morality, an area in which the Catholic Church became increasingly involved during the 1970s. Fr Liam Ryan has argued, in the course of a brilliant survey, that 'the Church is increasingly becoming an institution of social criticism . . . '[41] It might perhaps be contended that the Church had always been an institution of social criticism, but that it saw little to criticise in many earlier social or moral conditions that it had accepted with complacency, but that now seem to some bishops to outrage the Catholic version of the christian conscience. If it was not until the pastoral on Justice in 1977 that the bishops chose to refer to jobbery as a moral issue, this was hardly because jobbery had been hitherto unknown but because their concept of public morality was changing in the face of the challenges posed by economic growth, the end of emigration, television, and the Vatican Council.

The institutional church has naturally always been vulnerable to short term manipulation by the dominant elements in society. The hierarchy faced widespread incomprehension, at least from the older generation, once it expanded the concept of conscience in the direction of public morality. The beauty of 'traditional' morality was that the area to which it applied was so conveniently circumscribed. 'Traditional' Irish society achieved singular success in excluding ethics from the sphere of religion, largely confining the concept of morality to sexual morality and banishing from the agenda of moral discourse doctrines potentially subversive of the material interests of the dominant social elements. 'Traditionalists' naturally strove to divert hierarchical concern away from the dangerous area of public morality, and revert to the safe ground of sexual morality.

Opinions vary on how effectively the Church has responded to the challenge of 'the materialism of affluence' and 'political violence',[42] which have been identified as the two most serious threats to the christian witness. The decline in the number of recorded vocations restricted the room for manoeuvre of the institutional church on educational issues in particular. Just when the number of children began to increase, the number of available clergy began to decline. It must remain conjectural, however, whether this can be equated with a decline in *real* vocations. It may even be that the number of true vocations increased after the Council. 'Traditional' Irish culture exerted enormous pressure on the child in the seminary to stay in the seminary. Popular castigation of the 'spoiled priest' reflected the bitter

11

disappointment at a gilt-edged family investment turned sour – incomprehensibly, wilfully, ungratefully sour. That attitude would seem to be much less prevalent now than twenty five years ago, if only, the cynic might say, because the investment no longer appears gilt-edged, and alternative investment prospects have become more attractive.

There was, as ever, much that did not change. A glance at the 'agony' columns, making all appropriate allowance for the limitations of the genre, conveys some sense of the torment still inflicted on the sensitive young by hell fire preachers. Nevertheless, the fear of hell may not now be as central to the Catholic vision as it was a generation ago, being superseded by 'the optimistic view of one's own salvation . . . the Church's role is today increasingly seen not as that of the agent of salvation but as an instrument which enables people to live out the salvation which Christ has bestowed on them.'[43]

At the level of high politics, potential church/state conflict has been mediated with remarkable skill. The potentially explosive education issue was largely resolved in the 1960s, following an extraordinary surge of activity by the previously moribund Department of Education. If the strong feelings roused on both sides have not yet fully subsided, the observer must remain impressed with the relative smoothness of so striking a change in educational power structures. The contraception issue has also been handled with considerable political sophistication. Mr. C. J. Haughey's cunningly contrived 'Irish solution to an Irish problem', however abhorrent to the purists, was a nimble piece of political gymnastics.

The demographic data indicate that a growing proportion of the younger generation of Irish women are planning their families. The longer term consequences of the silent revolution of the sixties, which has resulted in a sharply reduced average completed family size, and in a much younger age of mother at birth of the last child, have yet to work themselves fully through. The implications for women will only begin to be felt in the next two decades. Then, for the first time, a substantial number of Irish women will have reared their families by their mid-40s rather than their mid-50s. Better educated than any previous generation of Irish women, they may not be prepared to suffer in silence the sense of unfulfilled lives that some of their mothers apparently felt.[44]

Formal religious observance remains high. Nevertheless, evidence indicating a sharp decline among the younger urbanised generation has deeply disturbed some observers, who detect 'shallow' religious roots and a church suffering from 'spiritual malnutrition'. The more comforting conclusion that 'what the Church is experiencing is less a crisis of faith than a crisis of culture' may be a shade optimistic in a society where faith and culture are so intimately intertwined. It is precisely this close connection that makes the civic culture so vulnerable to a sudden decline in the role of institutional religion. However confined the role religion may play in shaping standards of public morality, however long it may have been domesticated in Ireland as 'convention rather than conviction',[45] the very shallowness of 'traditional' civic culture leaves religion as the main bulwark between reasonably civilised social control and the untrammelled predatory instincts of sectoral and individual selfishness. If religion no longer fulfils its historic civilising mission as a substitute for internalised values of civic responsibility, the consequences for society no less than for the institutional church are potentially disruptive, particularly at a time when 'exit' no longer offers an alternative to 'voice' as a 'solution' to Irish problems.[46]

A sense of cultural identity itself constitutes a bonding power in most societies. Ireland suffers from a peculiarly weak sense of identity by European criteria in this respect. The failure of the language revival may have cost the country more than it realises in the meanest mercenary terms. Recent policy appears to have been increasingly geared towards the euthanasia of the language. The abolition of 'compulsory Irish' in the Leaving Certificate and civil service examinations since 1973 has at least reduced the level of hypocrisy, and did not mark any significant change of trend in teaching practices. Of course were there any serious political commitment, the procedure would have been to build on 'compulsory Irish' in the wider society, rather that to abolish it in the schools. The decline of Irish in the training colleges means that many teachers will soon be incapable of properly teaching the language.[47] Television offered the revival a chance as well as a threat, if only there were a national revival policy.[48] There was none. RTE has done rather better than the Review Group on Higher Remuneration in the Public Service, which revealed its sense of values by recommending 'after weighing all the evidence' that the remuneration of the chief executives of Bord na nGaeilge and Bord na gCon should be identical.[49] It rated the language every bit as important a national asset as the greyhound! Out of the mouths of Review Groups. . . !

The speed with which 'traditional' society succumbed to the temptations of affluence provides an eloquent commentary on the resilience of 'traditional' values. One may wonder how wholesome the 'traditional' culture was when such modest prosperity – for Ireland remains the poorest country in northern Europe – went so quickly to so many heads. The combination of shallowness, selfishness and exhibitionism is nicely caught in the ad man's philosophy, 'If you've got it – flaunt it'. This is also, of course, a recipe for rousing resentment among those who haven't[50] – a resentment which may in turn threaten to upset the social stability necessary for those who 'have it' to enjoy 'it' – but then the social consequences of the ad man's philosophy have not yet impinged on the horizons of our leaders.

But this refrain threatens to become too recriminatory. Skilfully though it has concealed it from itself, Ireland has been an extraordinarily lucky country since the tragedy of the Great Famine. It has been put to the stretch of its own vivid imagination to continue fertilising its sense of grievance when in reality it has had a charmed existence, thanks to the accident of geographical location, compared with most countries in Europe, not to mention the less fortunate continents. As a scathingly sympathetic critic observed in 1957, 'the truth is that Ireland has had an almost fatally easy time of it, at least in this century'. While the Ulster problem has since assumed a new degree of virulence, thanks in large measure to the primitiveness of the British nationalistic tradition, it remains as true in 1982 as in 1957 that 'Ireland has no right to be sick'.[51] The leadership cadre of 1957 did make a historic breakthrough. It did succeed in bringing to an end the emigration that for more than a century had been the main scar on the social anatomy. Since 1957 a bridgehead has been established in the direction of a viable community. The past twenty five years have seen the creation of a dual society, a dualism that has resulted from the, however halting, advance of the productive forces and despite the resolute resistance of the parasitic forces. A new Irishman does not have to be forged. He already exists. But there is still much travail ahead before he establishes his dominance. In business, agriculture, administration, scholarship, politics, or the media – right across the main areas of Irish life – high class achievers jostle cheek by jowl with high class dossers.[52] No society can be all one or all the other. It is a question of where the balance falls. In 1982 that balance falls far more than in 1957 on the productive side, but not yet sufficiently decisively to wrench the limpets clinging to their free ride completely loose from the ship of state.

The result of the past twenty five years is that Irish experience in 1982 is much less unrepresentative of the European norm than in 1957. The nature of Irish problems has shifted towards 'normalcy'! Consider the following remarks selected at random from recent literature:

> We seem to be . . . in a cultural crisis which may be the greatest challenge that confronts western society, in as much as our incapacity to develop appropriate decision making mechanisms – the ungovernability of our society – is a cultural failure.[53]

> Policy orientated research seems to have little or no direct impact on policy making.[54]

> The inability of parliaments to offer constructive comments upon economic plans or public expenditure plans is well known.[55]

> The political economy of the welfare state . . . is now confronted with new problems and demands which seem to challenge its continuing viability. The resulting crisis of transition may lead into political regression and even catastrophe unless political systems increased both their capacity for policy innovation and their ability to avoid dramatic policy failures.[56]

> The individual's loyalties are traditionally towards family rather than community, and civic cooperation in the Anglo-Saxon sense is not highly developed. Public initiatives are expected to come from the state and the authorities, rather than from ad hoc citizen groups . . . [57]

> Institutionally we have become spastic, and culturally we have lost our way.[58]

None of these comments was made with specific reference to Ireland, but all obviously apply with considerable force to our current circumstances.

Ireland now shares serious problems with other countries.

The prospects, however, are far more promising than in 1957. The problems are at least partly the problems of success rather than of almost unbroken failure. The dual culture offers a major opportunity to a leadership cadre capable of grasping it. That a variety of values are jostling side by side in a malleable culture, selflessness and selfishness, dedication and opportunism, energy and laziness, intelligence and stupidity, the psychology of tidy towns as well as dirty dumps, makes leadership vital in moulding the ethos of the wider society. 'We can manage our way out of our problems provided the leadership is there to create the *will,* unleash the *energy* and support the *courage* that coming times will require'.[59] Whether the political and administrative systems can now throw up the creative leadership to harness the potential is the major question mark hanging over Irish society in the early 1980s.

Our politicians have often been wiser than their media critics. The political stability of Irish society in the past twenty five years, as in the previous thirty five, has been no mean achievement. The potential disruption inherent in both economic change and in the northern problem has been incubated remarkably successfully within the existing party system. Irish politicians have continued to prove masterly party managers. And party management, however distasteful fastidious spirits may find the techniques of management, has a central role to play in maintaining political stability in an ideologically vacuous society. The pressures placed on Irish political leaders, even if partly of their own making, should not be underrated and may be all the greater for the feeble cultural bonding in the society. The lack of a hard core of Irish identity compels the politicians to work even harder at creating communities of interest. It is in this sense that the state now bears so heavy a burden in sustaining the identity of the society, rather than vice versa.[60] It is therefore particularly disturbing that the ship of state seems to have begun to drift increasingly out of control, in rather rudderless fashion, in recent years. Some would even fear that profligate leadership may be squandering the national capital that had begun to be stored up between 1957 and the mid 1970s.

It has been always an exciting, and sometimes a disturbing twenty five years. Whether it will historically come to be seen as a self-contained time period, or whether historians will date a significant shift – the ebbing of the rising tide of the sixties – from some time in the seventies, remains to be seen. Only then will it be possible to determine whether the culture was too fragile to cope with the shock of rapid economic change, with the challenge posed by the end of emigration. Or could a fugitive sense of identity survive only in a culture of national poverty? That would be a sad epitaph for even 'a trouble of fools'.

16

Notes to Article

1 'Favourable aspects of the Irish economy', *Irish Banking Review,* (Dec. 1958) pp. 5-9

2 David Thornley 'Ireland: the end of an era' *Studies* (Spring, 1964) p. 3

3 Mary Robinson, in M. Healy and J. Davis (eds) *The control and management of technology in society* (Dublin, 1981) p. 91

4 A. Dale Tussing *Irish education expenditures – past, present and future* ESRI Paper No. 92 (Dublin, 1978) p. 178

5 NESC *Irish social policies: priorities for future development* No. 61 (July 1981) pp. 3, 48

6 R. Fanning, *The Irish Department of Finance 1922-58* (Dublin, 1976)

7 D. F. Keogh 'Ireland: the Department of Foreign Affairs' in Z. Steiner (ed.) *The Times Survey of Foreign Offices of the World* (London, 1982)

8 P. Lynch, 'The economist and public policy' *Studies* (1953)

9 P. J. Mooney 'Incomes policy' in B. R. Dowling and J. Durcan (eds) *Irish economic policy: a review of major issues* (Dublin, 1978) pp. 260-1

10 J. Kavanagh 'Reflections on some areas of Irish society' in *ESRI The economic and social state of the nation* (Dublin, 1982) p. 66

11 L. Crowley *Cork Examiner* 1 May 1982

12 C. O Briain 'Broadcasting today: a status report' *Irish Broadcasting Review* 1 (Spring 1978) pp. 5-6

13 *Irish Times* 18 June 1979, p. 9

14 M. P. Gallagher 'What Hope for Irish Faith?' *The Furrow* xxix, 10 (October 1978) p. 608

15 As the present writer is inclined to argue! See J. J. Lee 'Continuity and change in Ireland, 1945-70' in J. J. Lee (ed.) *Ireland 1945-70* (Dublin, 1979) p. 177

16 E. Randles *Post primary education in*

Ireland 1957-1970 (Dublin, 1975) pp. 77-80

17 D. Fennell 'The Irish cultural prospect' *Social Studies* 1 (December 1972) p. 684

18 D. Bell 'Communication technology – for better or for worse' *Harvard Business Review* (May-June 1979) p. 36

19 P. Lynch 'Whither science policy?' *Administration* 27, 3 (Autumn 1979) pp. 255-81. See also C. Cooper and N. Whelan, *Science, Technology and Industry in Ireland* (Dublin, 1973)

20 M. Healy and J. Davis (eds) *The control and management of technology in society* (Dublin, 1981)

21 An Foras Forbartha *Ireland in the year 2000* (Dublin, 1980) p. 80

22 *Administration* 28, 2 (1980) p. 236

23 Quoted in E. M. Walsh 'Science, technology and education' in *Ireland in the year 2000* (Dublin, 1980) p. 32

24 OECD *Facing the future* (Paris, 1979) p. 187-8

25 N. Whelan 'Ireland's National and Regional Development – Issues for Consideration' *Administration* 28, 4 (1980) p. 380

26 J. Ardagh *The new France* (London, 1977) p. 679

27 G. E. Rusconi and S. Scamuzzi 'Italy: an eccentric society' *Current Sociology* 29, 1 (Spring 1981) p. 1

28 P. J. Moriarty 'My experience in Irish broadcasting' *Irish Broadcasting Review* xi (Summer 1981) p. 7

29 S. Gaffney 'A look across the Atlantic: how the Americans are pursuing public service reforms' *Seirbhís Phoiblí* 1, 2 (Samhain (1980) p. 19

30 Moriarty, 'Irish Broadcasting' p. 8

31 NESC *Enterprise in the public sector* No. 49 (1980) pp. 24-5, 79

32 S. F. Lemass 'The role of state sponsored bodies' *Administration* 6, 4, (1959) reprinted in B. Chubb and P. Lynch (eds) *Economic Development and Planning* (Dublin, 1969) p. 189

33 Review Body on Higher Remuneration in the Public Sector *Report No. 20* (Dublin, 1979) 10.45, 10.70. The occasional references to merit scattered through the text seem rather meaningless in the overall context.

34 For a wide-ranging review of many relevant issues, see K. Murphy 'Raising productivity in the civil service' *Seirbhís Phoiblí* 3, 1 (Meitheamh 1982) pp. 2-14

35 D. B. Rottman, D. F. Hannan, N. Hardiman, M. M. Wiley, *The distribution of income in the Republic of Ireland: a study in social class and family-cycle inequalities* (Dublin, 1982) p. 2

36 S. O Cinnéide 'Poverty and inequality in Ireland' in V. George and R. Lawson (eds) *Poverty and inequality in Common Market countries* (London, 1980) p. 156

37 *Cork Examiner* 1 May 1982

38 G. A. Bermingham *An Irishman looks at his world* (London, 1919) p. 236

39 *Cork Examiner* 1 May 1982

40 *Irish Press* 18 January 1957

41 Liam Ryan 'Church and politics: the last twenty five years' *The Furrow* xxx, 1 (1979) p. 7

42 Peter R. Connolly 'The Church in Ireland since Vatican II' *The Furrow* xxx, 12 (December 1979) p. 755

43 Liam Ryan 'The Church now' *The Furrow* xxxii, 2 (Feb. 1981) p. 82

44 M. Finucane 'Making women real' *Irish Broadcasting Review* 9 (Autumn/Winter 1980) p. 35

45 M. P. Gallagher 'What Hope for Irish Faith?' p. 609, 611. See also P. R. Connolly 'The Church in Ireland' pp. 756-8; L. McRedmond 'The Church of the visit' *The Furrow* xxx, 10 (Oct. 1979) pp. 620-4

46 To use the now familiar Hirschman vocabulary. See, in particular, 'Exit, voice, and the state' in A. Hirschman *Essays in trespassing: economics to politics*

and beyond (C.U.P., 1981) pp. 246-65

47 S. O Buachalla, 'The language in the classroom' *Crane Bag* 5, 2 (1981) p. 29

48 Nollaig O Gadhra 'Craoladh i nGaeilge: fadhb no faill?' *Irish Broadcasting Review* 1 (Spring, 1978) p. 28; Breandán O hEithir 'Thuas seal, thíos seal' *Irish Broadcasting Review* 9 (Autumn, 1980) p. 47; Liam O Murchú 'An Ghailge sna seirbhísí craolta' *Irish Broadcasting Review* 11 (Summer, 1981) p. 57

49 Review Body on Higher Remuneration in the Public Service pp. 192-3

50 J. Kavanagh 'Some areas of Irish Society' pp. 62, 71

51 John V. Kelleher 'Ireland . . . and where does she stand?' *Foreign Affairs* 35 (April, 1957) p. 491

52 For the situation in agriculture, a graphic case of dualism, see T. F. Raftery *The Dr Henry Kennedy Memorial Lecture* (1982)

53 M. Crozier 'Western Europe' in M. Crozier, S. P. Huntington and J Watanuki *The crisis of democracy* (New York, 1975) p. 30

54 B. Wittrock 'Social knowledge, public policy and social betterment' *European Journal of Political Research* xx (1982) p. 83

55 P. Self 'Planning: rational or political?' in P. R. Baehr and B. Wittrock (eds) *Policy analysis and policy innovation* (London, 1981) p. 224

56 F. W. Scharpf 'Public organisation and the waning of the welfare state' *European Journal of Political Research* 5 (1977) Abstract, p. 334

57 J. Ardagh *The new France* p. 28

58 S. MacRéamoinN 'Crisis and challenge' *Irish Broadcasting Review* (Summer, 1981) p. 47

59 H. Kilroy quoted in *Cork Examiner* 1 May 1982

60 L. de Paor 'Ireland's identities' *The Crane Bag* 3, 1 (1979) p. 29

20

Change and the Political System

TOM GARVIN

In this essay I discuss some evidence of change and continuity in the constraints which shape our government. These constraints include the constitutional rules and customs which prescribe particular courses of action in public life. There are also other less formal constraints which enhance or hinder the pursuit of better government, including the way the representative system works, and the public assumptions about politics.

Change and continuity are tricky words. Some observers of Irish affairs are quite willing to speak of apparently enormous changes that have occurred in Irish political life in the past generation, but others are equally willing to inform us bluntly that very little change has occurred and that on the contrary, a very considerable continuity is evident in most areas of Irish public life.[1] Evidently, different observers have different ideas of what constitutes change, different notions of which changes are important, and varying perceptions of how much change has occurred.

One way of handling the idea of social and political change is to use the concept of behavioural *system*. A generation ago, Easton proposed that politics could be usefully thought of as the process by which policies for the community as a whole were decided and, in the last analysis, imposed on everybody.[2] Decision-makers were seen as being responsive to influences outside themselves such as organised public opinion, interest groups and information sources; the system had input as well as output processes and, in a polity with any level of stability and internal order, the process was routinised and structures developed to ensure that these routines were preserved. In non-revolutionary eras, the political and governmental process develops sets of rules which are stronger than the rulers themselves, the process becomes institutionalised and also develops systemic properties.[3] One interesting property of a behavioural system of this sort is its tendency to conserve routines and to resist change in them. Furthermore, change, if inevitable, is absorbed by the system and is disguised; old labels are used to legitimise political innovation. Thus, a well-institutionalised political system adapts to change subtly and smoothly, and the more often it does this the more remote it becomes from the intentions of its founders and the political values of the period of foundation. If the Solons are truly successful, their creation will eventually turn on their dearest preconceptions. This kind of process is widely recognised; one obvious example is the historical evolution of the British Cabinet, and another is the often-noticed propensity of successful political parties to remain unchanged in structure and symbols while going through enormous changes in their ideologies.[4]

We should, therefore, look at institutional continuities and changes in political structures, such as parliament, parties, government *apparats,* and also look at policy in areas such as social welfare, health, economic policy and education. Other articles in this issue examine some of these areas. However, it is also important to look at the changing external constraints on the governmental system generated by the social structure, by changes in the parliamentary system, the political culture and the party system. It is on these that this essay concentrates.

Social change and politics

The Republic of Ireland has undergone considerable economic, social and cultural change in the last quarter century.[5] These changes have not, however, been spectacular by the standards of many other countries, and look impressive only when viewed in relation to the stagnation of Irish society in previous generations. Economic production, for example, which had been almost static in gross terms for the first generation after independence, increased in the last twenty-five years at a rate which was close to the OECD average, but could scarcely be described as spectacular. Admittedly, a classic economic 'take-off' did occur in the late 1950s, GNP *per capita* perhaps doubling in the following quarter century.[6] The proportion of the workforce in agriculture had been well over 50 per cent in 1926, was still over one-third in 1961 but had dropped to under one-fifth by 1980. The industrial workforce increased from 16 to nearly 30 per cent between 1961 and 1980. The economy became clearly non-agrarian for the first time, and a political system founded on, and designed for, a mainly rural and small-town society was called upon to face up to the task of governing an increasingly urban country.

Popular culture was also revolutionised, in ways that are still imperfectly understood. The growth of second- and third-level education was spectacular during the period, and the older, rather academic styles of education came under increasing pressure from newer, applied and technologically-advanced styles and subjects. The development of a consumer culture was rapid, as was the expansion of the Anglo-American youth culture. The growth of television and radio services after 1960 accelerated this process; by 1965, it was obvious that older preoccupations, styles and assumptions were going, and going fast. It is perhaps disconcerting to find that the Ireland of the 1950s is already becoming the subject of what amounts to academic cultural archaeology. Economic take-off, cultural revolution and the ecclesiastical upheaval sometimes labelled as 'Vatican II' all occurred together, and had devastating effects. Survey research indicates clearly that vast changes in social attitudes have occurred, and are continuing to occur, in Irish society; there is, for example, a large and obvious ideological gap corresponding to the generations which came of age before and after the watershed of 1957-65. Echoing and anticipating these changes, the Irish Catholic Church went through a massive reorientation in the 1960s, similar in scale to the reconstruction it had gone through a century previously; the partial liberalisation of Irish Catholicism in the 1960s and 1970s reversed much of the *Gleichschaltung* of ecclesiastical life of the previous century.[7]

Political decision-makers contributed much to the wave of changes that occurred after 1957, and T. K. Whitaker's *Economic Development* of 1958 is often viewed as the symbol of state action in favour of change.[8] However, the role of the state has been historically far more ambiguous than is sometimes suggested; political action assisted the 1950s take-off, but it is rarely pointed out that misguided state policy had probably delayed that take-off by at least a decade and that political action in earlier times may have contributed much to the stagnation of Irish economic life after independence. Certainly, one of the main obstacles to the economic new departure of the late 1950s was the loyalty of an older generation of politicians to the irrelevant nostrums of Arthur Griffith.

Representation and political change

The relationship between social change and political change is by no means one-way. In many ways, there has been little apparent political change since the mid-1950s; formal structures are much as they were then. Above all, the system of political representation is unchanged. Proportional Representation by means of the Single Transferable Vote (PR-STV) triumphantly survived two sustained attempts to abolish it in 1959 and 1968. Although its abolition was proposed by Fianna Fail governments and opposed by Fine Gael and Labour, the prospect of changing the electoral system was viewed with secret sympathy by a large section of the opposition front bench, and with deep unease by a large proportion of Fianna Fáil's backbenchers. The appeal of the electoral system to backbenchers and its lack of appeal to front-benchers is a central theme of Irish democracy, although one that is rarely articulated; it reflects the primacy of the politics of local re-presentation over the politics of government, a primacy which is as strong in 1982 as it was in 1957 and possibly even more crippling. In both 1959 and 1968 the referendum vote against abolition was noticeably higher in the towns than in the countryside, and it was particularly weak in the western counties; apparently, these referendums were interesting early examples of the greater willingness of urban voters to separate party preferences from issue preferences.[9]

Minor changes in the electoral law have been permitted to occur. In 1964, a series of legislative reforms made it possible to print the names of political parties on the ballot paper after the candidates' names for the first time, thus encouraging a greater measure of party voting. This institutionalised a measure of mild discrimination against minor parties. Another change was the steady decline in the average size of constituencies. This introduced a substantially more important bias against the minor parties. The party (or parties) in power were increasingly prone to distort constituency boundaries in their own favour when these were periodically redrawn to take account of demographic changes. These tendencies were brought to a halt and reversed only after the 1977 election when the power to revise constituency boundaries was moved from the Minister for the Environment to a non-partisan electoral commission. The general effect of the institutional changes was to suppress minor groups for most of the period and to permit new minor groups to emerge in the last few years.[10]

Thirty-five years ago, Senator Michael Hayes described the role of the Dáil deputy as being essentially one of 'going about persecuting civil servants', a phrase which became the *leitmotiv* of a classic article

Table 1   Parliamentary Questions, Dáil Éireann, 1958-1979

Subject Matter of Index Citations of Parliamentary Questions, January-March, Selected Years

	1958 %	1966 %	1972 %	1979 %
Foreign Affairs, E.E.C., Northern Ireland	1.7	2.0	8.8	4.3
Agriculture, Fisheries, Land, Agriculture-related Trade	28.2	11.9	18.0	10.1
Trade, Industry, Finance, Banking, Taxation	16.0	17.0	13.1	16.1
Employment, Industrial Relations, Pay and Conditions	2.7	4.5	3.6	6.2
Environment, Planning, Water, Electricity, Fire, Sewage	5.2	9.8	9.2	7.0
Health Services, Preventive Medicine, Nurses	5.9	4.8	5.7	10.2
Security, Defence, Crime, Prisons, Subversion	5.1	4.9	6.5	3.9
Education, Teachers, Schools, Universities, etc.	7.1	8.4	5.7	8.0
General Administration, Semi-State bodies, Elections, Courts	3.3	9.7	6.5	14.7
Communications: Roads, Post, Telephones, Television, Radio	15.4	10.9	11.5	9.4
Culture, Irish Language, Sport, Censorship	1.6	1.1	2.1	2.1
Social Welfare, Pensions Unemployment Benefit	5.2	4.7	5.0	5.2
Housing, Local Authority Dwellings, Cottages, etc.	2.9	10.4	4.6	2.9
Total	905	1673	1790	1660

NB – *percentage totals add up to slightly over 100% due to rounding.*

by Basil Chubb published in 1963.[11] Since then, a huge literature has grown up around the theme of the TD as messenger-boy, grievance-man, articulator of local particular interests and, from a more jaundiced view-point, local political gombeenman.[12] The archetypal backbench TD is seen as the product of the combination of highly centralised bureaucratic government, PR-STV and the parochialism of the culture. He is unconcerned with general issues or the world outside his own constituency; he is conservative, materialist and unintellectual.[13] He leaves policy to the front bench, the civil servants, the interest groups and the clergy; he is deferential to tribal symbols such as The Language, 1916, the tricolour and anti-partitionism, but his deference is essentially verbal and is denied by his utterly pragmatic everyday behaviour.[14] Ironically, the frontbenchers are recruited from the back benches and resemble backbenchers closely. The dominance of backbencher concerns in the Dáil is best seen at Question Time, when the structure of Irish representative politics becomes, perhaps, most visible.

As Table 1 indicates, the last twenty-five years have probably seen far more continuity than change in the behaviour of Dáil deputies.[15] Very few parliamentary questions in the periods examined dealt with external affairs or matters of general policy. In fact, the percentages entered under the heading 'Foreign Affairs, European Community, Northern Ireland' considerably exaggerate the Dáil's interest in the outside world, as many of these questions actually dealt with local or individual matters such as European Community grant eligibility rules, the cratering of border roads by the British Army or the visa regulations of foreign countries.

The most obvious change since 1958 has, of course, been the relative decline of agriculture as a major preoccupation of TDs. Many of the questions in this category dealt with matters of individual concern; many in the earlier years actually dealt with individual cases of land division – the last echoes of the great land reforms of the late nineteenth century. The noticeable increase in interest in health matters appears to reflect the setting up of the regional health boards in the early 1970s and the consequent increased interest in hospitals and other local health institutions as sources of local employment and prestige. Underlying a very large proportion of the questions in the other categories was a concern with local employment prospects, the availability of state benefits and the myriad enquiries that local people might have of the state apparatus that impinged on their lives. The

Change and the Political System

localist tone of the Dáil is also perhaps reflected in the absence of any very persistent concern with security matters or crime, despite the continuing violence in Northern Ireland and a noticeable increase in political and violent crime in the Republic during the 1970s.[16]

Table 2   Occupations of Dáil Deputies, Dáils of 1957 and 1981

	Fianna Fáil		Fine Gael		Labour		Others		Dáil	
	1957 %	1981 %	1957 %	1981 %	1957 %	1981 %	1957 %	1981 %	1957 %	1981 %
Farming only	24	14	25	12	—	—	41	—	25	11
Auctioneering, with or without other occupation	4	12	5	8	—	—	—	—	3	8
Business, Company Director	3	12	10	14	—	—	18	—	8	11
Teaching only	13	12	8	9	—	—	6	12	10	10
Solicitor, Barrister	6	5	28	17	8	13	—	—	12	10
Worker, Artisan	3	4	8	5	—	20	6	38	3	7
Publican, Shopkeeper with or without other occupation	12	6	5	6	—	—	—	—	9	4
Trade Union Officer	—	—	—	—	58	20	—	—	5	2
Other professions	14	13	5	9	—	7	6	25	8	11
Other	13	12	—	5	26	7	23	25	12	12
Total	78	78	40	65	12	15	17	8	147	166

Table 2 summarises the reported occupations of TDs in the Dáils of 1957 and 1981. Unsurprisingly, farming became a much less common occupation during the 1960s and 1970s. The numbers of businessmen, auctioneers and company directors increased, particularly in Fianna Fáil. The proportion of TDs of working class background is small, although larger than a generation ago, and the old domination of Fine Gael by the legal profession has weakened considerably. A noticeable increase has occurred in the numbers of TDs who describe themselves as having no occupation other than politics. Possibly this shift reflects a decline in amateurism in parliamentary politics; if so, amateurism has suffered a particularly severe decline in Fine Gael, and that party has lost much of its old dilettante character. Fianna Fáil is still stronger in the other professions, particularly engineering. Labour has become far less of a trade union party and may be suffering some loss of identity as a result. A striking change has occurred among the minor parties and independents; there were more in this category in 1957, and they were

27

mainly rural, but in 1981 they were often working-class and urban. Two of them were H-Block representatives. The traditional independent farmer TD has disappeared.[17]

The continued weakness of the professions in the Dáil distinguishes it from most other western legislatures and is a long standing characteristic, dating from the 1930s. It also distinguishes the Dáil from the old Irish Party of pre-1918 days, which had been replete with men of professional background since the political demise of the Irish landlord class. The core of the Dáil in the 1980s was, as it had been in the 1960s, the farming and small business groups. Chubb, writing in the late 1960s, commented 'The industrial and commercial group are mostly owners of small businesses, local contractors, publicans . . . and shopkeepers, and there is a strong rural and small-community element among them. Together with the farmers, they form the solid core of the Dáil and comprise more than half its total membership.'[18] As Table 2 indicates, this is still largely true; at least 45 per cent of the 1957 Dáil had small business or farming backgrounds, and the equivalent figure for 1981 was 34 per cent. The professions remained static at about 30 per cent in both Dáils.[19] Gradual and unspectacular change is the pattern suggested by Table 2.

Table 3   Dáil Deputies and the Senate

a. Dáil Deputies who had sat in previous Senate

1943	1957	1965	1981
4	1	5	9

b. Senators who had sat in previous Dáils

1943	1957	1965	1981
19	22	18	9

The Senate, nominally the second house of the Oireachtas, is still a very subordinate body indeed, with no clear role in the representative system. It has traditionally been used as a repository for ex-deputies in temporary or permanent retirement from the Dáil. It was also used occasionally as a means of entering the Dáil, and this role has become more significant in recent years. One central characteristic of Irish party politics is the near-sovereign power of the local parties over Dáil nominations. The Senate has been used increasingly as a means of by-passing the local organisations; a senator can build up a political base quickly, using his office's prestige, and then move from his Senate seat into a Dáil seat.[20] The Senate has become somewhat less of an attic and more of an antechamber in the Irish legislative edifice.

Educational levels have improved in the Dáil in the last generation, echoing the general improvement in education in the society as a whole. In 1965, only 30 per cent of TDs had achieved some third-level education but the equivalent figure for 1981 is 53 per cent. The number attaining primary schooling only has sunk from 20 to 14 per cent.[21] Incidentally, the proportion of TDs with higher education had actually declined in the first generation after independence, as the relatively highly-educated veterans of the campaign for independence were replaced by more mundane local representatives. Table 4 compares the figures for 1965 with those for 1981, and is quite revealing; Fianna Fáil comes close, in both Dáils, to the 'average' for

Table 4   Education of Dáil Deputies 1965 and 1981, by Party

a. Dáil 1965

	FF	FG	LP	Others	Dáil
	%	%	%	%	%
Primary only	14	20	32	67	20
Secondary, Vocational	57	40	54	33	50
Third-level	29	40	14	—	30
Total	72	47	22	3	144

b. Dáil 1981

	FF	FG	LP	Others	Dáil
	%	%	%	%	%
Primary only	14	12	20	38	14
Secondary, Vocational	36	29	33	25	33
Third-level	50	59	47	38	53
Total	78	65	15	8	166

the Dáil as a whole, while Fine Gael is the most highly educated of the three major parties on both occasions. However, in 1965 Fine Gael was spectacularly ahead of the rest, and is far less so in 1981. Labour has perhaps made the most impressive educational advances since the 1960s. The decline of the rural backbench or independent TD is reflected indirectly in these figures. However, gradual change is suggested rather than any abrupt discontinuity, despite the many dramatic political events of the last fifteen years.

A changing political culture?

Chubb characterised Irish political culture thirteen years ago as conservative, authoritarian, loyal and anti-intellectual; it was also very nationalist, egalitarian and, of course, pious with a marked puritanism. This assessment was not based on survey evidence, as survey research was very much in its infancy at the time in Ireland. Surveys of Irish political attitudes prior to the 1970s are not only scarce, they are also methodologically rather primitive, few of them inquiring very deeply into political beliefs. However, one quite elaborate and very early survey was carried out in 1962, in the Dublin area only. It was confined to Catholics and dealt with attitudes toward religion and clerical authority.[22] It did, however deal with political matters in passing and contained a fairly elaborate battery of questions by the standards of the period. Unfortunately, the original data-set is lost.

The portrait of Dublin Catholic political culture revealed by this survey is quite startling. Attitudes to the Catholic Church and to clerical authority varied little by class, region of birth or by age, almost 90 per cent of the sample agreeing, for example, that the Catholic Church was the greatest force for good in Ireland. Priests were accepted willingly as the natural social, economic and political leaders of the country, and their status was so high that the politicians of Leinster House were overshadowed. Cynicism about politicians and an accompanying suspicion of laymen's attempts at social leadership were widespread, attitudes that had deep historical roots. One respondent conceded that the clergy 'might make mistakes' occasionally, but they were 'not out for themselves' and he would rather be wrong with his priest than 'right with those damn crooks in Dublin.' When asked what side they would take in the event of a clash between church and state, 87 per cent said that they would back their church.[23] The politicians were described as being helpless in the face of such a social climate, and most important legislation was cleared with the clerical authorities in advance, informally.[24] The Irish political process was heavily tinged by theocracy, because the culture willed it to be so.

However, even in 1962, incipient change was visible. Those few who had completed secondary education were far more willing to question clerical prerogatives and formed an important but isolated

30

and alienated group, denied political authority both by their clergy and by the mass of their fellows. Whereas an extraordinary 88 per cent of the sample endorsed the proposition that the Church was the greatest force for good in the country, an equally striking 83 per cent of the educated group disagreed with it.[25] The division between the educated and uneducated segments of the population was enormous; while the rank and file of the Church's membership still looked to the Church for political, social and intellectual leadership, there was a 'solid core of what we may call the intellectual elite who flatly deny the contention. . .' The researcher concluded that there was ' . . . a ferment of disillusionment among the intellectuals as to the efficacy of the Church in the performance of her social functions.'[26]

In the early 1960s, then, an undercurrent of anti-clericalism ran through the educated stratum of a relatively uneducated nation. Hindsight suggests that the resentment of Church power dated back much farther, perhaps to the Mother and Child incident of 1951; it may be that the bishops, in sweeping aside the nascent 'Christian Democrat' tendency in Irish Catholic lay society in 1951, damaged the prospects for a lay political Catholicism irretrievably. Certainly, in 1962, the better-educated resented the Church's social power bitterly. The researcher, an American Jesuit, commented worriedly that the Irish priest was caught in a dilemma; he was confronted by a slowly-emerging educated class which required more sophisticated answers to contemporary problems than the platitudes with which an older generation had been satisfied, but he was confronted on the other hand by 'the suspicious gaze' of the many simple people of the rural areas 'who were hostile to change of any kind.'[27] The researcher concluded that the Church avoided the problem by brooking no rivals:

> the Catholic church has progressively estranged the intellectual class, as our data conclusively indicated, and has deprived itself as well as Ireland of that vitality both so desperately need by almost forcing the talented intellectual to seek his fortunes in some other country.[28]

Evidently, much has changed since 1962. The educated segment of the population is far larger now than it was in 1962. Vocations to the priesthood fell off rapidly in the 1960s as prosperity increased and other careers became available. The process of secularisation, familiar elsewhere in the west, occurred belatedly but rapidly in Ireland, and the Church lost, almost without realising it, the role of intellectual and cultural arbiter that it once had. However, this secularisation has not

31

been accompanied by any strengthening of the lay 'political class' in the political system. Older habits of deference and passivity die hard, and politicians who do not recognise the phrase still behave as though they feared a belt of a crozier. The demise of the Church's secular leadership has left political society in the Republic in a curiously leaderless condition; it is not so much that Ireland is ungovernable as that there is no large group of people in the society who have the trust of the population, and can get its co-operation for medium- or long-term goals. In other words, Ireland has no political establishment; it combines the cultural problems of an advanced country with the politics of an underdeveloped country. The weakening of the Church's power has put an end to its role as moral and, in effect political, arbiter for society as a whole, while providing no replacement. This 'political lag' may yet be made good, but in the meantime Ireland presents the strange spectacle of a small country with the political alienation of a very large one.

The country is still in a state of transition. Changes in social and political attitudes are easiest to document by means of survey evidence and the most obvious changes have been in attitudes toward sexual and marital mores. Contraception, a taboo subject until the late 1960s, has had majority support for nearly a decade. More recently, traditional opposition to a divorce law has eroded; in 1971, only 22 per cent of the population favoured such a change, but the figure in 1982 is well over 40 per cent. Significantly, support for a change in the marriage law is closely related to age and to marital status, and the young married couples themselves are most in favour of such a change. Fianna Fáil supporters are far more resistant to change than supporters of other parties, and Fianna Fáil has placed itself firmly on the 'right' of the political spectrum, in this respect at least.[29] The recent public campaign against abortion appears to reflect an awareness of cultural change and a wish to anticipate the possible consequences of such change by using the device of a constitutional amendment to entrench the legal prohibition on abortion. Ironically, a major effect of the pro-life campaign will be to publicise the issue and to normalise it as a topic for public discussion while adding little to the legal armoury of prohibitions against it.

Attitudes toward the political process were less than benign twenty years ago, and the state's weak legitimacy was compensated for by the superabundant legitimacy of the Church. It is not clear that politicians are regarded any more favourably nowadays. Certainly, Ireland's traditional political scepticism was alive and well in 1972 when the Economic and Social Research Institute conducted an investigation into Irish political culture. They found that Irish people did not feel that the political authorities paid much attention to their opinions, and they were unsure of their ability to resist the implementation of policy by government; Chubb's authoritarianism was alive and well.[30] The local TD was still seen as the main point of access to the political system. In 1976, 35 per cent of the electorate felt that the best person to contact for political or administrative problems was the local TD, but attitudes toward politicians were rather unflattering, particularly in urban areas. Fine Gael supporters had a noticeably more positive view of their TDs.[31]

Whereas nearly 60 per cent of the voters surveyed in 1976 regarded their vote as being directed at choosing a government, a Taoiseach or a set of policies, over 40 per cent saw their franchise as being used to choose a TD to look after the needs of the constituency. More recent surveys indicate that the number of such 'localists' is gradually dropping, at a time when the number of TDs and candidates willing to pander to localism is quite possibly still on the increase. Surveys generally indicate that the Irish electorate have very great faith in the efficacy of government action and believe the political leaders can solve the nation's problems of economic and social development. It is as though the voters believed in the efficacy of government, while expressing less than total regard, in their own electoral behaviour, for the national political process.[32] It is not clear whether traditional 'brokerage' in politics is declining; some recent research suggests that it may even be increasing because of bottlenecks in the administrative apparatus.

There is little evidence that traditional attitudes toward nationalist ideology have changed very much in the last twenty-five years. The constitutional commitment to a united Ireland continues to be endorsed by public opinion in the Republic and there is, if anything, increased hostility in recent years toward proposed solutions to the Northern Ireland problem which would involve indefinitely long periods of direct rule from London. Between 1973 and 1978, the Republic's population developed slightly 'harder' views on the question of Irish unity rather than, as many had expected, turning away from the prospect of closer involvement with the political problems of Ulster. Such a turning-away did occur in the early 1970s, but was short-lived.[33] Similarly, there is little support for changing the irredentist features of the 1937 Constitution. Whatever about puritan Ireland being dead and gone, nationalist Ireland is alive and well.

Electoral behaviour

A commonplace of political journalism in recent years has been the claim that the Irish electorate has become increasingly volatile and less inclined to adhere to the traditional political allegiances. Underlying this generalisation is the idea that the nationalist and pious generalities that served Fianna Fáil and Fine Gael as ideologies are less satisfactory to the young and that the electorate is becoming increasingly 'unreliable' from the point of view of the larger parties. Sometimes there is a suggestion that media exposure, education, social mobility and affluence have made the electorate more 'available' to new kinds of politics, whether left-wing, fundamentalist-nationalist or 'community' in ideological content.

There has been an increase in electoral volatility in many western countries in recent years. Class voting and voting by religious affiliation have both decreased in the last thirty years, while support for rather small, single-issue parties has increased. Typically, these new parties are radical, nationalist or 'ecologist' in general ideological character. Electorates have become more fluid, partly because of the prosperity of the generations since 1945. The satisfaction of the material needs of entire populations to an historically unprecedented extent has, it is suggested, encouraged a drift towards 'post-materialist' issues, such as pollution, the environment, the 'quality of life', aesthetic improvement of cities and the democratisation of economic institutions.[34] However, Ireland appears to be relatively little affected by such issues as yet, with the partial exception of feminist causes, and the country's politics appear to be still broadly in the 'materialist' political phase; Irish politics are determinedly bread-and-butter in character.

A useful way of approaching this question of volatility is to look at broad regional variations in support for Irish political parties over the decades since the foundation of the state. Table 5 displays in summary form the regional variations in voter support for Fianna Fáil since the early 1920s.[35] Fianna Fáil is the largest party in the system, and it has been dominant for most of the period since 1927. The party's support has always oscillated in a characteristic fashion between the eastern regions and the western regions of the country, and it has had, historically, a pronounced bias toward the west, visible even today.

34

Change and the Political System

Survey research indicates that the party has a hard core of support that is derived to a great extent from traditional, inherited family loyalties, a fact reflected in the lack of violent variation in the party's vote in the last forty years or so.

The party's electoral history falls rather neatly into three phases: 1923 to 1938, 1943 to 1965 and 1969 to the present. In the first phase the party had a very strong western bias, at a time when the western areas were far more demographically dominant than they are now, and it was far weaker in the Dublin area at a time when Dublin was demographically less important. Gradually, the party's western vote waned, until by 1943 its support was distributed evenly across the

Table 5 Regional Variations in Voter Support for Fianna Fáil (Sinn Féin 1923), 1923-1982, in percentages, rounded

	a	b	c	d	e	f
Election Year	Total Vote	Centre (Dublin Area)	Heartland (Leinster, Munster less Dublin, Louth Clare, Kerry)	Western Periphery (Connacht, Clare, Kerry)	Northern Periphery (Ulster, Louth)	Difference between b and d
	%	%	%	%	%	%
1923	28	17	25	39	23	+22
1927 (1)	26	24	24	33	27	+9
1927 (2)	35	27	33	45	33	+18
1932	45	34	43	55	40	+21
1933	50	43	45	61	50	+18
1937	45	41	42	53	50	+12
1938	52	49	48	61	51	+12
1943	42	45	40	43	43	-2
1944	49	52	46	51	52	-1
1948	42	39	41	45	45	+6
1951	46	46	46	45	49	-1
1954	43	39	44	45	46	+6
1957	48	47	50	48	47	+1
1961	44	45	42	43	49	-2
1965	48	48	47	48	50	0
1969	46	40	46	52	48	+12
1973	46	40	47	53	46	+13
1977	51	47	52	55	43	+8
1981	45	41	45	52	42	+11
1982	47	43	47	55	46	+12

entire country. This 'national' profile persisted until the late 1960s, when the party reverted to a western 'tilt' reminiscent of its pre-war configuration. As column f indicates, the party's support was far more volatile in the pre-war period, but a new volatility has crept in since the late 1960s. As Peter Mair has suggested, this is far more an urban

35

phenomenon than a rural one; pre-war volatility was rural and agrarian, post-war volatility was urban. The renewed strength of Fianna Fáil in the rural areas in the last decade may be connected with the rise to dominance of a new generation of backbench TDs, flourishing in rural areas where brokerage politics are successful. The price for this new ruralism has been the detachment of some of its Dublin strength. However, overall volatility in the Fianna Fáil vote is not impressive.

In general, the same is true for Fine Gael, although the party's long-term volatility is greater than Fianna Fáil's, reflecting the different structure of its support. Fine Gael has a smaller hard core of loyalists and a larger floating support, particularly among farmers, perhaps reflecting the old Centre Party tradition. Fine Gael's electoral history also exhibits phases: gradual decline from the 1920s until the war years, and gradual reconstruction after the war on quite different lines. It has never had a clear regional bias, but has in recent years become increasingly strong in Dublin and the other large towns, thereby echoing a bias it had had as Cumann na nGael in the 1920s.

Volatility increases as the size of the party decreases; it is far more visible in the Labour Party's support and in the minor groups. While the Labour vote has usually been fairly stable at about ten per cent, it has been subject to pronounced peak-and-valley effects, with low points in the 1930s, 1950s and 1980s and high points in the 1940s and late 1960s. Minor parties, once very important in Irish politics, have been unimportant since the early 1960s but the recent emergence of the Workers' Party may change this. It is notable that the Workers' Party is a radical socialist party; previous radicalisms which won parliamentary representation in the Dáil were nationalist or 'Christian Democrat'.

The major political parties are becoming more rather than less dominant in the system; Fine Gael expands at the expense not so much of Fianna Fáil but of Labour and the others, while Labour is squeezed at the other side by the Workers' Party and the independent socialists. It may be that Fine Gael is growing not only electorally but also in organisational sophistication and internal discipline, just as Fianna Fáil is losing its fabled internal cohesion because of its leaders' apparent inability to solve the problem of the apostolic succession to Seán Lemass.[36] As Irish society grows more complex, more 'modern' and more mobile, the party system has been undergoing a great simplification. We are perhaps nearer to a two-party system than ever before. Such an outcome would be logical; as Irish society becomes more integrated by modern communications, it may be becoming less localist. Prior to the 1960s, most of the old minor parties had rather pronounced regional bases: Clann na Talmhan, for instance, was virtually a Connacht party, while Labour was strongest in the south-eastern regions. Even the large parties were forced to bend to this pressure, and became dominated by localist satraps. As local identities grow weaker and as the number of distinct social categories increases, the possibilities of building a tightly-organised, national 'catch-all' party increase, and the attractions of such a party also increase. There may be long-term pressures favouring the emergence of a two-party system.

Conclusion

1957 is conventionally thought of as the end of an era, as marking the final exhaustion of the ideas of the first generation of political leaders. In many ways, the twenty-five years since then have seen a similar exhaustion of political ideas. The nationalist 'social democracy' of Lemass appears to be working rather creakily, if at all, and the North-South good feelings of the mid-sixties appear remote indeed. In the late 1950s, the possibilities of action by the state to achieve social and economic goals appeared immense; such ideas were the conventional wisdom of 'advanced' or liberal political thought at the time. In 1982, however, the state appears to have entangled itself in political nets from which it cannot be extricated, and backbench politics rather than scientific government dominates much of its behaviour. 'Planning', for instance, was a vogue word in the 1950s, and conjured up images of rational, 'scientific' and 'Swedish' styles of social management. It now appears as irrelevant to Irish political life as does the 1930s concept of intellectual censorship which died in the 1950s.

The great changes which occurred in Irish life in the last twenty-five years have tended to occur independently of state action, beyond the control of state or ecclesiastical authorities. At the same time, the tightly-organised moral community centred on the church, so taken for granted in the 1950s, has given way to a more individualistic and impersonal mode of social organisation; the freedom and alienation of the rest of the West has come to Ireland. The 'corporate' style of labour relations fostered by governmental policy over the last two decades appears to have reached some limit of possibilities and will scarcely last much longer. Political life is still a matter of the parish pump writ large at national level, but the pressures to change this old-fashioned style of politics are getting stronger; certainly, localist politics have become very expensive.」

This exhaustion of political ideas resembles that of the 1950s, but has happened for different reasons. In the 1950s, the failure of much of the original nationalist programme forced a rethink, whereas it is the success of the new departures of the 1950s that have led to the vacuum now; they were so successful that it seemed they merely needed to be applied again and again indefinitely. The intellectual confusion engendered by success was compounded by the irruption of the North into the politics of the Republic since 1969. The North's refusal to go away has forced the political heirs of Sinn Féin in Dublin to take stock of their inherited political postures on partition, postures that many of them really do not wish to examine too closely. The internal disarray of Fianna Fáil has been aggravated by ideological confusion brought on by the Northern Ireland crisis. Furthermore, the concern of many of our best and most senior politicians with the North and with the constitutional consequences in the Republic of any *rapprochement* with Ulster and British political forces has distracted them from the task of thinking about how best the Republic can be governed in the 1980s.

I started this essay with the notion of political life as a behavioural system which becomes institutionalised, and I think it is obvious that social and cultural change has outstripped the Irish political system's capacity to adapt, at least in the short run. Politics and administration have become out of gear with each other, mainly because the different sets of principles that underlie representative politics on the one hand and bureaucratised administration on the other have come increasingly into conflict; politicians have come under increasing public pressure to deliver more in the traditional localist style, whereas civil servants attempt to achieve coherent administration by passive resistance to such pressures. On the input side again, politicians perceive that reform does not bring votes, at least in the short run, and the secretiveness of administrators, combined with this perception, ensures that the better government of Ireland never becomes an election issue. Perhaps a long tradition of secret government and a parallel tradition of little public discourse about government lies behind much of our present malaise. In Ireland, secrecy and politics go hand in hand; some things never change.

38

Change and the Political System

Notes to Article

1 Michael Gallagher 'Societal Change and Party Adaptation in the Republic of Ireland, 1960-1981' *European Journal of Political Research* IX No. 3 (September, 1981) 269-286; Tom Garvin 'Continuity and Change in Irish Electoral Politics, 1923-1969' *Economic and Social Review* III (1972), 359-372; Peter Mair 'Analysis of Results' in Ted Nealon *Guide: 22nd Dáil and Seanad Election '81* Dublin: Platform Press 1981, 150-154; V. Browne *The Magill Book of Irish Politics* Dublin: Magill 1981; Michael Marsh 'Electoral Volatility in Ireland, 1948-81' typescript article 1981.

2 David Easton *The Political System* New York: Knopf 1953. See H. Spiro 'An Evaluation of Systems Theory' in J. C. Charlesworth (ed.) *Contemporary Political Analysis* New York: Free Press 1967, 164-174.

3 S. P. Huntington *Political Order in Changing Societies* New Haven: Yale University Press 1968, 8-31.

4 *Ibid.* 420–432.

5 Gallagher *op. cit.* 269-271.

6 Walsh, B. 'Economic Growth and Development' in J. Lee (ed.) *Ireland 1945-70* Dublin: Gill and Macmillan 1979, 27-37.

7 *Ibid. passim.*

8 T. K. Whitaker *Economic Development* Dublin: Stationery Office 1958.

9 C. O'Leary *Irish Elections, 1918-1977* Dublin: Gill and Macmillan 1979, 46-59 and 66-74.

10 *Ibid.* See *Irish Times* 24 March, 1982.

11 Basil Chubb 'Going About Persecuting Civil Servants: the Role of the Irish Parliamentary Representative' *Political Studies* XI (1963), 272-286.

12 Paul Sacks *The Donegal Mafia* New Haven: Yale University Press 1976;

Mart Bax *Harpstrings and Confessions* Amsterdam: University of Amsterdam Press 1976; R. K. Carty *Party and Parish Pump* Waterloo, Ontario: Wilfred Laurier University Press 1981.

13 Basil Chubb *The Government and Politics of Ireland* Stanford: Stanford University Press 1969, 42-60.

14 Chubb 1963 *passim.*

15 Sources for Table 1: *Dáil Debates* Vols. 165, 166, 220, 221, 258, 259, 311, 312.

16 But see E. E. Davis and R. Sinnott *Attitudes in the Republic of Ireland Relevant to the Northern Ireland Problem: Vol. 1* Dublin: Economic and Social Research Institute 1979.

17 Sources for Table 2: Browne *passim; Flynn's Parliamentary Companion* Dublin: Stationery Office 1948; *Thom's Directory 1948.*

18 Chubb *op. cit.* 1969, 211. On the Irish Party's social composition, Tom Garvin 'Decolonisation, Nationalism and Electoral Politics in Ireland 1932-1945' in O. Büsch (ed.) *Wählerbewegung in der Europäischen Geschichte* Berlin: Colloquium Verlag 1980, 259-279.

19 Those figures are not directly comparable with those in Chubb 1969 or those in J. McCracken *Representative Government in Ireland* London: Oxford University Press 1958, as slightly different rules-of-thumb have been used. In particular, both authors classified all ministers as politicians whereas I have taken their ascribed former occupation. This has the effect of inflating the professions category.

20 Sources for Table 3: Tom Garvin *The Irish Senate in Theory and Practice,* MA thesis, University College Dublin 1966 and Browne *op. cit.* 1981 both *passim.*

21 Chubb 1969, 209. Browne 1981.

These are also sources for Table 4.

22 Biever, B. F. *Religion, Culture and Values: a Cross-Cultural Analysis of Motivational Factors in Native Irish and American Irish Catholicism* New York: Arno Press 1976.

23 Biever 270-71, 306.

24 Biever 397.

25 Biever 226-27.

26 Biever 227.

27 Biever 278.

28 Biever 497, 503.

29 Irish Marketing Surveys *Report on Attitudes to Proposals for Constitutional Change* 1981 (October) 2-3, 15.

30 J. Raven, C. Whelan *et al. Political Culture in Ireland* Dublin: Institute of Public Administration 1976, 26-27

31 Irish Marketing Surveys *Research Report RTE 'Survey' – Politics* 1976 (September), Table 30B

32 Irish Marketing Surveys Report – *Political Opinion Poll June 7-8 1981* Table 30

33 Richard Rose, Ian McAllister and Peter Mair *Is There a Concurrent Majority about Northern Ireland?* Glasgow: University of Strathclyde 1978, 36-39

34 Maria Maguire *The Freezing of Party Systems Revisited: Aspects of Electoral Change in Western European Party Systems, 1948-1978,* MA thesis, University College, Dublin, 1979, 138

35 Cf. Mair 'Analysis of Results', in Nealon, *op. cit.* Sources for Table 5: Tom Garvin, *The Evolution of Irish Nationalist Politics* Dublin: Gill and Macmillan 1981, 162-165; Browne *op cit.* 981; *Irish Times* February 22, 1982; M. Marsh 'Electoral Volatility in Ireland, 1948-81'. The regions are those proposed in my 'Nationalist Elites, Irish Voters and Irish Political Development: A Comparative Perspective' *Economic and Social Review* VIII, (April, 1977), 161-186

36 Tom Garvin 'The Growth of Faction in the Fianna Fail Party, 1966-80', in *Parliamentary Affairs* XXXIV, No. 1 (Winter, 1981), 110-123

Aer Rianta. International Airports for an International Ireland.

At first glance, the role of Aer Rianta might seem simple. To ensure that Ireland's three international airports at Dublin, Cork and Shannon operate effectively and efficiently.

That alone takes some doing.

Already we cope with over 4 million passengers a year. By 1990, Dublin alone may well have to cater for 5½ million. Planning for that scale of expansion demands skill, enterprise and courage.

But Aer Rianta doesn't stop there.

We earn money – for ourselves and for Ireland. Our total turnover is now touching £60 million. Duty-Free and Mail Order sales and overseas consultancy training programmes earn valuable foreign revenue. Our catering staff at Shannon turn out in-flight meals for a dozen different airlines. Our tourism activities bring in over 20,000 tourists.

That's Aer Rianta in a nutshell.

Working today. Planning for tomorrow. Helping Ireland become more and more international.

41

42

Government, Economy and Society

JOHN BLACKWELL

Twenty five years ago, the Irish economy had many features of a 'less developed country'. These included a high dependence on agriculture for output and employment, high unemployment and emigration and a low standard of living. In addition, we lacked many natural resources and made poor use of those we had; the skills used in our industries were low level; and there was little evidence of that most intangible of resources, enterprise.

The economy was vulnerable to outside events as both imports and exports were significant relative to output. Imports were 33 per cent of output and exports were 29 per cent of output. Both capital and labour moved outside the economy in significant quantities. Between 1951 and 1961 net emigration was 409,000. This meant that, on average 4 per cent of the labour force left the country each year – an exceptionally high figure. When this figure is put together with the unemployment figure (in 1957 59,000 were on the unemployed register) a large disparity between the potential labour force and the level of employment emerges.

Output and living standards

In the period 1957-80 matters improved considerably: Gross National Product, the total output of goods and services, more than doubled. The average annual rate of increase in Gross National Product was 3.7 percent per annum over the period. This was almost double the rate of increase of 2.0 percent which occurred in the 1947-57 period. Expressing output per head of population, the difference in growth rates between the periods is less: 3.3 percent per annum over 1957-80 by contrast with 2.3 percent over 1947-57. The break in economic performance does not coincide exactly with the first year of the

43

Economic Programme of 1958-63. Nineteen sixty-one marks a turning point as the years between 1958 and 1961 marked a recovery from depression. The growth rate of output over 1961-73 was more than double that over each of the two periods 1947-57 and 1955-61 (Kennedy and Dowling, 1975). Since 1957, two contrasting periods can be identified. In 1957-73, the average annual growth of GNP was 4.0 percent per annum while in 1973-80, the average annual growth of output was 3.2 percent. The rate of increase in population was higher in the later period, hence output per head grew at an average annual rate of 2.1 percent over 1973-80 by contrast with a growth rate of 3.9 percent for output per head over 1957-73. Not only was the growth rate lower in the period since 1973 but output was more volatile: the growth rate ranged from 1.2 percent in 1976 to 6.1 percent in 1977.

Despite the higher growth rate in Ireland since the late 1950's , our living standard still lags behind those of our European neighbours. Indeed, in the period 1960-79, the gap between the Irish GNP per capita and those of other EEC countries widened. Living standards in the other EEC countries are between twice and three times the Irish. There is one exception, the United Kingdom. In 1960 the output per head in Ireland was just over half that in the UK, in 1979 it was two thirds the UK figure. (World Bank 1981; Ferris, 1981).

It is worthwhile to look at the output trends in the broader context, provided by the economic performance of the principal industrial market economies in the period since 1870. In the period 1870-1950 the average annual rate of growth of Gross Domestic Product (GNP less net property income from abroad) in sixteen advanced capitalist countries was 2.3 per cent (Maddison 1980). By contrast, in the period 1950-70 the average annual rate of growth in these countries was 4.9 per cent. There was a break in performance in 1973, with the rate of growth being 3.2 per cent a year over 1970-79 as a whole and 2.4 per cent a year over 1973-79. It is quite likely, therefore, that the 1950s and the 1960s will come to mark a 'golden age' in the economy of advanced capitalist countries taken as a whole. That period was marked by reductions in barriers to trade, government promotion of demand, relatively modest increases in consumer prices and a backlog of projects to be undertaken; since 1973 there has been more rapid inflation, a decline in commitment by governments to increase demand and a fall in productivity (Maddison, 1980).

The rise in output per head is an indication of the increase in living standards in our period. The eighty percent rise in personal consumption per head in real terms over 1957-80 (or an average annual increase of 2.6 percent per annum) is another. Disposable personal income (that is, income from the labour market *plus* transfer payments, mainly from government, less direct taxes on income and wealth) has increased. In real terms, it doubled over the twenty-three years between 1957 and 1980. To what extent does this add up to a genuine increase in economic well-being? There are many dimensions to human well-being which even the broadest economic measure will not capture. Even as a measure of economic well-being, there are well-known deficiencies in output per person. For instance, it does not take account of changes in the distribution of income over time. Irish statistics on the distribution of income are lamentably deficient in coverage and frequency, but the fragmentary evidence which is available shows no indication of a tendency towards greater equality in the distribution of income. The available data shows that there was little change in the degree of inequality in the decade up to 1975. If anything, the distribution of income became more unequal (Stark, 1977).

The output per head measure takes no account of the disutilities which come with economic 'development' – pollution, urban blight, congestion, noise. Moreover, some output, such as that of the security industry and of policing, can be classed as 'regrettable necessities'. These points suggest that an increase in output per head overstates the 'true' increase in well being. It can also be argued that it under-estimates it in another respect. An increase in output can mean that people do not have to work so hard. As the average work-week shortens, and holidays extend, people enjoy an increase in leisure which should be counted as an increase in well-being. Between 1957 and 1981, the average hours worked in transportable goods industries by adult males fell from 46.5 to 43.0, a relatively small decline over a period of twenty-four years. Moreover, to the extent that 'moon-lighting' could have increased in the interim, there may have been little decline in the average work week. Thus, individuals have not tended to 'purchase' leisure by giving up money income. This is explicable given relative earnings in Ireland compared to other countries, the relatively small number of multi-earner households compared with other countries and the larger family size in Ireland. On the other hand, there has been a shift in employment towards 'white-collar' services where average hours worked are less than in

45

other sectors. (In 1979, average hours worked per week in public administration were 40.9 by comparison with 43.2 in all industry – Eurostat, 1981.) On balance, though, the measure of output per person is likely to overstate the 'true' increase in economic well-being.

Even if all correction could be made, would households perceive that their lot was a better one? Not necessarily, for two reasons. First, wants or 'needs' tend to increase over time. Second, households may relate their satisfaction to their relative income position. A study of 30 surveys from 19 developed and less developed countries showed that:

In all societies, more money for the individual typically means more individual happiness. However, raising the incomes of all does not increase the happiness of all. . . individuals assess their material well-being not in terms of the absolute amount of goods they have, but relative to a social norm of what goods they ought to have (Easterlin, 1973, p.4).

Economic growth can increase discontent. In a society as unequal as that of Ireland, it is difficult not to ascribe the evident rise in tension over income shares to frustrated expectations about the benefits of economic growth, an increasing perception of the extent of economic inequality and the capricious redistribution of income and wealth which occurs as a result of a sharply higher rate of inflation.

Finally, there is need to consider the impact of the rise in the price of imports relative to the price of exports between 1973 and 1980. This happened largely because the price of oil increased faster than agricultural prices in some years. When this happens, the change in GNP is no longer a good indicator of the change in the volume of resources which are available for domestic spending in the form of domestic consumption (both private and public) and domestic investment. This is because a greater proportion of output must be exported in order to purchase the same quantity of imports. When a correction is made for this, the average annual increase in real GNP per head in the 1973-80 period was a negligible 0.3 per cent per annum. The disparity between this and the average annual increase of 2.6 per cent per annum in real disposable personal income in this period is explained as follows. The extent of the increase in living standards in 1973-80 was made possible only by a huge increase in the current balance of payments. This was, in turn, financed largely by substantial borrowing abroad and by a decline in the official external reserves.

This borrowing has to be serviced and ultimately repaid. It is in this sense that the increase in living standards which occurred over 1973-80 is 'unsustainable'.

Some of the increase in personal incomes which occurred in the 1960s and 1970s was due to an increase in transfer payments. In 1957, transfer payments by government accounted for 7.6 per cent of personal incomes in aggregate; in 1979 the figure was 12.7 per cent.

One of the features of the period since 1957 has been the acceleration in the rate of price inflation. Over the entire period 1957-81, the average annual rate of price inflation was 8.6 per cent (Consumer Price Index). There was, however, a marked contrast between the period 1960-70, with an inflation rate of 4.8 per cent a year, and the period 1970-81 when the inflation rate was 14.4 per cent a year. Some of this reflected inflation in the rest of the world. In particular, up to the break in the link with sterling in 1979, the rate of inflation was heavily influenced by that of the United Kingdom.

Output and Employment by Sector
Significant changes occurred in output and in employment by sector in the period 1957-80. In 1957, 433,000 people or 38 per cent of total employment worked in agriculture. By 1980, employment in the sector had fallen to 220,000 or 19 per cent of all employment. This amounts to an average annual decline of 9,300 per annum. By contrast, employment in industry in 1957 accounted for 25 per cent of total employment; by 1980 it accounted for 32 per cent of all employment. The average annual increase in employment in industry over 1957-80 was 1,300. Thus, the increase in employment in industry compensated for only a fraction of the decline in employment in agriculture. Most of the increase in employment in industry over the period – 61,000 out of 91,000 – occurred in manufacturing industry. By far the biggest increase in employment occurred in the service sector: an average annual increase of 6,500 per annum, pushing up the share of employment in this sector from 37 per cent in 1957 to 49 per cent in 1980. However, this cloaks another change which occurred, that is a shift towards 'service-type' jobs – work in the service sector together with the 'non-productive' occupations within agriculture and industry (eg transport and financial occupations). Over 50 per cent of the increase in employment outside the agricultural sector between 1961 and 1971 occurred in service-type employment, of which one-third was in industrial services (NESC 1977).

In 1958, output of agriculture accounted for 26 per cent of total output, while industry produced 29 per cent of all output. By 1980, the share of agriculture had fallen to 14 per cent. The share of the service sector increased slightly, to 48 per cent in 1981. These trends are typical of the change from a less developed or developing economy to a more developed one. (Ireland is now classed as one of the eighteen industrial market economies by the World Bank). In the typical pattern of development, the economy moves from a position where agriculture accounts for a large proportion of employment but a lower proportion of output indicating a sector with low income and low productivity. As a shift in employment between agriculture and other sectors occurs, there is an increase in output per person in agriculture. Output per person in industry is higher than in agriculture, hence the shift in employment towards industry gives rise to an increase in aggregate output. Eventually the income per head in agriculture will be closer to that of industry, as the employment income shares of agriculture converge. Over the period 1958-80, output per person in agriculture increased by 5.3 per cent per annum on average – this is likely to understate the 'true' underlying rate, as 1979 and 1980 were depressed years in agriculture. In this twenty-two year period, output per person in industry increased by 4.2 per cent per annum, on average.

Population, labour force and employment
Between the late 1840s and 1961 the population had more or less continuously declined, reaching a low point of 2,818 million in 1961. Between 1961 and 1979 the population increased at an accelerating rate. In the 1971-79 period there was an exceptionally high rate of increase in population of 1.5 per cent a year on average. This rate of increase comes around mid-way between that for a western European country and that of less developed country. For the first time ever, there was net immigration – of 109,000 between 1971 and 1979. A further increase in population of 1.1 per cent a year occurred between 1979 and 1981.

The labour force increased by 1.6 per cent a year over 1971-79 including an increase in the female labour force by 2.2 per cent a year. This reflected the rise in population and an increase in labour force participation rates in some age groups among women (although this was offset by marked declines in participation among those aged 55 and over).

48

In the period 1957-80, the increase in total employment has been only 26,000 or a little over a thousand a year on average. In this period there was a big increase in public sector employment: from 117,600 in 1961 to 214,300 in 1979; in the eight year period 1971-79 alone, the rise in public sector employment was 56 per cent (Sexton, 1982). Job losses in manufacturing industry in the 1970s (many were associated with an increase in imports) were greater than anticipated. Much of these increased imports resulted from *either* the trade liberalisation which began with unilateral tariff reductions in 1963 and 1964, continued with the Anglo-Irish Free Trade Area of 1965 and ended with accession to the EEC in 1973, *or* losses in competitiveness. Many firms were driven to increase investment or to change techniques of production in order to withstand competition but these changes were often associated with reductions in employment. At mid 1982, under the impact of a recession, unemployment was 150,000 or higher than at any time in the period since 1957.

Women in the economy
The change in the role of women has been one of the most striking features of the past twenty five years but equally notable has been the resistance to changes in their role. Up to the early 1970s it was widely accepted that the prime role of women was in the home. This was exemplified by the marriage bar in the public service, the denial to women of entry to certain skilled occupations and professions and the small number of females receiving third level education particularly in science and technology. The results of this interaction of values, regulations and response to economic incentives were manifold. In 1961 only 29 per cent of all women and only 5 per cent of married women were in the labour force. There was a high degree of 'sex segregation' in employment: in 1962, 22 per cent of women were in occupations where women accounted for 90 per cent or more of all persons and 36 per cent of women were in occupations where women accounted for 70 per cent or more of all persons. In 1957, the average hourly earnings of women in transportable goods industries were 57 per cent of the male wage. In 1971, only 4,500 women had a scie.. 'fic or technological qualification by contrast with 17,400 men.

While legislation hastened change, attitudes were at least as important. Changes in regulation occurred in the latter half of the last 25 years. The ending of the marriage bar in the public service was operative from 31 July 1973. The Anti-Discrimination (Pay) Act,

49

1974, came into operation on December 1975 and established the right of men and women employed on life-work by the same employer to equal pay. The Employment Equality Act, 1977 came into operation on 1 July 1977, prohibiting discrimination on grounds of sex or marital status in recruitment, training or provision of opportunities for promotion. While participation rates in the labour force increased between 1961 and 1979 (for women aged 20-54) these rates are still much lower than the Western European average. If the labour force participation rate for women in Ireland were equal to that of the EEC as a whole in 1979, there would be another 90,400 in the female labour force.

In 1981, average hourly earnings of women in transportable goods industries were 68 per cent of those of males. The increased number of women in the labour force has many causes. These include a decline in average family size (the average number of children is now three (1981) compared to four in 1971), the availability of labour-saving devices for the home and increased employment in public service (which offers greater employment opportunities for women and a shorter average work week). In other words, not only have there been changes in attitudes to women working but women have responded to economic incentives in the form of increased real earnings and an increase in productivity of household goods.

Agriculture
The growth rate in agriculture since 1957 is disappointing by comparison with potential although it is respectable if compared with the stagnation of the preceding decades. From 1977 to 1978, gross output in agriculture (including changes in livestock numbers) increased at an annual rate of 2.8 per cent. These figures overstate the position. The increase in output was matched by an increase in inputs. When these are accounted for, the average growth rate comes out as 1.8 per cent per annum. A good deal of interest centres on the impact of EEC membership on agriculture. While the response of Irish farmers to the higher EEC prices has been a matter of no little controversy, EEC accession seems to have had little effect on the growth rate of gross agricultural output (Sheehy, 1980).

The lack of discernible effects of EEC entry is all the more notable given the huge capital investment which occurred in agriculture in that period. At 1980 prices, total investment in agriculture in the 1970s was over £1,600 million, yet at the end of the decade the cattle herd had not increased (Matthews, 1981). Furthermore state expenditure on agriculture (eg. on disease eradication) has had a demonstrably poor return. It is likely that a duality exists in agriculture as it exists in industry. There is some evidence that the increase in output which did occur was confined to a minority of farms; the remainder showed no growth or even a decline (Matthews, 1981).

Little effort has been made to address these problems. Almost all land transfers are within the farm family through inheritance thereby making the entry of enterprising operators who are outside the family almost impossible. There has been little move towards performance criteria for state aids. While a Government White Paper of 1979 (Ireland 1979) said that 'the Government are in favour of a resource tax in principle', nothing has happened, even though such a land tax would lead to a more efficient use of land.

Industry

There has been a growth of 5.7 per cent per annum in output of transportable goods industries over 1957-58, and an increase of 4.0 per cent a year in output per person in these industries. This has been associated with a marked rise in manufactured goods exports: between 1963 and 1978, manufactured exports increased from 7.3 per cent to 24.9 per cent of Gross Domestic Product (Nolan, 1981). In the face of a sluggish growth in world trade in the 1970s, Ireland's export share of developed countries manufactured goods exports increased by two and a half times between 1970 and 1980.

Much of this has been due to an influx of new firms stimulated by investment incentives, government factory building and tax reliefs dating from the late 1950s. The 'active policy period' in the case of industrial policy has been held to date from 1958 (Moore, Rhodes and Traling, 1978). By 1974 new industry (which received new industry grants) accounted for over 60 per cent of industrial exports (McAleese, 1977). There is a duality in Irish industry, with domestic industry concentrating on the home market and contributing relatively little to the increase in output, exports and employment. Hence, the changes in nature of industry *within* the industrial sector have been as notable as the changes *between* one sector and another.

Planning in the 1960s and 1970s

At around the nadir of the depression in December 1957 the work which culminated in *Economic Development* of 1958 was initiated. This

51

study of national development problems and opportunities (Ireland, 1958B) was prepared by the Secretary of the Department of Finance in co-operation with others and was completed in May 1958. This laid the foundations for the first economic programme. In retrospect, it is striking that *Economic Development* laid much stress on what would now be called 'supply side measures': on the need to stimulate output and efficiency and to encourage enterprise, in part by avoiding unduly high rates of taxation. High taxation was seen as 'one of the greatest impediments to economic progress because of its adverse effects on saving and on enterprise' (p. 21). There was little mention of employment as an increase in the rate of growth of output was the way in which employment could be increased. 'There would be nothing to be gained by setting up fanciful employment targets: failure to reach such targets would only produce disillusionment' (p.207). In these and in many other respects, *Economic Development* reads as a startlingly modern tract for our times. It puts a commendable emphasis on agriculture as a potential source of output.

The first *Programme for Economic Expansion* (Ireland 1958A), which covered the period 1959 to 1963 inclusive expected that its implementation would lead to an increase of real national income of some 2 per cent per annum or twice that of the period 1949-1956. The programme put much emphasis on 'productive' expenditure and sought an increase in national output of marketed goods which would be sold in export markets. The programme expected a fall in social capital expenditure. In this regard it echoed *Economic Development* which stated:

Positive action by the Government, a slowing down in housing and certain other forms of social investment will occur from now on because needs are virtually satisfied over wide areas of the State. (Ireland, 1958B, pp.3-4).

The programme anticipated free trade and stressed the need to move away from protection and to promote exports. Thus, the programme was firmly committed to 'outward-looking' policies which were to influence industrial policy throughout the next two and a half decades. The emphasis was to be on export promotion rather than the substitution of imports: in this respect policy differs from the many less developed countries which emphasise import substitution. Foreign investment was welcomed in the first programme whereas formerly foreign ownership had been discouraged. Another feature of the programme was the emphasis on the private sector. 'The Government favours the system of private ownership of industry and will not be disposed to enter any manufacturing field in which private enterprise is already operating successfully'. (Ireland, 1958A, paragraph 108)

The emphasis on 'productive' investment can be seen from the attitude to foreign borrowing: 'Any external borrowing will be confined to the financing of productive projects'. (Paragraph 136)

The target for real output growth in the first programme was comfortably exceeded and the *Second Programme for Economic Expansion* (Ireland 1963, 1964A) was issued: its chief objective was to raise the aggregate real income by 50 per cent over the 1960-70 period. The Programme was intended to cover the years 1964 to 1970 but was effectively abandoned by early 1968. This programme was a more detailed exercise in setting targets.

From 1964 to 1967, there was a respectable growth in the volume of output although less than that envisaged under the programme. Imports increased more rapidly than had been anticipated and the employment target was not reached. The *Third Programme: Economic and Social Development* (Ireland, 1969) was due to run to the end of 1972. It was drawn up against the background of the National Industrial Economic Council's report on full employment and there was more emphasis on employment targets. While the second programme's target of a 50 per cent increase in real income in the 1960s was realised in a *52 per cent* growth – the target for output for the third programme was below that projected. Employment was less than projected in all sectors and job losses in manufacturing industry were higher than expected. The other unexpected result was that the increases in current and capital public expenditure were much greater than anticipated. To sum up the period of the second and third programmes: there was a respectable growth in output even if it was below expectations, there was little increase in employment and a sharper fall in agricultural employment than had been expected. Increased productivity contributed more to the increases in output than had been expected. The most significant divergence occurred in the public sector. Ironically, while the programmes set out targets for the private sector, they were unable to ensure that the 'plans' had an impact on the public sector itself.

The Irish planning experience of the 1960s and early 1970s is similar to that of Britain in the 1960s: an early enthusiasm gives way to disillusion as plan targets fail to be achieved. Too much was expected of the plans in both cases, given that policy instruments were either not available to correct deviations from target – or if available were regar ied as unpalatable. In Ireland there was an increasing pre-occupation with specifying detailed targets: the apogee of this was the report on agriculture in the second programme where extraordinarily detailed targets were given (Ireland, 1964). Planning is eventually about policies. The reviews of the second and third programmes tended to concentrate on comparisons of target with outcome rather than on policy. In a number of instances, targets were not achieved for reasons which were largely outside the influence of the planners. For example, the second programme was drawn up on assumptions of favourable external trade conditions and the avoidance of inflationary pressures. These assumptions were not realised in practice.

The changes in policy required in order to achieve targets should have been examined. The failure of the public sector to achieve its own targets can be blamed on the lack of coordination between the annual budget and the programmes. The second and third programmes had little influence over central and local government and state-sponsored bodies. 'Indicative planning' of the second and third programme type is designed to reduce uncertainty and to lower risk among those who undertake investment. Yet there is no indication that the planning influences the investment decisions of the public utilities (Bristow, 1979). In an economy as open as the Irish, it is difficult to say to what extent the outcomes were any different from what would have resulted without any attempts at planning. It has been widely agreed that the effects of the first programme were mainly achieved by its psychological impact, increasing public confidence. This is virtually an untestable proposition. If there were psychological effects, they can hardly have lasted more than a few years.

The problems of planning, and the difficulties of choosing between the different and conflicting objectives of economic growth, reducing economic fluctuations, increasing employment and reducing the rate of inflation applied equally to the succession of the Green and White Papers which were issued between 1976 (Ireland, 1976) and 1980 (Ireland, 1980). This period saw the inexorable rise of public expenditure. The Green and White Papers of the second half of the 1970s were unable to avoid the ever widening balance in public finances which led to a rapid increase in the exchequer borrowing requirement.

Pay and the search for an incomes policy

Issues of pay and of pay differences were a constant source of discontent: one of the themes of the period was and is the search for an effective pay policy.

As less developed economies develop pay differences which are associated with varying skills generally widen and then become narrower as development matures (Philips, Brown, 1977). As development takes off, the demand for skills which were previously little used increases. This is followed by increases in the supply of skilled workers, together with a rise in capital investment per worker and an increase in the proportion of less skilled workers who are members of trade unions. In the Irish case, this narrowing of wage differences could be expected to be less due to the open labour market. The flexibility of the labour force is such that at times of high demand for labour it is augmented by former migrants who return to Ireland in response to the increased job opportunities – as occurred in the 1970s. For the period 1947-66, there is little evidence of a change in the distribution of earnings in transportable goods industries for males (Geary and Ó Muircheartaigh, 1974) and there are no data after 1966. There is another reason why inequality could decline as the economy grows. The work force tends to shift from self employment to wage and salary employment where there is less inequality but, as indicated above, there is little evidence that this has had an effect in Ireland.

In the 1960s the government tried to achieve wage restraint by exhortation. The main feature of the 1970s was centralised pay bargaining. The government was involved in moves which led to the first National Wage Agreement in December 1970; a succession of national Agreements followed. In 1979 there was a change to the first National Agreements followed. In 1979 there was a change to the first National Understanding, which marked the incorporation of significant elements other than pay: elements such as employment and National Understandings raised a number of contentious issues. In particular how the role of the government as an employer (bargaining on pay) could be reconciled with the role of the government as manager of the public finances (in bargaining on issues other than pay). The National Agreements might have been expected to compress wage differences as, for instance, minimum increases were set in flat rate terms in a number of cases. However this must remain a supposition until the distribution of earnings is examined. A low pay problem persists, as indicated by the wage minima set under Joint Labour Committees. Finally, no policy has emerged to integrate tax and social security.

Some Current Problems

The limitations of policy in a small open economy under free trade has been one lesson of the past twenty five years.

The increased integration of the world economy sets limits to the ability of countries like Ireland to influence their economies. Indeed, an eminent economist has remarked that 'the nation state is just about through as an economic unit' (Kindleberger, 1969, p.207). To sustain his case he points to the increase in the speed and volume of communications, trade liberalisation, the rise of trans-national corporations and an increase in mobility of capital and labour across countries; these all lead to a decline in self-sufficiency for any individual country. Trans-national companies – that is, those which operate or control output in more than one country – are increasingly important to the Irish economy. Trans-national companies which commenced operation in the 1952-73 period with assistance from the Industrial Development Authority employed 45,000 by 1977 or about 25 per cent of the total work force in manufacturing (McAleese, 1978). These overseas firms accounted for 40 per cent of exports of manufacturing industry in 1974 and accounted for two-thirds of exports of Irish manufacturing industry to markets outside the UK.

The main difficulties which concern what used to be confidently called *the management of the economy* arise from the state of the public finances. A series of unbalanced budgets since 1974 has led to a huge increase in exchequer borrowing for current purposes. The public Capital Programme has given rise to additional borrowing. Much of this borrowing has been external, with the result that at June 1982 the external government debt was £4,713 million against which could be set official external resources of £1,465 million. This situation not only reduces the room to manoeuvre in budgetary policy but the servicing and repayment of the debt will reduce living standards. Further room for action in budgetary policy is limited by an exceedingly high current balance of payments deficit related to output.

The absence of any formal evaluation of the public capital programme, including its distributive impact, has been one of the biggest policy failures. Between 1957 and 1981 the public capital programme in *real* terms increased seven-fold. Associated with this, the ratio of investment to Gross Domestic Product increased from 16 per cent in 1958 to around 30 per cent in the late 1970s and early 1980s, yet the return from the additional capital investment has fallen. Despite the increase in the Public Capital Programme (38 per cent in real terms over 1978-81 alone) there has been little evidence of improvement in facilities such as transport. The restoration or increase of the previous level of social amenities, for example in transport and in urban amenities, is likely to be a policy issue given the continual increase in population around the larger urban areas. Yet this is likely to require a diversion of resources from current consumption at a time when little or no increase in real personal incomes is likely to occur.

It will also be more difficult to achieve social policy aims without a more precise articulation of aims and a greater concentration on distributive issues. The 'dividend', in the form of increased tax receipts, from economic growth is unlikely to be available to the same extent to fund social programmes.

A final set of problems concerns industrial policy. The importation of international technology has enabled a steady rise in output per head to be achieved but the domestic firms which concentrate on the home market have been much less successful. The policy problem is whether these domestic firms will continue to suffer the adverse effects of import competition, including that from the newly industrialising countries.

One notable irony arises from any examination of public policy and the economy over the past two and half decades. The issues of the aggregate economy received a lot of attention but policies were often directed to areas where there was a limited possibility of influence or where they were inappropriate (as in the case of fiscal policy boosts at times of high activity). At the same time little or no effort was made on matters such as pricing, public investment criteria, taxes and subsidies, the integration of taxation and social security. All of these matters were within the government's sphere of influence and policies directed towards them could have had substantial results.

A Note on Statistical Sources

Population

Report on Vital Statistics 1978,
Census of Population 1981, Vol. I

Net emigration

Statistical Abstract of Ireland

Aggregate output, output by sector and personal income

Kenney (1971)
For data up to 1946, *National Income and Expenditure* for subsequent periods.

Output and employment in transportable goods industries

Kennedy (1971) for data for 1957, for other years see *Irish Statistical Bulletin* and Central Statistics Office.

Labour Force

Census of Population 1961

Employment

The Trend of Employment and Unemployment,
Economic Review and Outlook Summer 1982

Earnings

Statistics of Wages, Earnings and Houses of Work 1962 Irish Statistical Bulletin

In other cases, sources are given in the text.

References

John Bristow 'Aspects of economic planning' *Administration* 27/2, pp. 192-200, 1979

Richard A. Easterlin 'Does money bring happiness?' *The Public Interest,* No. 30, pp. 3-10, 1972

Eurostat, 1981 *Labour Force Samples Survey 1979*

Tom Ferris 'Comparisons of productivity and living standards: Ireland and other EEC countries' *Irish Bank Review* 7-15, 1981

R.C. Geary and F.S. Ó Muircheartaigh *Equalization of Opportunity in Ireland: Statistics Aspects Broadsheet No. 10* Dublin: ESRI

Ireland (1958A) *Programme for Economic Expansion* Dublin: Stationery Office

Ireland (1958B) *Economic Development* Dublin: Stationery Office

Ireland 1963 *Second Programme for Economic Expansion* Dublin: Stationery Office

Ireland 1964A *Second Programme for Economic Expansion Part II* Dublin: Stationery Office

Ireland 1964B *Agriculture in the Second Programme for Economic Expansion* Dublin: Stationery Office

Ireland 1976 *Economic and Social Development, 1976-1980* Dublin: Stationery Office

Ireland 1979 *Third Programme: Economic and Social Development 1969-72* Dublin: Stationery Office

Ireland 1980 *Investment and National Development 1979-1983* Dublin: Stationery Office

Kieran A. Kennedy *Productivity and industrial growth: the Irish experience* Oxford: Clarendon Press, 1971

Kieran A. Kennedy and Brendan R. Dowling *Economic Growth in Ireland: The Experience Since 1947* Dublin: Gill and Macmillan, 1975

Charles P. Kindleberger *American business abroad: Six lectures on direct investment* London: Yale University Press, 1969

Dermot McAleese *A profile of grant-aided industry in Ireland* Dublin: Industrial Development Authority, 1977

Dermot McAleese 'Overseas industry in the Irish economy' *Irish Banking Review,* June 11-17

A. Maddison, 'Western economic performance in the 1970s: a perspective and assessment' *Banca Nazionale del Lavoro Quarterly Review,* No. 134, pp. 247-289, 1980

Alan Matthews 'Agriculture and the Jobs Crisis' Paper to Annual Economic Conference of Irish Congress of Trade Unions (mimeo),

1981

Barry Moore, John Rhodes and Roger Tarline 'Industrial Policy and Economic Development: The Experience of Northern Ireland and the Republic of Ireland' *Cambridge Journal of Economics* Vol. 2, pp. 99-114

NESC *Report on Public Expenditure,* Report No. 21, Dublin: Stationery Office, 1976

NESC National Economic and Social Council, 1977 *Service-type employment and regional development,* Report No. 28, Dublin: Stationery Office

Brian Nolan 'The Personal Distribution of Income in the Republic of Ireland' *Journal of the Statistical and Social Inquiry Society of Ireland,* XXIII (v) pp. 91-144, 1977-8

J. Nolan 'Economic Growth' in: ed. J.W. O'Hagan *The economy of Ireland: policy and performance* Dublin: Irish Management Institute, 1981

Philips, Brown 1977 *The inequality of pay* Oxford: Oxford University Press

J.J. Sexton 'Sectoral changes in the labour force over the period 1961-1980 with particular reference to public sector and services employment' *Quarterly Economic Commentary,* August pp. 36-45, 1982

Seamus J. Sheehy 'The impact of EEC membership on Irish agriculture' *Journal of Agricultural Economics* 31/3, pp. 297-310, 1980

Thomas Stark *The distribution of income in eight countries,* background paper No. 4 Royal Commission on the Distribution of Income and Wealth, London: HMSO, 1977

World Bank 1981 *World Development Report 1981* Washington, DC: The World Bank

Irish Agricultural Museum

Ireland's dairy industry has come a long way since.

The days of dairymaids and horse-drawn creameries have passed. In their place has emerged one of the world's most modern and dynamic dairy industries. Today Ireland turns the greenest grass in Europe into a diverse range of the best-known dairy products in the world.

From Honduras to Hong Kong, from Trinidad to Tokyo you will find Irish cream, milk powder, chocolate crumb, cheese, casein and a great variety of other products, many of them sold under the Kerrygold brand name.

Irish dairy exports this year are expected to be worth well over £600m. Which gives you some idea just how far the industry has come since the days of the dairymaid.

AN BORD BAINNE
IRISH DAIRY BOARD

61

If you're travelling in Ireland we have the best service!

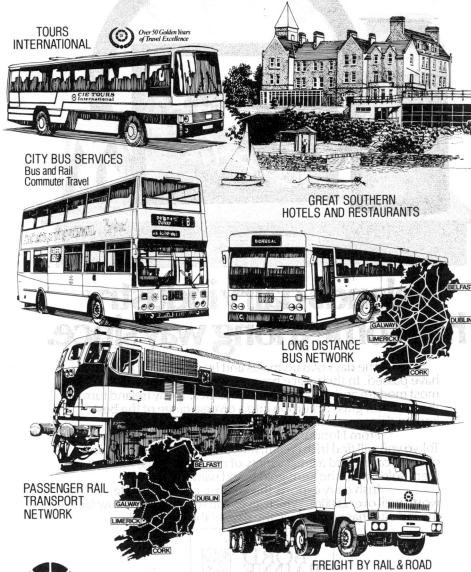

TOURS INTERNATIONAL

Over 50 Golden Years of Travel Excellence

CIE TOURS International

CITY BUS SERVICES
Bus and Rail Commuter Travel

GREAT SOUTHERN HOTELS AND RESTAURANTS

LONG DISTANCE BUS NETWORK

BELFAST
GALWAY
DUBLIN
LIMERICK
CORK

PASSENGER RAIL TRANSPORT NETWORK

BELFAST
GALWAY
DUBLIN
LIMERICK
CORK

FREIGHT BY RAIL & ROAD

CIE Ireland's total transport and hotel network.

The Changing Social Structure*

DAVID B. ROTTMAN and PHILIP J. O'CONNELL

This is an interpretation of the transformation Ireland has experienced since the mid-1950s. It sets out the essential features, as we see them, of a rapidly industrialising society. The specific items of change have been well chronicled: new forms of work force participation, altered family relationships, an emphasis on education, and a higher level of material well-being, among many others. As sociologists, however, our interest is in the basic pattern which allows a multitude of people and groups to operate as a totality in these changed circumstances. That pattern is not adequately captured by simply describing Ireland as an industrial society. Though Ireland exhibits many characteristics of such a society, its development has differed in some important respects from that which is associated with other western countries, because it took place in the context of disengagement from unilateral dependence on the British economy and a simultaneous integration with the international economy. It is a difference that is too rarely acknowledged.

The structures of Irish society in the 1950s were viable only insofar as they linked with those of the United Kingdom; they were appropriate to one of the peripheral regions of the British Isles. British capital was the most substantial foreign investor in Ireland, the migration of Irish labour to Britain was increasing, and two-thirds of total exports was destined for the British market. By the late 1960s state induced economic growth, through the expansion of the industrial and service sectors of production, had industrialised an economy formerly dominated by agriculture, and appeared to promise full employment. If so, for the first time, the massive redundancies

*We gratefully acknowledge the critical comments made on an earlier draft of this chapter by Frank Litton, Ciaran McCullagh, James Raftery, and Joseph Ruane.

created by the century-long restructuring of agricultural production could be absorbed.

It was a transformation set in motion as an act of will. Through state policy the outflow of labour in the 1950s has been replaced by the inflow of foreign capital. Policies adopted by successive governments re-oriented Ireland away from Britain and toward the world economy and made it possible for the national economy to capture most of each generation as it entered the workforce. Those policies released new forces in Irish society and accelerated processes, like farm mechanisation, which had been gathering momentum since the late 1940s. But by intervening so significantly the state had introduced changes whose logic would be worked out within the social structure, and over which no individual or government could retain control.

Structural change alters the ways in which the life chances of individuals are allocated – that is why it is so important a topic for study. By life chances we refer to inequalities in the opportunity people have of sharing 'in the socially created economic or cultural "goods" which typically exist in any given society'.[1] A transformation has taken place since 1957 in the allocation of life chances. What we offer is an explanation that treats social class as the most important indicator of a person's life chances, and we put emphasis on the specific life chances involved in migration flows and demographic patterns, which were dramatic reflections of class inequalities during the 1950s. Our basic theme is how the determination of life chances has over the past twenty-five years become for the most part self-contained within Ireland: the workforce no longer spans the Irish Sea, emigration has virtually ceased, and demography has been shaped by natural increase and immigration.

Because the change in social structure was so closely linked to policy choices, however unintended their consequences may have been, we begin our examination with an assessment of the development strategies adopted and the economic problems which they were designed to solve. The policies adopted had two crucial effects on the class structure: (1) the availability of various types of positions for economic participation and (2) the rules governing competition for vacancies in those positions.

The context of structural change

The search for economic independence that dominated policy-making since the state's foundation had obviously failed by the late 1950s.

Agriculture, then the dominant form of economic activity, especially as a source of foreign exchange, was dependent on exports of dairy products and cattle to Britain. Agricultural production had expanded only slightly, and the long-standing process by which agricultural labourers and small farmers were forced off the land, and into the British labour market, continued unabated, even becoming more vigorous in the 1950s. The industrial growth fostered to serve the domestic market during the protectionist 1930s had been exhausted decades earlier. Insulated by high tariffs, one of the legacies of the 1930s, from competition with foreign manufacturers, domestic industry was inefficient and produced for the restricted home market. A generally low level of linkages among firms, a further consequence of protection, and a distinct reluctance by private investors to provide capital offered little potential for any expansion of industry without effective state intervention.

By the late 1950s Ireland's ability to continue as a viable economic and social entity was in question. The 1950s had seen economic stagnation, continual balance of payments crises, rising unemployment and 400,000 emigrants. Gross national product (GNP) had increased by 8 per cent between 1949 and 1956, in contrast to the 21 per cent increase recorded in Britain and the 42 per cent recorded by the combined countries of the Organisation for European Economic Cooperation.[2] Left on that course, Ireland's future could only be grim. The value of gross agricultural output was rising by one-third the rate characteristic of the combined OEEC countries and the volume of industrial production grew at one-half the rate experienced in those countries.

The publication of the first *Programme for Economic Expansion* in November 1958 was a direct response to that critical situation, and marked a turning point in Irish economic policy. It followed closely the recommendations of the Department of Finance's major study of the national development problems and opportunities, *Economic Development*. These and subsequent planning documents marked the abandonment of the pursuit of self-sufficiency and turned the economy outwards with two inter-related strategies. First, agriculture, retaining its pre-eminence as the likely vehicle to prosperity, could increase production by integrating with the European market and its higher food prices. But increased agricultural production demanded the consolidation of small farms into larger, commercially viable units and more mechanisation – success in agriculture would yield less, not more, employment. Development strategy thus required a second focus: the attraction of foreign capital to invest in export-oriented manufacturing, an expansion of industry to be massively underwritten by state intervention. The main direct beneficiaries of development strategy therefore would be large farmers and overseas investors. An improved structure of living for all was promised for the not too distant future.

The pursuit of this dual strategy in 1958 was indeed a turning point. While certain of the institutions central to the success of the industrial development strategy had already been established – the Industrial Development Authority in 1949, An Foras Tionscal in 1952, and the Industrial Credit Company in 1933 – it was not until 1958 that the Irish economy was opened to the international market; protectionism was abandoned, and formal economic planning was initiated. This radical departure from former policies coincided with a major increase in the internationalisation of trade and investment.[3]

Such international developments ensured that foreign investment became the linchpin of Irish development strategies, although the invitation to foreign capital made in the first Programme was perhaps but one of several options at the initial stages of policy formation. Nevertheless, the influx of foreign capital was sufficient to provide 80 per cent of new private investment in the first six years of planning, contributing much to the success of the first Programme.[4] The second and third Programmes were far more optimistic, anticipating that the inflow of capital from overseas would make a major contribution, not simply in the form of direct investment but also in subscriptions to national loans and in loans to semi-state companies.

It was a bold development strategy. The growth in new industrial investment had to take place in tandem with a general shift to integration with the European economy, a move likely to result in a sharp contraction of the traditional domestic industries as protective tariffs were gradually removed. Adaptation grants were provided in order to improve the competitiveness of domestic industries, and their decline was compensated for, at least during the 1960s and early 1970s, by firms attracted from abroad. The strategy also incurred certain costs. Industrialisation through foreign capital required the state to provide a wide range of incentives and services to industry: direct aid in the form of investment grants, the provision and upgrading of infrastructural facilities, transport and communications, financing of research and development, as well as subsidising the education and training for an industrial work force. A range of tax incentives, including export profits tax relief, accelerated depreciation allowances and investment allowances for certain areas, enhanced Ireland's attractiveness as a location for both foreign and native investment.

These strategies enacted in pursuit of economic independence and stability generated an accelerated rate of growth during the 1960s and early 1970s. The resulting restructuring of the economy can be gauged in the changing shares which the main economic sectors contribute to gross domestic product (GDP). Between 1960 and 1979, the share of agriculture in GDP dropped from 22 per cent to 15 per cent of the total, while industry's share grew from 28 per cent to 38 per cent, and that of services dropped slightly, from 49 per cent to 48 per cent.[5] Changes in employment were also significant. Total employment in industry fell from 282,000 in 1951 to 257,000 in 1961 and increased thereafter to 319,000 in 1978, an increase since 1961 of 24 per cent. Employment in agriculture fell from 496,000 in 1951 to 379,500 in 1961 and 229,000 in 1978, a drop of 40 per cent between 1961 and 1978. Total employment in services grew by 20 per cent from 416,000 in 1961 to 500,000 in 1978, when it represented the largest employment sector. Public service employment expanded by 62 per cent between 1960 and 1980, from 182,000 to 295,000.[6] Over the same period, the Irish economy was successfully disengaged from its heavy reliance on Britain. British-owned companies, which in the period from 1960–1970 represented 22 per cent of new industry investment, accounted for less than 2 per cent in 1980, and the proportion of total exports destined for the British market fell from two-thirds of the total in 1956 to one-third in 1981.[7]

While the transformation since 1958 can hardly be regarded as a 'social revolution', the period did mark a watershed for the structure of Irish society. Nevertheless, Ireland remains a society with problems embedded in that structure, some of which had motivated the economic planners of the late 1950s. Though oriented toward the world economy as a coherent economic unit, the problem of dependence may in fact have been diffused rather than removed. And now that Ireland has largely withdrawn from participation in the British labour market, rising unemployment rather than increasing emigration threatens the society's viability.

Formal economic planning in the late 1950s emerged through the conviction held by a relatively small number of higher civil servants and academics that through the intelligent utilisation of fiscal policy and selective state interventions, the destiny of a society could be directed and controlled. Such assumptions underlay not only the publication of *Economic Development* and the subsequent *Programme for Economic Expansion*, but also the establishment of a number of organisations oriented toward the application of expertise, particularly of the economic variety, to the pursuit of national progress. Notable among these organisations were: the Institute of Public Administration, founded in 1957 to promote the study and improve the standard of public administration; the Economic Research Institute (later the Economic and Social Research Institute), founded in 1960 to conduct research and advance the knowledge of economics and other social sciences with particular reference to Ireland; An Foras Taluntais, founded in 1958 to undertake and assist agricultural research; and the National Industrial and Economic Council, the forerunner of the National Economic and Social Council, established in 1963 to report on the requirements for economic development and full employment.

These agents of economic development, like the planning documents, were the instruments of a decisive break with the past. Such significant interventions to a society release social forces which subsequently become independent of their immediate authors. The emergence of a wide range of organised interests during the next two decades, itself a consequence of economic restructuring, has involved the state in a complex network of relationships, often with conflicting interests, and considerably reduced the room for manoeuvre in any further state interventions. The success of the initial planning exercises both transformed the social structure and severely restricted the prospect that the same group of planners or another could intervene so decisively again in Irish society.

The transformation of the class structure
By the mid-1960s, industrial expansion and economic growth generally were forging dramatic changes to the Irish class structure. A class consists of families that have a similar set of economic resources which they use to generate income. The life chances of individuals depend, by and large, on the quality of such resources, whether in the form of property, as in farmland, or in qualifications for wage employment. Thus, a changing class structure alters the relative advantage of possessing different forms of economic resources. In Ireland, as in other industrialising countries, this took the form of

68

continuous contraction of employment possibilities for semi- or un-skilled manual work and declining viability for small farm enterprises and work thereon; the converse was growth in employment prospects for those with credentials required for white collar and service occupations, and the still more rapid expansion of opportunities for those trained in skilled industrial work. Yet the change in class structure was to be less complete in Ireland than in most European countries, and the implications for equality of opportunity less substantial than is often believed.

Still, a contrast of the class structure of the early 1950s, as portrayed in the 1951 census, with that of today, as revealed in the 1979 Labour Force Survey, denotes the passing of an era and the emergence of a new order. Table 1, which traces the changing class composition of the male labour force in 1951, 1961, 1971 and 1979,[8] includes both the number of workers in each class category and the percentage of the total male workforce it represents. It is a total workforce that has been steadily declining in size since the mid-nineteenth century. Such was the devastation sustained through emigration during the 1950s that the 1979 labour force of 883,000 men was 50,000 fewer than that in 1951. So it is possible for a category to have increased its percentage share since 1951 though remaining unchanged in the number of workers it contains. Simple stability in numbers reflected economic viability for a class.

Slightly less than one-half of the early 1950s workforce fell within class categories which derived income from property-ownership: 38 per cent of the workforce were either employers or self-employed in agriculture with an additional 8 per cent so engaged in non-agricultural pursuits. Professionals, managers and senior administrative workers, 48,000 in number, represented only 5 per cent of the 1951 workforce. A further 11 per cent were skilled manual workers. One fourth of the workforce was involved in semi-skilled or unskilled manual work – typically as labourers; there were 125,000 agricultural labourers in 1951, nearly one worker out of seven. For the children of these individuals life chances centred on the prospects for inheriting the family business and the accompanying house and household goods. Realistically, education or training could secure a livelihood within Ireland for only a minority of those aspiring to the workforce. Of those born between 1936 and 1941, by 1961 only 59 per cent remained in Ireland, and of those remaining, one in four were at work in some form of family employment.[9]

Table 1: Distribution of males at work by class categories, 1951 to 1979.

	1951		1961		1971		1979	
	No.	%	No.	%	No.	%	No.	%
Agriculture:								
(i) employers	27,832	3.1	14,000	1.8	212,950[1]	27.4	8,700	1.0
(ii) self-employed and relatives assisting	314,422	35.0	265,436	34.3			166,800	20.1
Non-agricultural activities:								
(i) employers	19,701	2.2	12,583	1.6	64,656[1]	8.3	27,900	3.4
(ii) self-employed and relatives assisting	52,898	5.9	47,985	6.2			53,800	6.5
Employers and Self-employed	414,853	46.2	340,004	43.9	279,606	35.6	257,200	31.1
(i) upper middle class (higher and lower professions managers and salaried employees)	47,780	5.3	58,934	7.6	84,512	10.9	110,200	13.3
(ii) lower middle class (intermediate and other non-manual)	123,011	13.7	121,159	15.6	139,991	18.0	169,300	20.5
(iii) skilled manual	95,308	10.6	96,050	12.4	130,625	16.8	167,400	20.2
(iv) semi and unskilled manual								
(a) agricultural	90,049	10.0	61,335	7.9	37,676	4.9	24,700	3.0
(b) non-agricultural	124,789	13.9	96,731	12.5	105,384	13.6	98,300	11.9
Employees:	480,937	53.6	434,209	56.1	498,188	64.2	569,900	68.8
Total at work[2]	897,465	100.0	774,540	100.0	776,507	100.0	827,800	100.0
Total out of work	36,115		46,989		55,157		55,600	
Total out of work as % of gainfully occupied		3.9		5.7		6.6		6.3

Sources: 1951, 1961, and 1971: *Census of Population*, Various Volumes; 1979: Derived from data specially provided to the ESRI by the Central Statistics Office from unpublished *Labour Force Survey* statistics.

1. Number of employers and self-employed were not disaggregated in the 1971 Census.
2. Total at work includes other and undefined workers, which are not separately given in the table above. The total excludes "theological students", "professional students" and "articled clerks" and in 1951, those in hospitals.

70

The Changing Social Structure

For the 1951–61 period, the spectre of emigration overshadowed all trends by reducing the size of the male labour force by one-seventh. Lower middle class and skilled manual categories retained constant levels of employment but became more considerable proportions of the total workforce. Where an actual increase in numbers was recorded, as for senior white collar employees, the effects of emigration accentuated the importance of the change for class structure. Perhaps the most basic of life chances in the 1950s was expressed as pressure to emigrate, and the viability of the class to which one belonged or could aspire to was of great relevance.

By the mid-1970s, wage bargaining in a class system sharply differentiated by skills and credentials became the dominant factor in determining one's life chances. Employers and the self-employed represented less than one-third of the 1979 total workforce, with proprietors in agriculture outnumbering those in other pursuits by 2 to 1. The declining size of proprietorial categories, however, is attributable to depletion of those engaged in agricultural production, with a proportionately greater decline for employers than for the self-employed. In contrast, non-agricultural proprietors have increased their share of the workforce over the past thirty years, and that growth in numbers was concentrated among employers (20,000 in 1951 and 28,000 in 1979). By 1979, Ireland had clearly ceased to be characterised as petit bourgeois: the predominant categories were of large scale employers and of well-qualified employees.

The distribution of employees among class categories in 1979 and the contrast with earlier years are shown clearly in Table 1. Employed professionals formed some 13 per cent of the workforce, more than doubling their representation since 1951; skilled manual employees also grew markedly over that period, from 11 per cent to 20 per cent of the workforce, rising in numbers from 95,000 in 1951 to 167,000 in 1979. The number of 'lower' middle class workers – commercial travellers and junior clerks – also increased, but less dramatically, from 14 per cent to 21 per cent. Semi-skilled and unskilled manual workers represented nearly one quarter of the workforce in 1951 and 14 per cent in 1979, representing in particular a massive decline (from 90,000 to 25,000) in the number of agricultural labourers.

The 1979 employee workforce, 570,000 strong, was one-half middle class (though this covers a diverse range of occupations) and 29 per cent skilled manual; professionals, managers and senior salaried employees alone represented nearly one-fifth of the total employed,

71

whereas in 1951 they represented one-tenth. The weight of family inheritance as a factor in life chance allocation had diminished. Only 15 per cent of young men aged 20–24 in 1971 relied on family employment; one third had been so employed in 1951.

We can observe two overarching trends: (1) the dwindling away of the viability of self-employment and the growing salience of wage employment and (2) the shift in the balance in the employed workforce from semi-skilled and unskilled labour toward white collar and skilled manual work. By 1971 the new hierarchy of class positions was apparent. The value of various forms of economic resources had shifted, changing the balance of advantage or disadvantage associated with particular skills, qualifications, land, and businesses. Inequalities of income, opportunity, and wealth were distributed in accordance with the new pattern. The contraction of the agricultural labour force and the expansion of senior white collar work were continuous processes. Most changes were not. The real growth in skilled manual and junior white collar work only commenced in the 1960s and continued unabated through the 1970s, as far as can be judged from census-type data.

The changes in the class composition of the Irish workforce emerged from industrial development that was later, more rapid and more state-inspired than in most western societies. So intense were the changes that it is easy to overlook their incompleteness. Even in 1979, a substantial share of the workforce was in residual classes stranded in the course of industrial development, especially farmers on marginal holdings and labourers without skills. The only European parallels for such a presence are in Greece, Portugal and Spain.[10] People in these marginal categories have little opportunity to transfer to the more favourably placed categories; their children's chances are little better, perpetuating marginality within families. So today's class structure contains a substantial number of positions that are viable only insofar as they are underwritten by state social welfare programmes and from which, especially given present economic circumstances, there appears to be no exit. In the mid-1970s, such positions accounted for more than one twelfth of the workforce.

Allocating and negotiating economic rewards

A strategy to industrialise generally comprises the upgrading of the labour force as well as of infrastructure and machinery. Education was elevated to particular prominence in the *Second Programme*, published in 1963. Development and education were to have reciprocal links: the heightened levels of economic performance achieved under the programme could finance improvements in education and training, to be proposed by the 'Investment in Education' study commissioned in that year, and those improvements would ' . . . support and stimulate continued economic expansion. Even the economic returns from investment in education and training are likely to be as high in the long-run as those from investment in physical capital.'[11] Decisions on revitalising Irish education, made and implemented over the next two decades, helped to set the definitive cast to the class structure. Irish society became more meritocratic. Entry to the positions opened up by the new order now depends on evidence of success in second and third level educational institutions.

It should not be assumed that a clear relationship exists between the attributes to which such credentials attest and the nature of the work to be done in the position that requires them. All hierarchies require objective criteria for evaluation and industrial hierarchies require criteria that are based on achievement and can be applied universally. The credentials of scholarly and technical accomplishment have become the general resource by which aspirants to the labour force are differentiated – the currency of social evaluation.

If educational credentials give a general sense of the quality of a workforce, then Ireland by the mid-1970s was on the road to having one of the finest in Europe. By then, Irish participation rates in second-level education exceeded those in Great Britain. The rise was dramatic. In 1964, one-quarter of 17 year olds remained in full-time education, a participation rate that grew to one-half in 1979. A two-thirds growth in participation rates had occurred over that period in third-level education, with some 20 per cent of each cohort of young people entering a third-level institution.[12]

The consequences of this education explosion were equally dramatic. The importance of educational institutions within the society was greatly enhanced, the population better or at least more extensively educated, and the content of that education greatly altered.[13] But the expansion of education, and particularly the opening of opportunities through 'free education' in the 1960s and 1970s, did more to consolidate the advantages of propertied and professional middle class families than to facilitate social mobility: the strong encouragement to educational accomplishment was disproportionately taken up by children from middle class backgrounds. The qualifications so obtained were used to secure for those families the bulk of opportunities becoming available in white collar and skilled industrial employment and self-employment. Participation in second and third-level education was and remained severely restricted along social class lines, with children from substantial proprietorial and upper-middle class professional families forming a share of the student population at higher levels which vastly exceeded their share of the student-aged population. Middle class dominance is strongly evident at the Leaving Certificate standard and in the late 1970s nearly three-quarters of the children of members of the major professions entered a third-level institution, in contrast to less than four per cent of the children of unskilled workers. [14]

The result is a virtual upper middle class monopoly of the advantages that depend on education. If, as in Table 2, we treat the major professions, employers, and managers as constituting the upper

Table 2: Social class selectivities among university entrants

Social Class	1971 Population Aged 0–13	1979 University Entrants
	%	%
Farmers	19.6	16.6
Upper middle class	9.8	37.9
Lower middle class	15.3	26.9
Working class	51.9	14.3
Unknown	3.5	4.2
Total	100.0	100.0

Source: Population percentages are from Census of Population of Ireland 1971 Volume IV *Occupations* (Dublin: Stationery Office 1975) p. 146. University entrants are as stated in The Higher Education Authority *Accounts 1979 and Student Statistics 1979/80* (Dublin: The HEA 1981), p. 64. Upper middle class includes higher professionals and employers and managers; lower middle class includes lower professionals, salaried employees, and intermediate non-manual workers; the working class includes other agricultural occupations, other non-manual, and all three manual categories of the CSO socio-economic groups.

middle class, we find 38 per cent of university entrants in 1979 came from such a background. Working class children, who represented 52 per cent of those of university age, formed only 14 per cent of the university entrants. Certainly a Leaving Certificate or even a third-level degree no longer guarantees privileged employment. But the expected standard of preparation for candidates for a range of opportunities, such as recruitment grades in the civil service or even apprenticeships, has risen, sharpening the divide based on education and thus on class.

So class transformation, which fundamentally altered the hierarchy of positions within the class structure, coincided with processes that acted to ensure an essential stability in the distribution of privileges. The same families, by and large, occupied the most advantaged positions in the old and the new class structures. This is not to deny the gains recorded in working class and small farm families over recent years in educational participation – but so minute was their participation until recently and so extensive the middle class dominance of higher education, that the educational system today is a barrier to social mobility. Similarly, improvements in standards of living have been almost universally experienced, but the differentials between the top and the bottom of the class structure remain. Large scale property-holdings or professional qualifications in the 1950s were able to secure a comparable level of advantage for the children born to such families in the 1960s and 1970s, either through inheritance or through disproportionate shares in the educational credentials that had the greatest labour market value. Those without such resources emigrated or remained in marginal positions within Ireland. Economic growth did not secure the promised social progress.

A new hierarchy also implies a greatly altered set of organisations established or sponsored by class interests to preserve their relative positions. A transformed class hierarchy is thus reflected in the distribution of power within the society. The shift towards wage employment generally and skilled and white collar work particularly is reflected in greater numerical strength of trade union membership and its changing composition. From 328,000 trade union members in 1961, 51 per cent of all employees, membership expanded by 1979 to 499,000 – 65 per cent of all employees. That expansion was more marked – at more than twice the rate – in the 1970s than in the 1960s, with the bulk of the growth occurring in white collar unions. By the 1970s, Ireland had one of the highest levels of trade union membership in the EEC and the highest rate of union growth of any EEC country.[15]

Changes in trade union strength were complemented by extensive consolidation and expansion in the numerical and organisational strength of employer representative bodies over those years, and in the services they provided. The Federated Union of Employers had 1,497 firms as members in 1965; 3,000 firms were on its membership rolls by the end of 1980, together employing more than 50% of all non-agricultural/non-public service employers. Other specialised employer representative organisations, such as the Construction Industry Federation, represented the bulk of the relevant industries by the late 1970s.[16] Similar endeavours by organised agricultural interests have met with less success of late, a reflection of the reduced significance of that economic sector.

The changing population structure

Economic prosperity and changed opportunities affect more than the way people earn their livelihoods. The frameworks within which people reach decisions – on whether to emigrate, on when to marry, or on the ideal family size – will be affected by the new forces governing life chances. For example, the declining significance of inheritance to life chances and the desire to ensure a full education for children, a costly and lengthy enterprise, cannot but influence the strategies people adopt – influence, not determine. Ultimately, the consequences of such altered perspectives become evident in the population structure.

The demographic consequences of Irish economic expansion were soon evident. The first sustained population growth since the Famine was recorded after 1961, and the ages at marriage and family size began to approximate the European norm. The total population of the twenty-six counties had declined steadily from 6.5 million in 1841 to 3.2 million in 1901, and stood at 2.8 million in 1961. That long decline had coincided with a population explosion in the rest of Europe. In the 1960s and 1970s, as the population elsewhere in Europe stabilised, that of Ireland grew, to nearly 3 million in 1971 and 3.4 million in 1981.

The post-1961 reversal reflects the virtual cessation of emigration and an accelerated rate of natural increase. The annual rate of net emigration fell to less than 0.6 per cent of the population between 1961 and 1966, from the 2 per cent experienced in some years during the 1950s, and in the 1971–79 period there was an annual net inflow of

0.4 per cent. The average annual rate of natural increase (the excess of births over deaths) rose from 0.9 per cent in the 1950s to 1 per cent in the 1960s and 1.1 per cent in the 1970s, a significant actual growth in population.[17]

The natural increase component of the growth in population was established by two offsetting trends; a rising marriage rate and a declining marriage fertility rate. Ireland in the early part of this century was characterised by high levels of celibacy and extremely late average age at marriage: 'in the generation born between 1896 and 1905 almost 30 per cent of the males and 25 per cent of the females remaining in Ireland never married, while for those who did marry the mean age of marriage was about 33 years for men and 27 years for women'. Infrequent and late marriages persisted through the economic depression of the 1930s, the Second World War, and agricultural restructuring. But by 1966 the median age at marriage had dropped to 24 for women and 27 for men, and subsequently levelled off in the 1970s at 23 for women and 25 for men. The number of marriages per 1,000 of population peaked at 7.4 in 1973 (as compared with a rate of 8.1 in England and Wales) and declined thereafter to 6.1 in 1977 in Ireland. The impact of economic recession and rising unemployment is in part responsible, but the Irish trend follows the general decline in the popularity of early marriage in the western world.[18]

If the rate of marriage earlier in the century was very low, the fertility of marriage was exceptionally high by European standards. By the middle of the century, Irish families were, on average, twice as large as those in other European countries. This pattern persisted until 'the sharp decline in fertility that occurred in the mid-1960s halted temporarily at the end of the decade, and accelerated during the 1970s'.[19] The falling number of families with four or more children is the most marked change. That decline seems likely to persist: the temporary halt in fertility decline between 1969 and 1971 may have been a response to the Roman Catholic Church's opposition to 'artificial' birth control, but there is no evidence that the 1968 Encyclical *Humanae Vitae* effected a more permanent halt to the declining prevalence of large families. The number of legitimate births per 1,000 married women between the ages of 15 and 44 dropped from 269 in 1946 to 245 in both 1951 and 1961. By 1971 this rate had fallen to 240, and in 1979 stood at 189 per 1,000 married women of child bearing age. As the effects of an increasing rate of marriage and a declining marriage fertility counterbalance, only minor fluctuations in the overall birth rate have occurred.[20]

Emigration, however, had the most decisive impact on Irish demography. Its consequences are manifest today as distortions in the population's age distribution. Approximately one person out of every five born since the foundation of the state and resident in 1951 had emigrated by the end of that decade. The ranks of the young were particularly diminished: of the 502,000 persons aged 10 to 19 in 1951, only 303,000 remained in the country by 1961. While some emigrants were to return during the post-1960 period of sustained employment growth, a large proportion of the generation, now in early middle age, was lost. That disproportion in the age distribution was accentuated by natural increase so that by 1979, 31 per cent of the population was less than 15 years old and 11 per cent was over 65 years of age (see Figure 1). The result is a dependency ratio far higher than that of any other EEC country and a rapidly expanding labour force.[21]

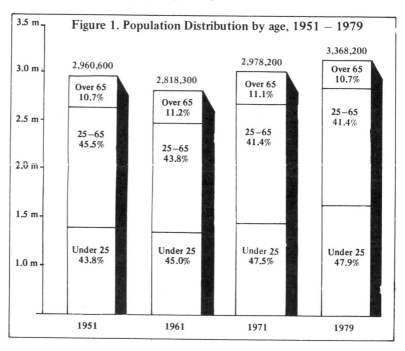

Figure 1. Population Distribution by age, 1951 – 1979

Because emigration was so selective in the social origins of those who left, it was a major force in shaping the post-1960 class structure.

Equally, the selectivities as to which emigrants returned in the 1970s – and at least 100,000 did in the decade – proved important.

First, who emigrated? A full portrait is impossible but the broad answer is clear. The *Investment in Education* report noted that some 82 per cent of Irish-born British residents in 1961 had left school at the age of 15 or earlier. Those leaving in the 1950s and early 1960s were predominantly young, and drawn from agriculture – farm labourers, children of small farmers, and owners of small farms – and from unskilled or semi-skilled manual labouring families. Many were unemployed or never employed before emigrating. Even in the mid-1960s, over two-thirds of recent male emigrants to Britain became manual workers, with another 14 per cent in occupations that paid little better. Female emigrants tended to work in slightly more advantageous occupations, 71 per cent in non-manual work, generally of a routine nature.[22]

The strongest break with the past came in the 1970s with a flow of former emigrants returning to take advantage of opportunities in Ireland. Most were aged 30 to 44 when returning and many reported having improved their occupational skills while in Britain. The limited evidence available suggests that while nearly one-half of the men had left Ireland as unskilled manual workers, only 28% returned as such; 16 per cent left with skills and 27 per cent were working in skilled manual work on their return. One in five returned to farm though only one in eight had been engaged in farming before emigrating.[23] Like their counterparts who had remained in Ireland throughout, those with some minimal level of skill or educational credential were able to improve their life chances and those without were consequently severely restricted.

A less heartening flow of migrants was taking the reverse journey throughout the 1970s. Smaller in number than those returning, the new emigrants were young, mainly in the 20 to 24 age group; some 13,000 individuals emigrated to Britain between 1971 and 1977. But the weight of the relationship between labour markets had clearly shifted, with aspiring emigrants in most years far outnumbering those returning from Britain.[24]

Increasing marriage rates, decreasing age at marriage, and returning emigrants were not evenly experienced by all class categories. Small farmers and unskilled manual workers in the 1970s were demographically as well as economically marginal. Heads of households in such categories were on average far older, fewer were married, and very few households in the categories were at the child-rearing stages of the family cycle. Their situation still reflected the life chances of the 1950s.

The regional pattern

The geographic as well as the class distribution of opportunities shifted in the course of economic development. Industrial location decisions and agricultural support policies established the strength of forces pushing individuals and families away from some areas and pulling them toward others. The results were to be found in the amount of rural depopulation and the influx to urban centres after 1958, as well as in the life chances of individuals and the balance of power between regions and between urban and rural in Irish society. The most basic consequence is that Ireland, unlike other European countries, did not experience a mass inflow of migrants into its largest cities, emigration to Britain was not replaced by migration to Dublin.

The late 1950s marked an important shift in regional development policy. Decentralisation of industrial employment was favoured earlier in the decade as a way of countering the severe regional inequalities in opportunities. The first planning exercise questioned that approach, and thereafter state investment was concentrated in special growth centres, though the desired number of centres remained controversial. The 1968 Buchanan Report expressed a preference for a small number of centres, but was never implemented; consistent policy on whether to seek dispersed or centralised industrial development did not emerge until the early 1970s.

State policy showed greater consistency after 1972, with the IDA's Regional Industrial Plans forming the centrepiece. New employment would be distributed so as to moderate the rate of growth in the Dublin region, encourage substantial industrial development in the other main urban centres, and make lesser population centres the nucleus for small industry concentrations. Development in the West was emphasised.[25] Since the vast bulk of net industrial employment gains during the 1960s and 1970s was through IDA subsidised schemes, the distribution of new employment opportunities closely followed the IDA's regional objectives. Regional shares of total manufacturing employment in 1961 and 1977 index the effect: the Dublin region accounted for 52 per cent in 1961 and 44 per cent in 1977; the combined share of the three most undeveloped planning regions – Donegal, North West, and West – grew from 7 per cent to

10 per cent of the national total. Concern over the rate of unemployment in the Dublin region, however, led to an IDA policy reversal in 1978; 19,000 jobs were targeted for the Eastern Region for 1978-82, to compensate for the net loss in employment the region had previously experienced.[26]

Manufacturing represents, even today, one-fifth of total national employment. A failure to challenge the concentration of administrative and service employment in Dublin, for example, maintained overall employment levels there. That concentration became even more marked in the 1970s. In rural areas, the continuing outflow from agriculture was only partially counterbalanced by the combined employment growth generated from manufacturing, other industry, services and the public sector. So, attention to the imbalance in manufacturing, though successful in dispersing new industrial growth to a degree which has few international precedents, left other imbalances unchanged. Over the 1960s, the Dublin area experienced a net employment gain of 44,000 jobs, while the South-East and the Midlands/West lost, respectively, 8,000 and 33,000 net jobs.[27] And this occurred despite an apparent slowing of the decline in agricultural employment. Thus, even in the 1960s, the exodus from farming was shaping the class structure of individual regions.

Though economic trends and demographic patterns shifted the population to a more urban, Eastern, profile, suburbanisation is perhaps the most significant change of the recent past. The proportion of the population dwelling in urban areas stood at 42 per cent in 1951, 46 per cent in 1961, and became the majority in 1971 at 52 per cent. That growth reflects more the demographic realities of rural and urban areas as expressed in natural increases than internal migration, which is exceptionally low by international standards. But within the Dublin area there was a decisive transfer of population to suburbs. Over the 1970s the Dublin county borough actually declined in population; yet so dynamic were the trends of natural increase and net migration in the remaining areas of the county that its total population grew by 18 per cent over 1971–81 to stand at 1,002,000.[28]

But the Dublin area is populated overwhelmingly by the Dublin-born, an insularity rare among capital cities. If migrants to Dublin are more conspicuous than their numbers would lead one to expect, it is perhaps because they are better educated and of higher socio-economic status than their Dublin-born contemporaries.[29] Migration to Dublin was highly selective; the poorly educated rural-born with restricted life chances emigrated, and settling in Dublin indicated favoured life chances.

The role of the state

The principle that economic expansion was to draw primarily on private enterprise was inscribed at the onset of economic planning.[30] Despite that commitment, the state sector has grown at an accelerated rate over the last two decades. State expenditure on economic services, with the exception of agriculture and fisheries, expanded at a rate faster than GNP during the 1960s and 1970s.[31] State involvement in the provision of social services grew still more rapidly, increasing from the equivalent of 14 per cent of GNP in 1961 to 29 per cent in 1980. Social welfare payments formed the largest component of social expenditure (6 per cent of GNP in 1961 and 11 per cent in 1980), although total expenditure on health services increased more rapidly over that period, rising from 3 per cent to 8 per cent of GNP.[32]

In distributing these vast sums and in levelling taxation to obtain the revenue for doing so, the state increasingly impinged on the life chances of individuals and of families. The state has become a major source of income through its various cash transfer programmes such as unemployment assistance, pensions, and occupational injuries compensation. In 1973, nearly one household in four relied on state transfer payments for more than 30 per cent of its gross income. One half of marginal farmers and 41 per cent of unskilled manual workers were dependent on the state to that extent or greater. The state's responsibilities for income support increased during the 1970s: for urban families, by 1978 state transfers averaged £9.67 weekly, equivalent to nearly ten per cent of average gross income; in 1973, state support amounted to 8.2 per cent of average gross income.[32]

Through the provision of services in health, education, and housing, the state can redistribute income, mitigating inequalities between classes and across the life cycle. Expenditure on health and housing was progressive in 1973, benefiting lower income families more than higher income families. State support for education, on the other hand, was of greatest benefit to higher income families, enhancing the life chances of those already advantaged.[34]

The taxation burden imposed by expanding state responsibilities has been unevenly distributed. Taxation policy has shifted the tax burden on to families. The contribution from taxes on goods and services has been maintained at an exceptionally high level, falling slightly from 53 per cent of total tax revenue in 1965 to 47 per cent in 1978 when the average contribution in EEC countries was 30 per cent.[35] At the same time income taxation has risen rapidly, increasing its contribution to total tax revenue from 17 per cent in 1965 to 29 per cent in 1978. On the other hand, the state has been highly sensitive to the interests of the corporate sector and property owners, both of whose shares in total tax revenue dropped significantly between 1965 and 1978.

The most significant increase in taxation has occurred in income tax. As incomes rose steadily with inflation during the last two decades, personal tax allowances and the starting points of tax bands were left virtually undisturbed, yielding increasing amounts of tax, and capturing a larger proportion of income earners. As a result the average direct taxation taken from urban households grew from 8 per cent of direct income in 1965 to 14 per cent in 1973 and to 18 per cent in 1978. Increases in income taxation have seen certain class categories lose more than others. The effective rate of direct tax levied on semi- and unskilled manual households grew from 14 per cent to 18 per cent between 1973 and 1978, and the rates increased from 17 per cent to 20 per cent in the case of professionals and managers. Households headed by employers and proprietors fared rather better; direct taxes rose from 9 per cent of direct incomes to only 11 per cent between 1973 and 1978. Despite this important anomaly, income taxation is in general progressive, taking a greater proportion from higher incomes than from lower incomes. All other forms of taxation, however, were found to be regressive in 1973, taking a greater proportion from lower than from higher incomes.[36]

State expenditure and taxation as experienced over the 1960s and 1970s raise questions of equity. Working class households assume a substantially greater share of the tax burden. Yet what they receive from the state basically compensates for their disadvantages in the market place. Proprietors and employers, in contrast, are taxed at a far lower rate – facilitating private investment that will enhance their own life chances. Middle class employees, although they are more heavily taxed than proprietors and employers, are not taxed at a rate which would be expected in a rigorously progressive tax system, while they receive a major subsidy in the form of education, significantly improving the prospects of their children in the labour market.

The state also increasingly performs a mediating role in the market between organised interests. Conflicts between employers and employees have led to the creation of institutions for centralised collective bargaining over National Wage Agreements, and these dominated industrial relations from 1970 until 1981. That policy involves the state as a facilitator, but also as the underwriter, through the use of fiscal policy, of peaceful relations both between capital and labour and between the state and its own employees. State induced economic growth, by changing the balance between economic sectors, has allowed the interests of those in the more dynamic non-agricultural sectors to come to the fore. This has had the unintended consequence of displacing the formerly dominant agricultural interests, as evidenced, for instance, by the decline in farm incomes in recent years, the declining proportion of state expenditure on agriculture, and the attempted taxation of farm incomes.

Prospects for the 1980s: stability and change
Ireland entered the 1980s vastly changed from two decades of industrial development. Ironically, that transformation culminated in a narrowing of the possibilities for future development. Constrained by a newly consolidated class structure, a demographic pattern that ensures high levels of dependency within the population for the foreseeable future and a safety valve of emigration that is all but closed, as well as by regional and urban/rural imbalances, the structure of Irish society seems fixed for the 1980s. Moreover, the state has come ever-increasingly to underwrite the status quo through its expenditure commitments. Relativities cannot be altered.

Changes in class structure have altered the bases for the distribution of resources and rewards, but this has not meant that the high level of inequality prevalent in Irish society has been substantially reduced. Income and wealth continue to be highly concentrated, in spite of official promises that social progress would follow economic progress. Perhaps the major change has been the extent of state social intervention to counteract disadvantages thrown up by the market.

Class differences at present are self-perpetuating. The kinds of skills and credentials that offer the possibility of upward mobility are remaining within those families already possessing substantial resources. Even a dramatic expansion in economic growth would not guarantee substantial improvement in equality of opportunity.

The demographic vitality of the 1960s and 1970s was more universally experienced and made natural increase, rather than emigration, the main influence on the population structure. But it imposed major responsibilities: subsidies to ease the burden of

84

dependency within families, a massive investment in education, and, above all, a need to improve employment prospects within Ireland. The concentration of natural increase within urban areas accentuated the imbalance in population between regions and between urban and rural areas. The resources to compensate regions for the outflow from the agricultural workforce through alternative employment are not available. The less developed an area, the greater the resources required to redress the imbalance. But given competition for resources, all in the form of plausible assertions of need, the demands from the urban centres are likely to carry the greatest weight.

The transformation we have described was shaped by economic development that had to redress the kind of distortions usually found in the social structure of post-colonial societies. Dispersed economic dependence has replaced dependence on a single country and many of the problems of an industrialised society have come to replace those of a predominantly agricultural one. It is unlikely, however, that the 1980s will be a period of stagnation or even of stability. One effect of the transformation is to create a highly complex society that is more vulnerable to international events and beyond the effective intervention of any single group. It is striking that today, in contrast to the late 1950s, there is no confidence in Ireland's ability to control its future. No new organisations are being proposed to assist in the task of national development and the experts can only warn of the limits to what state policy can achieve.

Notes to Article

1 Anthony Giddens, *The Class Structure of the Advanced Societies* (London: Hutchinson 1973) pp. 130–131.

2 *Economic Development* Dublin: Stationery Office 1958 p. 11.

3 The argument for importance of the international economic environment is developed in J. Wickham 'The politics of dependent capitalism: international capital and the nation state' in A. Morgan and B. Purdie (eds.) *Ireland: Divided Nation, Divided Class* London: Ink Links 1980.

4 See Loraine Donaldson, *Development Planning in Ireland* (New York: Praeger 1965) p. 39.

5 Gross Domestic Product is derived from Eoin O'Malley, *Industrial Policy and Development: A Survey of the Literature from the Early 1960s* (NESC Report No. 56) Dublin: Stationery Office 1980 p. 21 Table 3.

6 Employment statistics are obtained from *Trend in Employment and Unemployment* (Dublin: Stationery Office various years); public service figures are working estimates from a project on public sector employment being carried out by Miceal Ross at the Economic and Social Research Institute.

7 Investment statistics are from Industrial Development Authority *Annual Report* (Dublin: IDA Ireland various years), exports to Britain are

derived from *Trade Statistics of Ireland* (Dublin: Stationery Office various years).

8 The Census of Population provides far more detailed information on occupations of men than it does for women. As a result, it is not possible to re-classify the female labour force statistics into adequate class categories.

9 Cohort emigration and family employment rates are calculated from Census of Population of Ireland volumes as follows: 1946: Vol. V (Parts I and II) 1951: Vol III, Part II 1961: Volumes II and V 1971: Volumes II and V.

10 The comparable statistics are published in Eurostat *Basic Statistics of the Community* (Luxembourg, Statistical Office of the European Communities 1980) p. 17 and p. 19.

11 *Second Programme for Economic Expansion Part I*. Dublin, Stationery Office, 1963, p. 13.

12 The participation rate for 17 year olds is from *Investment in Education* (Dublin: Stationery Office 1966) p. 4; the 1979 rate is from Department of Education *Statistical Report 1979/80* (Dublin: Stationery Office 1981 p. 2. Third level participation rate is estimated for 1964 in Investment in Education p. 4 at 5.9%; a 1979 rate of 10.1% for 18–24 year olds, the same base as the 1964 estimate, is calculated from Department of Education, *Statistical Report 1979/80* and Census of Population of Ireland 1979 *Volume II* p. 16. The estimate of a 20% entrance rate to third level institutions is from David Rottman, Damian Hannan, Niamh Hardiman, and Miriam Wiley, *The Distribution of Income in the Republic of Ireland: A Study of Social Class and Family Cycle Inequalities*, (Dublin: The Economic and Social Research Institute 1982) p.

61.

13 A. Dale Tussing, *Irish Educational Expenditures – Past, Present and Future* (Dublin: The Economic and Social Research Institute 1978) p. 58. Tussing notes that in the 1950s and before, Irish first and second level education was concentrated on an 'arts' curriculum, with little scientific technical content: 'until fairly recently the schools have not been viewed principally in terms of their role in preparing youth for employment; rather, their role has been more moral, intellectual and religious.'

14 Rottman et al. pp. 50–66.

15 Statistics on trade union membership are derived from three sources: James F. O'Brien, *A Study of National Wage Agreements in Ireland* (Dublin: The Economic and Social Research Institute Paper No. 104 1981) p. 21; Commission of Inquiry on Industrial Relations *Report* (Dublin) 1981 pp. 21–24; Christopher T. Whelan *Worker Priorities, Trust in Management and Prospects for Workers' Participation* (Dublin: Economic and Social Research Institute, draft report 1982) pp. 5.7–5.8.

16 The Federated Union of Employers *Annual Report for 1966* (Dublin: FUE 1967; The Federated Union of Employers *Annual Report for 1980* (Dublin, FUE, 1981); Commission of Inquiry on Industrial Relations *Report* pp. 41–45.

17 Central Statistics Office *Census of Population of Ireland 1981: Preliminary Report* (Dublin, Stationery Office 1981) p. xi.

18 Quote from Brendan Walsh 'Recent demographic trends in the Republic of Ireland', *Population Trends* (Autumn, 1980) p. 5; median ages at marriage are from Walsh 1980 p. 7. Marriages per 1,000 population are

from Central Statistics Office, *Report on Vital Statistics 1977* (Dublin: Stationery Office, 1981) with England and Wales comparisons from Central Statistical Office, *Annual Abstract of Statnstics 1982* (London: HMSO 1982).

19 Historical material and quote from Walsh 1980 pp. 6–7.

20 Information on births was derived from the following sources *Statistical Abstract of Ireland 1946; Report on Vital Statistics* 1966, 1977; *Quarterly Report on Births, Deaths and Marriages* December 1980. The number of men and women aged 15 – 44 is from the Census of Population of Ireland 1979 *Volume 11* Table 1C. More generally, see Walsh 1980.

21 Central Statistics Office, Census of Population of Ireland 1979; Volume II, *Ages and Marital Status Classified by Areas* (Dublin: Stationery Office 1981). Comparative dependency ratios are given in Laraine Joyce and A. McCashin, *Poverty and Social Policy* (Dublin: The Institute of Public Administration 1982) p. 7.

22 Economist Intelligence Unit, *Studies on Immigration from the Commonwealth* (London, Economist Intelligence Unit, 1963); reproduced in *Investment in Education,* 1963, p. 180 and J. G. Hughes and B. M. Walsh, 'Migration flows between Ireland, the United Kingdom and the Rest of the world, 1966–71', *European Demographic Information Bulletin* 7, No. 4 (1976), pp. 125–149.

23 Age 30–44 is from F. X. Kirwan 'Recent Anglo-Irish migration – the evidence of the British Labour Force Surveys' *Economic and Social Review* Vol. 13 No. 3 (1982) p. 202. Other data are from an EEC funded Study of Housing Conditions of Migrant Workers, sponsored by the Directorate for Social Affairs in 1974; the data

cited are produced in B.J. Whelan and J.G. Hughes *A Survey of Returned and Intending Emigrants in Ireland* (Dublin, The Economic and Social Research Institute, draft report 1976) Tables 3A.4 and 3B.10.

24 Kirwan 'Recent Anglo-Irish migration' p. 203.

25 Miceal Ross, 'Comprehensiveness in regional policy', in B. Dowling and J. Durkan (eds.) *Irish Economic Policy: A Review of Major Issues* (Dublin: The Economic and Social Research Institute 1978) pp. 306–317.

26 Employment data for the 1961–71 period are from Patrick N. O'Farrell, *Regional Industrial Development Trends in Ireland 1960–1973* (Dublin, The Industrial Development Authority 1975) p. 15, data from 1971–77 are taken from M. Ross and B. Walsh *Regional Policy and the Full-Employment Target* (Dublin, The Economic and Social Research Institute, Policy Paper No. 1 1979) p. 24. IDA targets are stated in *IDA Industrial Plan 1978–82* Dublin, IDA Ireland 1979.

27 Miceal Ross, 'Comprehensiveness in regional policy' 1979 p. 313.

28 1951 to 1971 urbanisation trends are from P. N. O'Farrell *Urbanisation and Regional Development in Ireland* The National Economic and Social Council Report No. 45 (Dublin, Stationery Office 1979) p. 30, and the changes between 1971–81 in County Dublin are from *Census of Population of Ireland 1981 Preliminary Results* 1981.

29 Bertram Hutchinson *Social Status and Inter-Generational Social Mobility in Dublin* (Dublin: The Economic and Social Research Institute 1969) pp. 7–9.

30 *Programme for Economic Expansion* (Dublin, Stationery Office 1958) p. 8.

31 F. Gould 'The growth of Irish public expenditure 1947–77' *Administration* Vol. 29 No. 2 (1981) p. 128.

32 Kieran A. Kennedy, 'Poverty and changes in the socio-economic environment in Ireland 1971–81' Paper read to the Council for Social Welfare Conference, Kilkenny, 6–8 November 1981 p. 15.

33 Rottman et al. p. 84; D. Rottman and D. Hannan, 'Fiscal welfare and inflation: winners and losers' in *The Irish Economy and Society in the 1980s: Proceedings of the 21st Anniversary Conference* (Dublin: The Economic and Social Research Institute 1981) p. 97.

34 Philip O'Connell, 'The distribution and redistribution of income in the Republic of Ireland' *Economic and Social Review* Vol. 13 No. 4 (1982) p. 268.

35 Organisation for Economic Co-operation and Development *Revenue Statistics of OECD Member Countries 1965–1980* (Paris: OECD 1981).

36 Central Statistics Office, Household Budget Inquiry/Survey 1966; 1973; Vol. 3 1978. Rottman and Hannan p. 97; O'Connell p. 276.

Whatever Happened to Irish Government?

THOMAS J. BARRINGTON

Why Government?

Why is government necessary? What is its role? How can it be more effective? How does one fairly judge its performance?

This last is just what the plain people of Ireland do every few years or so: those politicians who have been entrusted with the duty of government give an account of their stewardship and, amid all the passion and shouting, are judged accordingly. But in the longer run, over a quarter of a century or more, when the conflicts of party and personality have been muted, what criteria does one use? And in any event, how relevant are these questions in assessing Irish public administration over the past twenty-five years?

Government is a complex affair in a free society, entrusted only with tackling intractable issues of society that otherwise would not be solved at all, or badly solved, and providing those services that would not be provided, or badly provided, if there were no government. Thus, we have government providing internal order and external defence, communications, economic support, social services, cultural continuity, and institutions to underpin these. One has only to reflect on the great variety of these responsibilities to realise how great a role government plays in modern society and, of necessity, to enquire how much of what government does is necessary for the wellbeing of society and how much of what must be done is well done?

Government is, of its nature, a force making for a high, long-term rationality in society – as, for example, when the sum of individual and group decisions leads to social instability or injustice or endangers long-term security. An important criterion by which to judge the quality of government, therefore, is the level of rationality it seeks to achieve. Is it identifying the big underlying issues of society and concerning itself with clarifying and solving them so far as circumstances will permit? Is it showing itself competent to rise above the pressing short-term problems to engage itself with those long-term issues that will dominate the future? Is it gearing itself to command future events?

When we think of government we think not only of the well publicised world of politics but also of the quality of the administration of the public services. Government is a partnership, the partnership of politics and administration. That partnership, when things go well, can be seen as something like a successful marriage – the allocation of roles real and largely distinct, yet fluid when one partner or the other is under stress, wrapped in an envelope of mutual responsibility. This insight of mutual and reciprocal responsibility in the practice of government suggests that when something goes wrong it is not a question of whose is the blame: the responsibility, and the responsibility to do all one can to put things right, becomes joint and several.

So, if we think now – as so many do – that Irish government has for many years been going through a bad patch, it is useless to look for scapegoats: what is important is to learn what has gone wrong and to try to devise means of putting things to rights.

If we in Ireland look back over the performance of government in the past twenty five years we can see three fairly distinct periods – the first ten years or so, when things promised well; an intervening period of 5 years when the clouds began to gather; and a final period of ten years when unsolved difficulties have continued to mount. Many of the difficulties were wholly or largely outside our control – the troubles in the North of Ireland, the cost of energy, world recession and inflation. Some, like our especially high level of inflation and unemployment, have been partly within our control. Others have been basically within our own control, such as the state of the public finances, capital and current; the ruthlessness of the special interests; the collapse of planning and of other administrative techniques; the quality of many public services; the disarray of administrative institutions, central, local and functional; the failure to engage in institutional modernisation and reform.

Twenty-five years ago the country was sunk in a crisis of morale; it went through, in the phrase of an authoritative commentator,[1] "a dark night of the soul". It was government, both its political and administrative sides, that created a new spirit of hope, enterprise, and innovation. The harking back to an insular, rural past, was replaced by determination to look out into the western world, to learn from it, and to be a part of its enterprises. The new spirit worked like a charm. There *was* a future for the country. Material growth and possessions were there for – the grabbing? It all seemed so easy! Within a decade morale shot from the basement through the roof. As the difficulties began to close in the response was not to tackle them with that so recently acquired sense of realism and confidence but to let them accumulate and to let morale once again deflate. In that quarter century Irish society travelled a long way but, in terms of its own self-reliance, it has almost completed a full circle, becoming once more introspective, uncertain, apathetic.

There have been notable exceptions of course and, in the context of government, great preoccupations: the North, membership of the European Community, energy, to name but three that have heavily diverted the talents and time of the best; but overall, the response by government to the challenge of our capabilities has not been maintained.

The prepared mind

Towards the beginning of our period, Gerard Sweetman, then Minister for Finance, had taken the tough decision to recommend the appointment as Secretary to the Department of Finance of an exceptionally able, younger man, T.K. Whitaker, 'over the heads' as the saying goes, of a number of able, older ones. Two years later in 1958, with Sweetman out of office, his successor, James Ryan, could commend to the government a major fruit of that decision,[2] the study *Economic Development*[3] that Whitaker, with some close collaborators, had prepared. The document had a number of facets, notably its essentially *political* concern to restore morale by instilling confidence. The basis for overall progress could be laid by giving priority to economic growth, by adopting realistic objectives for that growth, and by firmly relating detailed decision-making and policies to that end. The *First Programme for Economic Expansion*[4] was, therefore, a document that aimed to achieve good government through both political and administrative means: the political concerned with leadership and morale, the administrative, at heart, concerned to get the public capital investment programme under control and geared to the objective of growth.

This, unlike Pallas Athene, did not spring full-panoplied from the progenitor's head: it was in gestation for a decade. As far back as 1949 Patrick Lynch as economic adviser to the Taoiseach had persuaded John Costello that as well as a current budget there should be a public capital one;[5] the Swedes had shown that this could be a powerful engine of growth. Unfortunately, the political and administrative techniques of operating that system had to be learned through the slow process of trial and error. The realisation that social Keynesianism as then understood would not do the trick in our kind of society was one reason for the disillusion of the mid fifties. What criteria for public capital investment could be devised? In 1956 the Capital Investment Advisory Committee under the chairmanship of John Leydon, was set up[6] and, in three vigorous reports helped to clarify the sorts of values that should, in the conditions of that time, govern public capital decisions.[7] Earlier, in 1956, Whitaker, in a notable paper to the Statistical and Social Inquiry Society of Ireland set out his own thinking on these matters.[8] *Economic Development* and the *First Programme for Economic Expansion* translated this thinking into a practical action programme. The process of idea, practical experiment, disillusion, review, and renewed thought had taken a decade to develop; but by then the intellectual foundations had been laid and decisive, rapid and successful building could begin so that Ireland, a decade late, could join the great post-war upsurge of economic development.

It was inevitable – and a good part of their strength – that the documents, prepared almost entirely in the Department of Finance, should rest mainly on rationalising the public capital programme. It was one of the retrogressions, as time went on, that this link between the planning system, the public capital programme and the annual budget should have become progressively weaker, notwithstanding that for nearly the whole of that time planning remained within the Department of Finance side by side with the normal administration of the public finances, a vivid example of that constant drift to particularism that is a besetting sin of Irish public administration.

The adoption of planning – or of 'programming' as it was cautiously called – was not the only major innovation of those years. In some ways the most remarkable change – because it represented a reversal not only of policies but of the whole way of thinking about Irish development – was the abandonment of protective self-sufficiency for the idea of export-led growth.[9]

So the Industrial Development Authority began to emerge from its civil service chrysalis and to take on something of its present form. Coras Trachtala, originally founded in 1952 to stimulate dollar exports, had its remit widened to cover all industrial exports. The remarkable experiment at Shannon began under the committed leadership of Brendan O'Regan. This turning towards the outside world flowed from the realisation of what was happening in Europe under the Treaty of Rome and that here was a chance to emerge from the isolation of our Atlantic mists into a more congenial clime. Not least of the attractions was the chance to escape from the British stranglehold on Irish agricultural development. It all took longer than seemed possible at the time; but the speed, drive and clearheadedness of this major piece of decision-making represented a remarkable example of politico-administrative leadership, that is, of effective government.

By one of those happy chances of history the 1957 crisis of morale did not find the governmental system unprepared. The momentum of what had been thought and discussed in darker times was sufficient to propel this society to successful economic performance throughout the sunny sixties. The lift-off, psychologically and economically, in the late fifties shows how, in the words of Louis Pasteur, 'fortune favours the prepared mind'.

The process of applied thinking in the economic area of government has not been matched by comparable activity in other areas – infrastructural, social, institutional, political. Indeed, the economic success, whilst obscuring the need for balanced development of those areas, made that development the more necessary. There is no respite in government – success, no less than failure, calls for constant initiative and action and, as government grows bigger and more complex, its successful practice calls for ever greater sophistication. It is clear that a major part of that sophistication is to be ahead of the immediate pressure of events, to be concerned with the 'oughts' well before they become the 'musts'.

The infrastructural debacle

This was soon illustrated in the infrastructural area. In conjunction with 'town and regional' the word 'planning' had long been a respectable term. Town and regional planning had been a responsibility of local government under two, curiously conditional, Acts of 1934 and 1939. Under these, each local authority adopting them had to prepare a plan setting out permissible physical or infrastructural development for, it seemed, all time. By the early 1950s, no such plan had been prepared. In 1953[10] however, the Courts, at the instance of a building contractor, required the Dublin Corporation to produce its plan. Only when this emerged was it seen that the law, if it were to be followed, required the production of intellectual monstrosities and administrative nightmares. The law clearly required drastic amendment, but not until another legal action was threatened did new proposals emerge in what became the Local Government (Planning and Development) Act, 1963.

A formidable legal and institutional apparatus was erected, but has proved extraordinarily sterile. What values was it intended to realise? What sorts of infrastructural and cultural policies should it implement? How were these to be shaped with prospects of success? The great engine found itself operating in a vast intellectual scrubland in which, in a whole generation, virtually no cultivation had taken place. To take the most dramatic example, what was to be done about the growth, the decay, and the redevelopment of Dublin? What was the role of government in relation to the capital city? (A group of students in Hume Street showed the limits of positive governmental vandalism; but overall?). What was to be the role of the city government itself, incapable of reversing the momentum of its own initial mistake at Wood Quay?

So much for the local and regional level, but what form of planning was devised to relate the positive developmental works of local authorities on roads, housing, and sanitary services – all financed by capital provided by central government – with a coherent form of national planning for infrastructural development with overall priorities and clearcut and real financial commitments? In the seventies as the long decline of population began to be reversed, a special priority was given to housing, and here some remarkable work was done. Other aspects of infrastructural development – such as transport, communications, industrial development, all largely financed from the public capital programme – were related together largely at haphazard. Policies were devised for the development of some infrastructural services but not for others; while planning – which is about the ordering and co-ordination of policies – simply did not take off.

What emerges is that 'planning' is a severe intellectual exercise and this requires, in the infrastructural area, at least as much commitment to hard thought, to unflinching review, and to conceptual development as in the economic area. For all its long and respectable pedigree and for all its vast capital needs, (in recent years some 60% of the Capital Programme[11]) infrastructural 'planning' has revealed a disconcerting side to the quality of Irish government. The recent frenetic attempt to tackle the telecommunications tangle and the sorry fate of the recent Roads Plan,[12] illustrate how far government has, in practice, fallen below the level of the 1960s. So far, there is nothing to show that anything has been learned for the practice of government from this experience.

Emerging social issues
For a third, newly emerged area, social development, one can paint a somewhat different, perhaps more hopeful, picture in that we can see the learning process of government at work – slowly and patchily, as is the way, but with some assurance. Social expenditure as a generator of growth in an open economy had failed in the fifties and the new thinking gave absolute priority in new spending and policies to generating economic growth. This, it was rightly argued, would provide the means for social spending which, in the words of the Third Programme,[13] would involve an 'equitable sharing' of what was going. But what was 'equitable'? Were there principles that might govern the process of social redistribution? A rapidly growing economic system could look after the rewards of those who participated in it. But even within that system how were those rewards to be shared? If the logic of the private enterprise system was greed, then everyone could shout for his share – and did. Government tried to devise what it called 'Incomes Policies' but with, on the whole, indifferent success. A new Department of Labour was set up and many improvements in labour law and conditions introduced. Nonetheless, the underlying malaise of a society unable to resolve this issue of redistribution, has continued to grow until it is now a big contributor to the increasing ungovernability of the society as a whole. We shall be coming back to this surprising challenge of relative affluence – but for now let us mention it as one major issue in the problem of social distribution.

The second issue was the development of specific social services, notably education and health. In 1965 there was published the report of an OECD group, under Patrick Lynch, *Investment in Education,*[14] that provided a blueprint from 1966 for a dynamic Minister for Education, Donogh O'Malley, and a stimulus for a Department long regarded as a passive facilitator of spontaneous educational growth but now, under the influence of these inspirations, to become a major force in educational development.[15] Earlier in 1966, O'Malley, then the Minister for Health, had published a white paper on the re-organisation of the health services.[16] This owed something to the discussions of a Dail Committee on those services that, apparently, never reported but largely reflected the thinking that had been going on within the Department of Health. O'Malley soon moved to Education but the impetus was maintained and led to the re-organisation and the major development of the health services under the Health Act, 1970.[17]

In these two services of education and health, and in others such as housing, 'equitable sharing' seemed to require that they be made available as freely or as cheaply to as many people as possible and, where this was not financially feasible, that the burden be eased by tax concessions.

A third issue was the transfer of resources from the haves to the havenots, both by increasing benefits and by extending their range. The early assumption was that 'equitable sharing' here would mean increasing benefits by about the same, relatively rapid, proportion as the total resources of the society were increasing. The discovery, launched at the famous 1971 Kilkenny 'Poverty' Conference of the Catholic Council for Social Welfare, of the incidence and extent of poverty in Ireland was a major shock;[18] for the future 'equity' clearly would mean – amongst a number of other changes – a rapid *increase* in the proportion transferred.

Improvements in individual social services – notably education and health – and in the transfers led to a rapid rise in total social expenditure and in its proportion – to about half of a rapidly rising expenditure by central government.[19] This at a time when, from 1973, the economy had begun to flounder and its overall management had already lost its sense of direction. The problems produced by this rise were compounded by the extent to which the social services were labour intensive and the rate at which labour costs in them were increasing.

Already, by the mid-1960s, the need to give some general thought to the principles of social development had become apparent. Following the Friis report,[20] sponsored by the Social Affairs Division of the United Nations for the Institute of Public Administration, the need for a programme of applied social research was accepted.

Accordingly, the Economic Research Institute was remodelled in 1966 to become the Economic and Social Research Institute. The third (and last) plan, the Third Programme for Economic and *Social* Development 1968-72, had, in its title and briefly in its text, formally recognised the principle, if not much else, of the complex relationship of getting and spending.[21]

It was not until the former advisory National Industrial and Economic Council (1960-72) (NIEC) was reconstituted in 1973 as the National Economic and *Social* Council (NESC) – this following pressure from the Council for Social Welfare – that real progress began to be made in the understanding of how haphazard and contradictory had been the growth of the social services. A series of notable NESC reports over the past decade has documented the extent to which, to take one example, indiscriminate subsidisation and taxation reliefs tend to benefit the better, rather than the worse, off.[22] This bears out the cogency of one of Gunnar Myrdal's arguments[23] that the sum of ad hoc governmental interventions in any area is wasteful and contradictory, and that, in consequence, planning is necessary for rationality, economy and effectiveness.

This illustrates that there is a subject of social development as part of the process of government; that it is concerned with great emotional and disruptive forces; that it raises issues transcending the development of individual social services; that it is concerned with the wise and humane – that is, planned – use of vast public expenditures; and that it takes a long time to tease out its main principles and, perhaps, a very long time to incorporate them into the year-to-year process of government.

Nolumus mutari

In a fourth area – institutional development – major issues have also emerged but progress in solving them has been wholly inadequate. The last quarter of a century has seen the state in Ireland take on a greatly enlarged role, qualitatively and quantitatively – qualitatively in the aspiration to 'plan for national development' and quantitatively by some doubling of the ratio of public expenditure to national income.[24] There has been institutional change in consequence, not by institutional *development* but by a combination of varying responses: in the legislative bodies, institutional paralysis; in the popularly elected local bodies, institutional decay; and in the rest, institutional proliferation – proliferation within the institutions and proliferation between them. These responses suggest drift, not the conscious development of the institutions of government for national development.

So far as the administrative side of government is concerned, the heart of the matter is at the level of the senior civil service where, under ministers, the problems of government are gathered together for analysis, policy formulation and control.

The growth of government over the past 25 years has been formidable. In real terms the growth of central government expenditure has been about sixfold.[25] The number of government departments (including the two large 'offices' of Revenue and Public Works) has risen from 15 to 20 and the number of civil servants has about doubled.[26] Even allowing for the 'hiving off' to state-sponsored bodies of work formerly done by civil servants, this does not seem to be a disproportionate rate of growth.

Contrast this with the growth in the higher civil service, taken here (somewhat arbitrarily) to mean the general service grades from secretary to assistant principal, plus the corresponding ranks in the Department of Foreign Affairs, in the 20 departments and major offices. The figures may be summarised as follows:

	1956-7	1982	% Increase
Deputy Secs. and higher	29	72	148
Asst. Secretaries	53	102	92
Principals	108	386	248
Asst. Principals	196	930	374
Totals	386	1490	286

In general, the administrative class has almost quadrupled in the past quarter of a century. It is instructive to compare this pattern with what has been happening at the level of overall administrative co-ordination; the centre of the thinking part of the administrative side of government. Here the three crucial departments are Taoiseach, Finance and Public Service:

Department	1956-7	1982	% Increase
	Administrative Staff (Nos)		
Taoiseach	4	35	
Finance	42	187	
Public Service		141	
Totals	46	363	700

While the administrative class, as defined, has risen almost fourfold, that part of it concerned with overall co-ordination has risen eightfold.

There has been, therefore, a great growth in that part of the civil service concerned with the *thinking* part of government and, especially dramatically, that part concerned with the co-ordination of that thinking; but, as is apparent, this has not been accompanied by increased thoughtfulness in the evolution of new policies and effective plans for its emerging dilemmas. Indeed, there is steadily mounting evidence to suggest that in *identifying* problems, in *appraisal* of projects, in *co-ordination* of policies, in *planning*, in *implementation* of decisions, in *management*, and even in concern for *safety*, there are some decisive indications of what one must deduce as decline. There is not space to illustrate this judgement in detail, but a few references to document it must be made.

Enough has been said above to illustrate the failure to *identify* soon enough, or at all, major problems of a long-term programme for national development. Below there is some discussion of the significance of the administrative failure to grasp the implications of the alienation of the people.

As to *appraisal*, consider the fate of the Public Capital Programme, the flagship of the whole enterprise. In recent years, Irish capital investment, has been, as a proportion of GNP, amongst the highest of the 24 members of the OECD, normally second only to that of Japan;[28] so relatively we have been investing very heavily. Of total capital formation the public sector contributes nearly half and directly influences a good part of the remainder.[29] Now, we have little or no economic growth *and* seriously deficient public services, a clear sign of poor appraisal. Various techniques – capital appraisal, cost benefit, programming planning budgeting – to improve the sophistication of appraisal were tried and because they did not fulfil (excessive) expectations were, like the toys of a wanton child, simply thrown away leaving an inadequate legacy of disciplined thinking.

One has only to look at the social services, at taxation, at the slow – and still partial – coming together of industrial, infrastructural, and educational development, to realise how ill-*coordinated* and haphazard in practice is the operation overall of so much of government activity.

Much of this might have been remedied if we had made a success of *planning* after the First Programme. The more ambitious Second and Third Programmes had to be abandoned and since then, apart from a flurry of documents[30] issued in a spirit of 'irrational optimism'[31] from the short-lived Department of Economic Planning and Development, there has been, to the time of writing, nothing at all.

A selective view tends to be taken about the *implementation* of governmental decisions. For example, the Third Programme for Economic and Social Development, 1968-72, said that each department would be equipped with a 'development unit'.[32] In 1970 the government adopted the Devlin proposal that each department should have four staff units, one of them for planning. Only now are these becoming general in the departments. (This is not to argue that organisation of itself will lead to policy formulation and its integration into planning. For example, the then Department of Transport and Power, to its credit, quickly set up a planning unit – yet look at what recent reports have to say about transport policy and planning!)[33] In 1967 the government announced the so-called 'decentralisation' of two government departments to provincial towns, and early in 1979 the dispersal of parts of others to 'about eight' provincial towns.[34] In the former context an inter-departmental committee was set up in 1975 to assist in implementing the Devlin proposal[35] for a 'very early examination' of the problems of the co-ordination of the field activities of all departments and of local authorities at regional level, what came to be called 'sub-national systems'; but nothing has emerged.

The quality of *management* in the telecommunications service and as between the Department of Finance on the one hand and the Department of Posts and Telegraphs on the other, has been documented in the Dargan Report.[36] The belated, and disastrous, introduction of automatic data processing in the Department of Social Welfare has resulted in much suffering for poor people.

Lastly, no one can read the Costello Report on the Whiddy Island disaster,[37] or the so far available newspaper reports of the Keane Report on the Stardust disaster, without being seriously concerned about the concern for safety of a number of public bodies in times of changing technology.

This recital illustrates some things that have gone wrong, but against that, of course, there are many things that have gone well. (Contrast, for example, the early and brilliant computerisation in Revenue with the Social Welfare story). One must always recognise the vast amount of dedicated work that goes on. But government is about problems and enough has emerged to the public eye that a great increase in the *size* of the administrative class seems to be far from matched by an

100

increase in its overall performance; to achieve better performance calls for much better organisation and especially for active administrative development to make better use of the vast human resources and qualities available in the public service.

In 1959 I argued that 'the next necessary thing' in ensuring adequate policy formulation was positive action to enhance the quality of the higher civil service by a sophisticated promotion and mobility policy for the grades from assistant principal upwards, so that talent be identified and developed.[38] Only now is some small progress being made in this crucial area – a quarter of a century lost through the inertia of civil service management and the narrow selfishness of civil service unions.[39]

Already in 1959, Professor (now Sir) Charles Carter, then a member of the Capital Investment Advisory Committee, said: 'It is unwise to enter the competitive world of Five Year Plans without putting the planning machinery right first. It is not only unwise; it is dangerous'.[40] By the mid-1960s some of these dangers were becoming evident in NIEC and elsewhere as anxiety about the outcome of the Second Programme began to mount. There followed the setting up, in 1966, of the Public Services Organisation Review Group under the chairmanship of Liam St J. Devlin. The Group's remit was:

> Having regard to the growing responsibilities of Government, to examine and report on the organisation of the Departments of State at the higher levels, including both the appropriate distribution of functions as between both Departments themselves and Departments and other bodies.

The Devlin Report of 1969 proposed a number of structural changes, mainly concerned to ensure that the higher civil service had a clear duty to see its primary role as policy formulation and planning and that it be freed and adequately equipped for that task. The three crucial Devlin recommendations – the setting up of the Department of the Public Service, the introduction of the four staff units (for planning finance, personnel and organisation) and the division of departments into policy units (aireachts) around ministers, and executive units on the lines of the state-sponsored bodies – were accepted by the government in 1970 and 1971. In the aireacht case there were to be experiments in four (later five) departments.

Now twelve years later, there is little to show, but the problems remain and grow. If Devlin is not the answer, what answers is the civil service system itself producing? If, as I would hold, the answer is 'little or none' the service has left itself open to very severe criticism indeed. The abortive 'sub-national' inquiry (P. 00 above) is a telling illustration of this failure.

The Devlin proposals offered, in some degree, a means of getting an increasingly complex governmental system under effective political and administrative control. The great growth in the tasks of Irish government has not been adequately reflected in the role of a minister as envisaged in the Ministers and Secretaries Act, 1924 – something similar to that of the owner of a village shop, directly relating to every customer and taking *all* the necessary decisions. But Irish government with this year a turnover of almost £6bn., now resembles in many ways a transnational firm. These, to survive, have had to adjust the role of top management to cope with extended responsibilities. Many politicians, especially those with experience of office, recognise the problem; but others, especially those without such experience, are deeply embedded in that village shop. Given this division on the political side, and the inertia – indeed some active hostility – on the administrative side, one can understand why those politicians who took the necessary decisions have been slow to demand that they be effectively implemented.

Less understandable is the gap between the legislature and the process of government, and the sense of unreality about the proceedings of the two Houses of the Oireachtas. Even the parliamentary question system has become so bloated as to be virtually useless. Procedural reform now gets some political thought, but there seems little momentum behind the idea that the legislature in this country, as in others, should play a more positive part in considering what ought to be done about the emerging problems and should exact a higher standard of public accountability.

The exception, the Joint Committee on State-Sponsored Bodies, has made a considerable number of reports on individual state-sponsored bodies raising issues of considerable public interest, but not one report has so far been discussed by either House. Similarly, the work of the Joint Committee on Secondary Legislation of the European Communities is impassively received.

In general, informed study and discussion of the problems of government occurs, not in the legislature, but in other institutional structures, formal and informal. For example, the principles, objectives, priorities and progress of planning have been the business not of the legislature but of two appointed bodies, the National Industrial and Economic Council and its successor the National Economic and Social Council. Similarly, strategic decisions about the society have been reached with the 'social partners' or with the great vocational and corporate interests, not with the legislature. One wonders how the democratic system can maintain itself when its central institution is content to be largely irrelevant to such major decision-making.

Least understandable of all is the fate that has befallen the local government system. In many countries local government is provided for under the national constitution and administration of local services under popularly elected representatives is regarded as a key-stone of democracy; but over the past 25 years that key-stone has, in this country, been so chipped away and the local representative system has been treated with such apparent contempt that either other countries are quite mistaken or at least part of our governmental edifice is in danger of collapse.

As one looks back over the past 25 years it becomes clear that just too many of the crucial institutions of our democracy have been, and are being, neglected. Given this widening gap in the degree of acceptance of change, it is no wonder that the gravest of all the domestic problems that have emerged in those years is that of our own governability, daily bedevilling the practice of politics and administration. It is as if an ice floe were to crack and break, leaving government on one part and the governed on the other, each drifting steadily, inexorably apart.

Social responsibility

In the long run government cannot operate without the consent of the governed or of some considerable section of them, as the government of Northern Ireland discovered. If popular consensus begins to be withdrawn and breaches grow in the sense of social cohesion, the foundations of healthy government are undermined. The larger government becomes and the more pervasive its operations, the more crucial become consensus and cohesion. This is not just a question of the degree of popular support that political parties can evoke: it applies to the whole structure, political and administrative. There is wholly inadequate recognition of this point both at the level of politics and, most particularly, at the level of administration. The consequence has been the hastening drift to ungovernability.

Our period opened with the recognition, at both political and administrative levels, that crucial to success was the raising of the morale of the people. Then we became, in Stalin's phrase, 'dizzy with success'. Then again, as over-confidence began to wane, arose a new problem – how to restore a reasonable degree of trust in the virtues of collective discipline and social morality, values essential to the effective practice of government.

As society develops the degree of interaction within it much increases. A local disruption, therefore, can have damaging effects far and wide. This point was made by the Irish bishops in an insufficiently discussed pastoral issued in 1977, which stressed:

In this new situation we just cannot continue to think and act in the old selfish and individualistic ways. Unless the new fact of interdependence is accompanied by a sense of community and brotherhood, then society is bound to get more and more violent and destructive.[41]

In a book published in 1980,[42] Professor J. J. Lee has this to say:

It would be hard to argue that even the most selfish group of workers like the maintenance men who went on strike in 1969, exhibit a cruder moral sense than the most selfish sectors of other, and more affluent, groups. Like those veterinary surgeons laden down with their trophies from the battle against brucellosis, or the big farmers wending their way in sombre procession to the poor house in Brussels, or the doyens of the Incorporated Law Society striving might and main to ensure fair entry to their profession, or the disciples of Hippocrates deluging the Revenue Commissioners with their tax returns. By the traditional standards of the society in which they find themselves, most Irish industrial workers, at least, may have some claim to consider themselves remarkably honest men.

Since then more examples have accumulated. Take, for example, the teachers. Professor Dale Tussing pointed out in a study published in 1978[43] that, thanks largely to the self-sacrifice and economical management of religious, there were large hidden economies in Irish education. The teachers soon swept that kitty clean. They now, there being nothing left for educational development, complain about the failure further to reduce class sizes!

104

But why particularise? What is being described is, of course, the law of the jungle. One is reminded of the famous piece by Thomas Hobbes on the quality of life in the state of nature, 'the life of man solitary, poor, nasty, brutish and short'. It is the glory of the State to have superseded the law of the jungle with order, peace and procedure, so far as individuals are concerned. But now, the war is not, as Hobbes described it, of 'every*one* against every*one*', but of more and more groups that pit themselves against the rest of society in a kind of institutional brigandage, free of the trammels of *collective* morality and patriotic responsibility.

Another of the symptoms of malaise has been the high number of working days lost through strikes, often for apparently trivial reasons and occasionally prompted by a death-wish. These symptoms suggest the alienation of the work force. In a number of places management was improved but the problem of alienation, if that is what it is, has not been tackled. Worker-participation seemed, in some countries, a remedy for alienation so this was tried, but in a typically trivialised way. No participation, of course, on the shop floor where the workers actually live and move and have their grievances, but in a selected number of state-sponsored bodies they are now empowered to elect some members to the board. Admirable in itself, but wholly inadequate to the scale of the problem. And what about the private sector? This is not government: it is cosmetics.

So too, in relation to the redress of citizens' grievances. By any standard, Irish government is in this area extraordinarily backward compared with other democracies and, indeed, some that are not democracies in our sense. Irish government is extremely complicated, it is usually remote, it is uninformative, it has limited procedures for orderly redress[44] and often operates badly those procedures it has.[45] One gets the impression that officials lack the imagination – or the democratic concern – to jump over the counter and look at themselves and their work through the eyes of their clients. Those who do have this opportunity – the practising politicians – are happy to act, to an ever increasing extent, as scavengers on the decaying system. There is no interest in establishing procedures for administrative simplification and justice such as exists in other countries except, again, at the level of the trivial and the cosmetic. So, when at length the Oireachtas got around to doing something in this area, it enacted the Ombudsman Act 1980. At best an ombudsman is the cap-stone of a proper system for redressing grievances; but, in the absence of such a system and given the limited functions of the office now created, it is in this case not more than, as it has been called, an 'ombudsmouse'. Even then, two years after the passing of the Act, no appointment has been made.

Irish government is remarkably centralised, and the steady drift away from local government makes it more centralised still. This is, of course, contrary to what is happening in most other European democracies where one of the remedies for Big Government and the problems that follow from it, is the renewal of local and regional governments and a transfer to them not only of massive functions but also of substantial democratic discretion. The purpose is not only to free central government for the overall tasks of government, but also to involve the people to a very considerable degree in the responsibility of governing themselves. In Ireland, however, when we talk of 'decentralisation' we mean dropping fragments of public bodies in provincial towns. This is to distribute goodies, but it has nothing whatever to do with 'decentralisation' which means to distribute discretion.[46] Similarly, 'regional development' in this country is usually held to mean something done *to* a region by a benign central authority, not done *by* a region for itself.

Our period has seen in this country, the rise of corporatism. This seems to be a feature of the modern world but we have here an especially virulent breed; virulent, I believe, because rather than develop a responsible democracy by effective systems for economic participation, for redressing grievances, for exercising responsibility – to name but three – we have shown, administratively, a terrifying complacency and, politically, an unerring instinct for the trivial. Now with the clouds gathering about us once again, with an over-centralised government unable to govern, with corporate bodies operating their feudal raids, with the taxpayers' revolt, and foreign borrowing no longer a soft option, our total neglect of *political development* has reached its nemesis.

We might have paid more heed to the world about us, particularly to another small country with its own difficulties. At about the time our troubles began to emerge in the late 1960s, the first of the tax revolts broke out in Denmark, a rich, very advanced social democracy with a population of about half as great again as ours and an area not much more than half of ours. It became clear that 'beyond the welfare state' lay the problem of the responsible society. The analysis was that the kind of irresponsibility inherent in the Danish protest could be countered by inviting the citizens into the closed world of government and by sharing responsibility with them over a wide area. This was done through an orderly programme extending over ten years from 1970. First a large number of small, archaic local authorities were reconstituted into 273 municipalities and 14 counties, plus the Greater Copenhagen Council. To this system, an orderly, massive transfer of central government functions was made insofar as they impinged directly on people and were thick on the ground. Now, about 70 per cent of governmental functions are handled by the new local authorities with a wide degree of discretion.[47] The problems of governing Denmark have not been solved – the problems of a government are perennial – but a grave danger to Danish government, such as we are facing, seems to have been averted by resolute and serious-minded action.

There is increasing acceptance in European countries that three great diseases of the modern state are alienation of the people, amoral centralised corporatism, and congested government. I think there can be no doubt but that, in this country, those three diseases are far advanced. The remedies now being adopted elsewhere in Europe are first, to counter alienation by involving the people in widely based participation; so secondly, setting up a democratic counteracting force to the abuses of corporatism; and thirdly, enabling central governments to shed much of their crippling loads. That is, they take steps to achieve a more democratic and more responsible society by diffusing responsibility through democratic institutions. In this country we drift in another direction – treating alienation with the political equivalent of the occasional aspirin, selling out to rapacious corporatism and loading still more on central government notwithstanding its declining level of performance. That is to say, we have chosen to drift steadily towards disaster.

Our period began with a brilliant demonstration in *Economic Development* and the *First Programme for Economic Expansion* of what positive, principled government can do for the country. The period ends with the pressing need for a comparable document setting out, in an equally serious and committed way, principles for political development to be embodied in a First Programme for Democratic Expansion.

Unfinished agenda

'I think it is true to say', said Sean Lemass to a conference of the Institute of Public Administration in 1961, 'that in some Government

Departments there is still a tendency to wait for new ideas to walk in through the door'.[48] From the review we have been making, we can, I think, conclude that this applies to the whole governmental system, that the ideas have been few, that when they have tried to cross the thresholds they have received a chilly reception, and that many of those that survived to be adopted were applied in routine, uncreative, even frivolous ways. The major conclusion that emerges is, after the initial period, of an extraordinary dearth of intellectual inquiry and ferment, and consequently, of the adoption and adaptation of ideas. 'I am not sure now if the biggest problem after all will not be one of organisation', said T. K. Whitaker to the same group – 'how Secretaries and other senior officers can organise their time and work so as to get away from their desks and the harassing experiences of every day sufficiently to read, consider, and consult with others in order to be able to give sound and comprehensive advice on future development policy'.[49]

Ideas are, basically, solutions to problems as perceived: good advice, therefore, depends on knowledge, persistent analysis, capacity for abstraction – and discussion. 'From the clash of ideas', said Patrick Lynch, 'minds ignite'. What is at stake here is the capacity to achieve creative thinking within necessarily rigid structures and to prevent minds from becoming dulled from the daily routine. This is, first, the task of mobilising the best of the talent that is, or that can be made, available. Of the overall urgency of getting creativity going at the thinking levels of government let there be no doubt whatever. The individual or group, whether by inaction or opposition, that impedes action on this commits a grave offence against the national interest.

This leads to the second point – that somehow the practice of government must be professionalised so that it will have continually before it the pursuit of excellence in the national interest, that there will be a lively concern for the advance of knowledge, for the quality of practice, and for the standards of commitment and performance. This is something only the members of the profession can do for themselves, a task for them of special urgency and of personal and patriotic responsibility. In particular, that there will be a wide acceptance of personal responsibility for getting decisions taken and for putting them promptly into effect.

Thirdly, thinking about government is different from thinking about economics, or sociology, or the environment, or organisation, or politics, or law, or whatever, although it depends greatly on the insights these studies can yield. It is concerned, in a way similar to medicine, with the implications of the relationships of these insights to the functioning of the corporate body and in optimising their moving, mutual balances in critical times. Of course for the best solutions there will also be required, as in medicine, outstanding flair; but in the hard graft of raising the effective level of government overall, there is no substitute for raising its level of rationality by a well developed planning system, so that throughout government there will be a common purpose and a number of bench marks of rationality against which more specific decisions and policies can be evolved and tested.

Fourthly, there is need to develop the learning process of government by the practice of orderly review for the purpose of building into future action the relevant lessons of experience. Here, one might think, is a major role for the legislature and for the elected representatives generally; but in any event, the administrative system must build an effective system so as to learn to remedy faults in a continuing, iterative process. Where review of this kind does not operate effectively there is the danger there will be *un*learning, as seems to have happened with the planning process and a number of financial techniques. Again, there is the ever present possibility that little or no learning will even begin, as seems to have happened with planning in the infrastructural area and development in the political one.

Fifthly, there is the clear need to accelerate this learning process. It is sobering to reflect that it took almost ten years to get capital budgeting under control and, after twice as long, social development is not yet at the operational stage.

Sixthly, there is urgent need to get ahead with institutional adaptation. Somebody must make up his mind sometime on how governmental structures are to be adapted to the problems of the present and the future – what part the legislature, ministers, civil service, local and regional government, and the state-sponsored bodies are to play in the governmental process and how their roles are to be defined in some clearcut and orderly way relevant to their responsibilities.

Finally, there is the question of actively working towards a more democratic and responsible society – where the people generally will be able to be closely involved in public affairs; where corporate bodies will operate within the constraints both of a moral and patriotic code and decentralised political institutions; and where public morale will be based on a spirit of informed realism – not to lose heart in bad times, not to lose head in good times and not to lose concern at all times.

In the last analysis, what matters is the health of our democracy. If there are to be plans or programmes or policies for national development these must relate in some way to a conscious public philosophy embodying the aspirations of most people and capable of being argued about by the rest. Our governmental system has lurched from hazard to hazard with no sufficient care for thought and discussion of principles and objectives. It is time to apply the experience of the past 25 years: thought and discussion achieve a great deal in the practical world; the descent from thought and discussion brings back the bad times.

Whatever happened to Irish government in the past 25 years? Alas, a loss of ideas and ideals, confidence and competence; but nothing that concern, vision and resolution cannot remedy. As we look towards the next 25 years and the new century, we see looming up the same unsolved problems, an unfinished agenda, compounded by delay. For that agenda, without doubt, many new problems will present themselves, to tax intelligence, thoughtfulness, creativity and resolution. This is, of course, the challenge, the exhilaration, of government.

Notes to Article

1 T. K. Whitaker 'Economic Development – The Irish Experience' *Irish Times* 28 September 1982

2 R. Fanning *The Irish Department of Finance 1922-58* IPA, 1978, Ch 11

3 *Economic Development* 1958, Pr 4803

4 *First Programme for Economic Expansion 1959-62*, 1958

5 Fanning, op. cit. pp 457-8

6 Ibid, pp 506-8. See also G. Fitzgerald 'Grey, White and Blue' *Administration* 6 (1958-9) 3, reprinted in Chubb, B and Lynch P (eds) *Economic Development and Planning* IPA 1969

7 Capital Investment Advisory Committee *First Report* 1957, *Second Report* 1957, *Third Report* 1958

8 T. K. Whitaker 'Capital Formation, Saving and Economic Progress' *Administration* 4 (1956) 2, reprinted in Chubb and Lynch, loc. cit.

9 T. K. Whitaker 'From Protection to Free Trade – The Irish Experience' Sean Lemass Memorial Lecture, *Administration* 21 (1973) 4

10 *State (Modern Homes) (Ireland) Ltd. v Dublin Corporation* 1953 IR 202 65

11 eg *Public Capital Programme* pl 449, 1982, Table I

12 Department of the Environment *Road Development Plan for the 1980s* 1979, Prl 7967. For a discussion in some detail of these issues see my 'Organisational Considerations' in *Ireland in the Year 2000: Infrastructure* Foras Forbartha, 1982

13 *Third Programme for Economic and Social*

Development 1969-72, 1969, Ch 2, para 3

14 OECD *Investment in Education* 2 vols, 1965 and 1966

15 See the striking, and courageous, article by Sean O'Connor 'Post Primary Education: Now and in the Future' *Studies* Autumn 1968

16 *The Health Services and their Further Development* 1966, pr 8653

17 B. Hensey *The Health Services of Ireland* IPA, 3rd edn 1979, Ch 4

18 An issue of *Social Studies* 1 (1972) 4, was devoted to the papers and documents thrown up by this Conference.

19 eg *Administration Yearbook and Diary* 1982, Tables 41 and 44

20 H. Friis: *Development of Social Research in Ireland* IPA, 1965

21 eg Ch 2, paras 5-6

22 National Economic and Social Council Report No 12 *Education Expenditure in Ireland* 1976 prl 4730; Report No 16 *Some Aspects of Finance for Owner-Occupied Housing* 1976. See also Kennedy, F. *Social Expenditure in Ireland* ESRI, 1975; Baker, T. J. and O'Brien, L. M. *The Irish Housing System: A Critical Overview* ESRI, 1979

23 Gunnar Myrdal *Beyond the Welfare State* Duckworth , 1960, ch 5

24 'In 1940 public sector expenditure in Ireland amounted to almost 30% of national income; in 1960 the percentage had risen to about 37% and by 1980 had increased sharply to represent some 73% of national income'. *A Better Way to Plan the Nation's Finances* 1981, p 2

25 *National Income and Expenditure* 1959, Table A12; 1979, Table A15; *Irish Statistical Bulletin* 49 (1974) 1, 20; 56 (1981) 1, 7

26 See P. D. Gaffey 'The Central Administration' in this collection.

27 *Sources:* 1956-7. Estimates for that year; 1982: *State Directory,* 1982.

There are considerable difficulties in arriving at accurate figures for the earlier year – those given must be taken as indicating orders of magnitude only. Staffs of smaller offices excluded for both years.

28 eg 1980: OECD *Observer* March 1982, pp 26-7

29 *National Income and Expenditure* 1979, Tables A13 and A17. On the need for better (or refurbished) financial techniques see Public Service Advisory Council, Report no 7 (1979-80) ch 1

30 *Development for Full Employment* 1978; *National Development* 1977-80, 1978; *Programme for National Development* 1978-81, 1979; *Investment and National Development* 979-83, 1980. The second of these documents seemed (para 7.1) to have forgotten what had been so painfully learned since the *First Programme* about redistribution.

31 T. K. Whitaker *Irish Times* 28 September 1982

32 Ch 19, para 20

33 See (eg) NESC 48 *Transport Policy* 1980; 59 *The Importance of Infrastructure to National Development,* 1981; Transport Consultative Commission *Passenger Transport Services in the Dublin Area* 1980, and *Road Freight Haulage,* 1981.

34 *Programme for National Development* 1978-81, para 4.62

35 Para 13.4.8

36 Posts and Telegraphs Review Group 1978-9, (Dargan) *Report,* 1979

37 Whiddy Island Disaster *Report,* 1980, ch 22

38 'The Next Necessary Thing' *Administration* 7 (1959) 2, reprinted in Chubb and Lynch, loc. cit.

39 For the limited progress after so long, see Public Services Advisory Council *Report* No 8 (1980-81) paras 6.6-12. For the Council's bounded enthusiasm at the rate of advance, see

para 2.3

40 C. F. Carter: 'A Problem of Economic Development' *Administration* 7 (1959) 2, reprinted in Chubb and Lynch loc. cit.

41 *The Work of Justice* Veritas, 1977, para 58

42 Nevin, D (ed) *Trade Unions and Change in Irish Society* Mercier/RTE, 1980, pp 23-4

43 A. Dale Tussing *Irish Educational Expenditure – Past, Present and Future* ESRI, 1978

44 Barrington, T. J. *The Irish Administrative System* 1980, p 177 ff

45 Coolock Community Law Centre *Social Welfare Appeals* 1980. The Public Service Advisory Council (*7th Report* ,

ch. 1.3) attempt to get this general issue back onto the rails.

46 Public Services Organisation Review Group *Report,* 10.5.3

47 Palle Mikkelsen 'Role of Regional Institutions in Balanced Development – Denmark', Paper to Conference on Regional Institutions and Policies for Development, Rome, January 1982

48 Sean Lemass: 'The Organisation behind the Economic Programme' *Administrtion* 9 (1961-2) p 5, reprinted in Chubb and Lynch, loc. cit . p 205

49 T. K. Whitaker, 'The Civil Service and Development' *Administration* 9 (1961-2) 2, p 87, reprinted in Chubb and Lynch, loc. cit., p 218

26 MOUNTJOY SQUARE DUBLIN 1
TELEPHONE (01) 741526/7/8

DIRECTOR PADRAIG MACDIARMADA

comhaiRle náisiúnta na gcáiliochtaí oíoeachaís

THE NATIONAL COUNCIL FOR EDUCATIONAL AWARDS

ORIGIN AND FUNCTIONS:

After 8 years of existence the National Council for Educational Awards was established on a statutory basis on the 16th July, 1980, following the passing of the N.C.E.A. Act (1979):

— To encourage, facilitate, promote, co-ordinate and develop Higher Education outside of the universities

— To approve and recognise courses

— To grant and confer National Awards on students who successfully complete approved courses

THE AWARD LEVELS OF COUNCIL ARE:

ONE-YEAR CERTIFICATE
NATIONAL CERTIFICATE
NATIONAL DIPLOMA
BACHELOR'S DEGREE
GRADUATE DIPLOMA
MASTER'S DEGREE

National Certificates and National Diplomas account for a high proportion of the total awards conferred. A National Certificate may be obtained after a two-year full-time course and a National Diploma after a further year. These awards may also be obtained through a comparable period of part-time study. A Degree course normally takes four years. Courses leading to the award of Graduate Diploma are designed for graduates seeking vocational 're-orientation' and are usually of one year's duration.

COURSES LEADING TO NCEA AWARDS ARE PROVIDED AT THE FOLLOWING LOCATIONS:

In Regional Technical Colleges, Colleges of Technology, National Institutes for Higher Education, Thomond College of Education, the National College of Art and Design, and other institutions of higher education throughout the country.

STANDARDS:

Council, through its Boards of Studies, specialist Assessors and Extern Examiners, at all times seeks to ensure that courses leading to its awards are analogous to academic standards elsewhere, and carry with them appropriate professional status.

FOR FURTHER INFORMATION:

Please refer to the **Directory of NCEA Approved Courses in Higher Education (2nd Edition)** for general information on all courses approved of by Council. Further related information may be obtained from time to time in various NCEA publications. Details of specific courses may be obtained directly from the educational institution concerned.

NATIONAL COUNCIL FOR EDUCATIONAL AWARDS
26 MOUNTJOY SQUARE
DUBLIN 1

CONGRATULATIONS TO A 25-YEAR OLD FROM A 21-YEAR OLD

In celebrating our 21st
we're delighted to congratulate
the IPA on its Silver Jubilee
and to welcome the publication
of this Special Issue of
"Administration".

RTE

1961-1982

The Central Administration

PETER GAFFEY

It is convenient, and now widely accepted, to regard the public administration in Ireland as a trinity comprising the central administration, the local authorities and the state-sponsored bodies. Following Section 1 of the Ministers and Secretaries Act, 1924, the central administration is concerned with the administration and business of the public services distributed among the departments of state assigned to and administered by ministers of the government; in effect, it is the functions and organisation of ministers and the civil service in their departments. A look at the numbers of people involved, however, suggests that this tripartite classification is not based on any natural order; it is, in fact, changing as we observe it. In 1957 there were less than 35,000 civil servants; to-day, there are over 60,000 but, next year, with the proposed departure of the postal and telecommunications services, there will be no more than 32,000.

In 1957 the boundaries of the central administration seemed reasonably settled. The civil service and departments were very like the institutions set up on the foundation of the state. Some functions had been redistributed since 1924; the numbers of non-industrial civil servants had grown from 21,000 in 1922 to 35,000 in 1957 but this increase was largely attributable to the increase in public business in that period. The Civil Service Commissioners Act and the Civil Service Regulation Act of 1956 consolidated the basic provisions governing recruitment and tenure of civil servants. Although many new functions had been assigned to state-sponsored bodies these bodies were seen as discharging functions different from those of the central administration.

In fact, the administrative outlook in 1957 was still mainly influenced by the philosophy of the founding fathers of the administration. That philosophy, as expressed in the Ministers and Secretaries Act, 1924, was predominantly centralist, bringing most functions of government under direct ministerial control and making provision for bringing under direct control almost every other function of government which had escaped the net. As described in the *Report of the Public Services Reorganisation Review Group*, such a system, concentrating total responsibility in the hands of a few ministers, proved unworkable and two devices were adopted to make it work – an informal delegation to civil servants and the invention of the state-sponsored body. In 1957, however, the state-sponsored bodies were mainly of the commercial type and were regarded more or less as companies owned by ministers and their departments; the scale of the non-commercial bodies was relatively small.

Formally, there has been little change in the constitutional and legal position since 1957. Under Article 28.2 of the Constitution,

'The executive power of the State shall, subject to the provisions of this Constitution, be exercised by or on the authority of the Government'

and Article 28.12 provides that 'the organisation of and distribution of business amongst Departments of State . . . ' shall be regulated by law.

The government and individual ministers through their departments are responsible for the administration and business of the public services as set out in the Ministers and Secretaries Acts. Most of the business assigned to state-sponsored bodies is new and is carried out on the authority of the government. Where such bodies perform commercial type functions, few would question that, with appropriate relationships to Ministers, they should form a sector of government business separate from the central administration. In regard to the non-commercial bodies, however, the existence both of state-sponsored bodies and executive branches of departments to perform comparable functions casts doubts on the whole organisation of the public business. In the consideration of central administration, therefore, it is necessary to consider why functions which formerly would have been handled by executive branches of government departments are increasingly assigned to non-commercial state-sponsored bodies.

Usually, the primary reason advanced is that civil service structure and status does not suit the particular activity to be discharged. It is argued that the more closely a new activity is related to the private sector, the more closely should its organisational forms and practices conform to those of the private sector.

It is also argued that the assignment of responsibility for overall management and direction to a board of directors follows normal commercial practice; the board has a mandate and, with the removal of an area of settled policy from day-to-day parliamentary scrutiny and from government accounting procedures, it should be able to get on with the job much more effectively than would an executive branch of a government department, subject to the normal constraints. What constraints are normal is, however, an open question. In recent years, much of the argument in this area has been concerned with the power of boards to fix staff pay levels without central co-ordination or direction, an issue with much wider social implications.

Finally, there is the functional argument in favour of single purpose organisations which devote themselves completely to the achievement of given objectives. Indeed, if staff can be transferred between different areas of the public service so that people of ability are not confined to restricted careers in small bodies, this argument has particular validity. One great virtue of the civil service type of organisation in the past, however, was the ease with which the resources of a single service could be diverted to meet urgent and unforeseen needs and steps must be taken to ensure that the activities of such bodies do not acquire a life of their own even when the need for their services has ceased to exist.

Since the foundation of the state, the number of civil service employees has grown from 21,000 to over 60,000 while the non-commercial state bodies have developed to a stage where they employ over 10,000 people. However, by next year, with the proposed assignment of the postal and telecommunications service to two commercial state-sponsored bodies, the civil service of the central administration will be almost halved to a strength of some 32,000. If such major changes can be made in the central services on the basis of decisions particular to individual parts of that service, the principles governing the organisation of the central administration need to be reconsidered. Broadly, the argument that follows is that, subject to overall strategic direction and control by the central administration, the state-sponsored body sector should be responsible for commercial type activities and local authorities for whatever functions it is decided to administer locally. The rest of the public business is for the central administration. The organisation of this business is the main concern of this article.

The *Report of the Public Services Organisation Review Group* in 1969 was the first comprehensive attempt since the Ministers and Secretaries Act 1924 to consider how the whole public sector might best be organised and managed. In looking at the whole area of the exercise of the executive power of the state, the Group were critical of the arbitrary way in which new functions of government were organised and concluded that 'every new decision to set up a state-sponsored body is an avoidance of the main issue involved and we suggest that the time has now come to rationalise the whole structure of the public service'. They also concluded that there was a unity in the public service as the instrument for the discharge of the executive power of the state. It was, however, organised on lines which were largely the result of historical accident and there was a need to rationalise functions and to secure a new division between what must be subject to political direction and control and what could be left to more independent units working through agreed systems towards defined objectives.

The Review Group envisaged the central co-ordination of all government business through the staff support functions of planning, finance, organisation and personnel. The central area would direct the activities of the various executive bodies in the public service 'executive counsel'. The concept of 'executive counsel' was designed to cover a wide range of relationships from the close control necessary in politically sensitive or temporarily badly managed bodies, to the much more liberal relationship with bodies whose discharge of their mandates was generally acceptable.

There have been changes in circumstances affecting the public service since 1969. The years of economic planning and unprecedented growth were succeeded by accession to the European Communities in 1973, followed by the oil crisis and general international recession. The problems facing the public service to-day are, as a result, somewhat different from those in the period 1966-69 during which the Review Group sat and must be taken into account when considering the relevance of their proposals to-day.

First, the scale and magnitude of international changes has altered the demands on public management systems. The effect on western economies of the increased demands of the oil-producing countries led to a significant increase in state involvement in the economy. A consequence for the management of public business has been that, instead of managing a system that was largely administrative, governments now have to manage a system that contains much more diverse elements, some of which were once the domain of the private sector. Following transition to the public sector, these elements no longer appear susceptible to management by traditional private sector methods. In moving into activities which were once run on a commercial basis, states often doubt whether they can legitimately enter the situation of making profit; without the profit and loss discipline, however, it is difficult to see by what criteria the business should be managed. At the same time, the tools traditionally used by the state to manage its affairs have been blunted by efforts to deal with the crises of the 1970s. Traditional financial and budgetary procedures were relaxed to deal on a short-term basis with what proved to be a long-term shift of resources to the oil producing countries. The much-vaunted PPBS systems of the 1960s were replaced in the 1970s by less confidently backed variations of management by objective systems. These, in turn, were gradually abandoned as belief in planning evaporated in the heat of crises which the planners had not built into their projections. The public management system to-day must recognise and attempt to deal with the greatly increased complexity of the business of government.

Secondly, this system must be designed to respond to the distribution of power between government and governed. Relationships have changed substantially in recent years with the emergence of highly organised interest groups, greater government involvement in everyday life and the disposal by government of the greater proportion of the national product. As a result, government is now in dialogue with a far wider range of organised interest groups about both the provision of services and the distribution of national resources. In relation to pay levels, for example, the type of generalised pay rounds which emerged in the post-war period had developed by the early 1970s into the National Pay Agreements and, by the end of the decade, into the National Understandings covering economic and social policies as well as pay. Although no National Understanding emerged in 1981, the whole process of government/ employer/trade union relationships in regard to pay and economic policies has been radically changed. At the same time, relationships between government and other organised groups have developed far beyond those which existed in 1957. A formal institutional response by government to emerging new forms of pressure has not yet emerged but the central administrative area is now regularly involved in discussion and negotiation with bodies representing various interests. Finally, and perhaps of the greatest importance, is the effect of technological developments both on employment generally and on the type of employment provided by the public service, particularly in the areas of central administration. It has become increasingly evident that in the more developed societies the new technology increasingly enables workers to be replaced by machines. A major problem is how to provide meaningful occupations for those displaced by technology.

One solution has been to accept the trend in the major economies and to move the displaced to the services sector and, in particular, to the public sector. Indeed, this approach was adopted here to some extent in the job creation approach for several years after 1977 resulting in a substantial increase in all areas of the public sector. However, while budgetary constraints have now come into play, the problem of technology-induced unemployment remains. It is difficult to escape the conclusion that if technology abolishes large areas of industrial work, a large number of people must either be maintained in perpetual idleness or provided with public service employment. If this is accepted, it must also be accepted that the cost of their maintenance or employment must be borne from the increased productivity provided by technology and those lucky enough to be retained in employment cannot appropriate to themselves the savings arising from disemploying their fellow workers. If, on the other hand, as we have witnessed in recent years, some sections in both the private and public sectors receive unreal productivity increases, the employment situation is exacerbated.

Few would dispute that if the state has to provide for the technologically displaced, it should do so by the offer of employment which would increase the total public welfare, at sustainable rates of pay. The second effect of technological development, unfortunately, comes into play here. Technology offers the possibility of eliminating large blocks not only of industrial work, but of clerical and administrative work also. In particular, jobs may disappear more rapidly in the area of central administration with the automation of functions such as filing, calculation and record-keeping. A major problem facing the public service for the remainder of this century will be how to provide worthwhile jobs for an increasing number of people. The pace of technological innovation is now so rapid that solutions to the enormous problems of how to identify and manage jobs and resources, to redeploy people and to ensure equity without destroying society in the process, must be worked out and planned. They will not just happen but will be a main concern of central administration in the future.

While there is a logic in dividing the administrative system into central, local and state-sponsored body sectors, the boundaries between these sectors depend on the current view of the allocation of power and responsibility between them. Recognising that this allocation must be largely arbitrary and influenced by political and administrative work also. In particular, jobs may disappear more things might best be organised; what follows, is mainly concerned with the organisation and operation of the central administration.

Even on current assumptions, only a fraction of the 300,000 public sector employees are employed in the central administration. The breakdown in the numbers employed in 1981 is as follows:

1	*Employees of Department of State*		
	non-industrial civil servants	60,500	
	industrial and contract staff	9,500	70,000
2	*State-sponsored body employees*		
	commercial bodies	57,000	
	non-commercial bodies	11,000	68,000
3	*Local authority employees*		35,400
4	*Health sector employees*		
	regional health boards	42,000	
	voluntary hospitals	16,000	
	miscellaneous health bodies	5,500	63,500
5	*Educational and security service employees*		
	teachers and third level education	47,400	
	Garda Síochána	9,900	
	defence forces	17,200	74,500
	Total		311,400

On current understandings, the central administration consists of ministers and the 60,500 staff of the non-industrial civil service; with the departure of the 28,000 civil servants employed in the Department of Posts and Telegraphs, this figure will fall to about 32,000. Almost all the remaining categories are by general agreement or definition not

121

part of the central administration. The commercial state-sponsored bodies have been placed at a remove from the centre. The local authorities are traditionally in a separate position and the health sector, although no longer strictly in the local administration area, is still nearer to that area than to the central administration. The three specialist service sectors of education, police and army are involved in the provision of discrete services rather than in central administration. The main problem arises with the non-commercial state-sponsored bodies. By law, they have been placed in the same positions as the commercial bodies although they discharge functions of central government which could just as well have been assigned to executive branches of departments of state.

As we have seen, the primary reasons for the establishment of these bodies and the assignment to them of central government functions are largely managerial. For an adequate consideration of the future organisation and functions of the central administration, the 11,000 staff of the non-commercial state-sponsored bodies should, therefore, be added to the 32,000 civil servants remaining after the post office reorganisation to see how this group of over 40,000 people might be organised and operated.

The present organisation is irrational. It is hard to see why some executive areas of government should be assigned to departments of state and others to non-commercial state-sponsored bodies. Why, for example, should the Department of Social Welfare administer unemployment benefit while AnCO is responsible for industrial training and the Department of Labour through the National Manpower Service looks after placement and occupational guidance? At the extremes, there are two alternatives. It would not be impossible, taking the area outlined as the central administration, to return to the concept in the Ministers and Secretaries Act, 1924, and bring all executive activities now discharged by the non-commercial state-sponsored bodies back into the departments of state staffed by civil servants with ministers carrying full responsibility. There are now fifteen ministers of state who could take much of the burden from ministers and indeed, the assignment of responsibility for limited areas of business to junior ministers could be a preparation for the position of Minister of the Government.

The other alternative would be to assign to state-sponsored bodies everything but the essential work which must be done by ministers – legislation, the financial business as required by the constitution and the general supervision of the executive business assigned to the state-sponsored bodies.

For practical reasons, the solution must be sought between these alternatives but it must have some rational basis if the system is to work effectively. Despite the various objections raised by sectional interests to the proposals of the Review Group, no credible alternative organisational proposals for the central administration have emerged since they reported in 1969. Taking the central administration as comprising 43,000 employees, the main features of this organisation would be:

1 the functions of government would be allocated on a rational basis between the departments of state headed by ministers;
2 the execution of settled policy would be assigned to a number of executive units in each department which would operate with more freedom and individual responsibility than existing executive branches of departments but would be subject to more systematic review than the existing non-commercial state-sponsored bodies;
3 commercial state-sponsored bodies, local authorities and health authorities would not be regarded as part of the central administration but would report separately to the appropriate ministers and departments;
4 the central area of a department, grouped around the minister, would be responsible for policy formulation and advice, the preparation of legislation, the determination of strategy for associated bodies and the review and appraisal of executive activities;
5. management and communications would flow through a system of staff support in the functions of planning, finance, organisation and personnel, co-ordinated at central level by the Departments of Finance and the Public Service, which would provide the staff support to government.

This system would have enormous benefits. The members of the government, freed from the burden of day-to-day tasks, would be able to devote more time to considering policy rather than minor cases; with the aid of the staff support systems, the government would produce the necessary plans and financial appraisals and organise resources to enable them to do what was needed, to cease doing what was no longer necessary and continuously to review, appraise and adjust course. The executive bodies, with clear mandates and freed from all but the essential controls, would push ahead to ensure continuous increases in the national well-being. That this vision is somewhat utopian and that the reality some thirteen years after the Review Group reported falls well short of its realisation should not obscure the potentiality.

In the current difficult circumstances worldwide, it is easy to despair about the administrative scene. Without denying the seriousness of the situation, we should also take our assets into account. In the administrative system, and particularly in the central administration, there is much on which future progress can be based.

To begin with, general levels of education and competence in the civil service are satisfactory and the administrative system is firmly established. Organisationally, there has been more development than is immediately apparent. In contrast to the more publicised development of the Aireacht system in the Departments of Health and Transport and Power in the early 1970s, there has been a steady programme of reform of institutions across a range of departments which, within the next year, should begin to be reflected in a real move towards the type of organisation envisaged by the Review Group. In the area of staff support, specialised units have been created in a number of departments and training has been developed and provided.

Although providing a base for progress, all this is far from the transformation which the Review Group envisaged being accomplished in a period of five years. It has been the experience of countries which began programmes of administrative reform in the past two decades that the system is far more complicated than was originally believed. Reform on the grand scale would have required great resolve and the allocation of large resources. The example of the United Kingdom administration shows that even to prune and curtail the administrative system needs unhesitating resolve and continuous effort. The constructive reform of a system is even more difficult and can only be secured by advances in particular areas where resources must be concentrated and problems faced and solved. Instead of the blanket advance on all fronts which was envisaged by the Review Group, concentration on a smaller number of programme areas offers a better prospect of progress.

Within the first area, which we might call horizontal rationalisation, is the unobtrusive business of the continuing organisation and management of the public service. To see that lines of authority and responsibility are clearly defined, that functions are grouped on a rational basis, that duplication and waste are eliminated, that schemes and programmes are not allowed to outlive their usefulness and relevance and that new services are subject to the same criteria are the concerns which will always inform this programme area and with particular emphasis to-day when demands for the reduction of the current deficit must be met. The immediate prospect, therefore, is for a reduction in the size of the public service through efficient administration and the elimination of schemes and programmes. If, as a result of this approach, the private sector can expand to provide the necessary jobs there can be little objection except on ideological grounds to the reduction in size of the public service. There is, however, an alternative prospect which will require a different response from the public service.

The shift of resources from the public to the private sector might not produce the required increase in employment. One reason might be the effects of technology in making large areas of manufacturing jobs redundant while services might not be able to expand fast enough to compensate. In such circumstances, it is hard to see how the public sector could escape responsibility for providing jobs. An expanded public service is at least a possibility for the future and its implications must be considered and planned for. While eliminating waste in its services, the state may also have to consider where new services can reasonably be provided and the question of redeployment of staff between public services arises to challenge existing interests. If such services cannot be financed within available resources, the question of the trade-off between pay rates and employment arises. A rationalisation programme, therefore, raises uncomfortable issues which will refuse to go away and the nature of the choices involved should be clearly understood and settled within the interests concerned. The management and negotiation of such issues will be a growing task of the central administration.

The second area might be termed vertical rationalisation – the settlement of the levels of authority between the government and its agencies. The Review Group suggested that there should be a central area in each department, grouped round the minister, which would be responsible for policy formulation and overall review and appraisal of executive activities whether in the commercial state-sponsored bodies, local authorities or other service areas. The activities of executive branches of departments and of non-commercial state-sponsored bodies would be assigned to executive units of the department staffed by civil servants with common conditions and mobility.

Two sets of problems arise in this area. The question of the assignment of ministerial functions to executive units has never been fully debated at the political level and, the precedent of the state-sponsored bodies notwithstanding, only the Oireachtas can finally decide the issue. The other problem is one of personnel. The Review Group's proposal that the staff of the non-commercial state-sponsored bodies should become members of the new civil service seems, more than anything else, to have disturbed the state-sponsored body sector. While the proposal seems to have emerged from the logic of the situation in the interests of staff mobility, and by comparison with countries which have a common staff grading system across the public service, it is not essential to the aim of vertical rationalisation. Executive units of departments and non-commercial state-sponsored bodies could continue to work side by side within the central administration without any change in the staffing structures of the state-sponsored bodies – the current programme operates on this basis. What is important is to secure an effective distribution of functions and responsibilities between the levels of the central administration. The questions of staff mobility, recruitment, status and pay levels are separate issues for separate resolution.

The third area for action is that of specialist staff support in the functions of planning, finance, organisation and personnel. Most departments and major offices now have units to discharge the functions of organisation and personnel in communication with the Department of the Public Service and finance units in communication with the Department of Finance; while some issues relating to skills and systems remain to be resolved, the main problem arises in the planning area. As seen by the Review Group, planning as a function is not readily separable from the finance function of the Department of Finance, but such is the urgency of financial pressures that the planning function in the Department tends to be subordinated to the budgetary process. Unless this dilemma is resolved, the rather elegant system proposed by the Review Group cannot work effectively. A central theme of the Group's report was that the business of government would be discharged by ministers and their departments in accordance with plans formulated with the assistance of planning units in departments, co-ordinated by the central planning function of the Department of Finance and tailored to available resources by the finance function in its budgetary role. The organisation of the human and technical resources necessary to carry out the plans would be done with the aid of the organisation function and the recruitment, development and maintenance of the personnel to fill the organisational structures would be done through the personnel function. Obviously, if the planning function does not operate satisfactorily, the whole concept is endangered and the planning function has not yet been perfected.

Up to 1977, it was apparent that the planning function in the Department of Finance remained subordinate to the budgetary function or was concerned only with macro-economic plans; indeed, after the 1973 oil crisis it became the official wisdom that, in such conditions of uncertainty, planning was not a meaningful exercise. With the creation of the Department of Economic Planning and Development in 1977, economic planning was accorded a major role in the administrative system but experience appears to have confirmed the Review Group's argument against separating the planning function from the Department of Finance. The Department of Economic Planning and Development and the Department of Finance did not achieve an effective distribution of functions between them and, in several areas, the impression was given that the two departments duplicated rather than complemented each other. Since the abolition of the Department of Economic Planning, the institutionalisation of the planning function still presents problems. A satisfactory balance is difficult to achieve and international experience is not helpful. A possible solution might be the appointment of two members of the government at the Department of Finance to ensure that, while planning and finance have separate voices at cabinet level, they operate in conjunction with each other at official level. What is becoming evident is that management of the public service and its response to the needs of the community are critically dependent on the institution of planning.

Finally, the fourth area for attention is that of management of people. Development of staff, particularly in relation to the specialist staff support functions, free movement within the public service and resolution of the long-standing administrator/professional problems are among the matters which must be pursued to successful conclusions. However, the greatest single issue is the determination of public sector pay. With the limits on public expenditure being reached or exceeded, it is becoming increasingly evident that there is a definite trade-off between pay and employment at a time when unemployment is a major national problem. The issue is common to the whole economy and its resolution in the public sector will have to be found in the context of some national consensus on incomes and pay. If present trends continue, it is likely that the future development of public administration will be constrained by harsh financial imperatives rather than rational considerations.

Conclusions

Where then does this discussion on the central administration lead? It is, admittedly, tendentious in that it is based on the belief that the public sector is in need of firm central direction and that the best organisation of the central administration is one in which ministers and their advisers are given the maximum freedom from relatively minor matters to deal with perhaps the greatest problems that have faced the state since its foundation. Furthermore, no attempt has been made to discuss the question of the allocation of functions between central and local government; that question is left to the consideration of the politicians. Within the limits of the space available, it has been necessary to be somewhat selective in the treatment of the subject, and, in the belief that if the structures are right, management and performance can more easily be improved, this treatment has concentrated on the size and shape of the central administration. Despite recent attention, public finance has not been a main theme. This is not to deny the importance of the subject but it is suggested that our financial procedures are adequate. What is needed is not so much better controls as better plans against which to operate them. Indeed, the development of the planning system offers the greatest possibilities for the reform of the system of public administration. The whole operation of the central administration should be involved in the development and promulgation of policy; without an integrated planning system, the effective translation of policy into action cannot be achieved.

Significant events in the Irish central administration, 1957-82

1958   *Programme for Economic Expansion, 1958 and Economic Development, 1958*
       The formal beginning of indicative planning and of the planning role of the Department of Finance.

1959   *Department of Transport and Power established*

128

The transport and energy functions were hived off from the Department of Industry and Commerce to a new Department.

1961 *Health (Corporate Bodies) Act, 1961*
A significant legislative innovation enabling the Minister to establish new corporate bodies by Order.

1963 *Second Programme for Economic Expansion*
With the success of the First Programme, the more ambitious Second Programme was intended to cover the period 1963-70. When it became apparent in the second half of the decade that its targets would not be achieved, the Second Programme was replaced by the Third Programme 1969-72.

First Computer installed in Civil Service
The acquisition of the first real computer by the Revenue Commissioners marked the beginning of electronic data processing in the civil service leading to the establishment of the Central Data Processing Services and other major installations and the adoption of a technology with ever-extending applications.

1965 *Investment in Education Report*

1967 *Report of the Commission on Higher Education*
These reports and the radical decisions on educational policies resulted in a major transfer of resources to education.

1966 *Department of Labour established*
The Department of Labour took over industrial relations and related functions from the Department of Industry and Commerce. For a brief period, it also administered the employment exchanges and it has since become involved on a large scale with training, manpower placement and youth employment.

1969 *Third Programme for Economic and Social Development, 1969-72*
The Third Programme attempted to correct some of the deficiencies in the Second Programme and also introduced a social dimension. Its expiry marked the decline of the first attempt at national economic planning.

Programme Budgeting
A major effort by the Department of Finance to introduce PPBS, which began in the late 1960s, finally took off about 1969. As in other countries, and in particular in the United States, the effort failed through over ambition and has left little permanent mark on public administration.

Report of the Public Services Organisation Review Group
Although the major reform of the public service proposed by the Group has not been achieved, the Report has significantly affected thinking about Irish public administration; it forms the basis for much of the current reform programme and has not been supplanted by any subsequent overall propositions for public service reform.

Political unrest in Northern Ireland
The events of 1969 in Northern Ireland marked the beginning of a new preoccupation by Government with Northern Ireland affairs and with a major increase in resources devoted to the security area.

1970   *Health Act, 1970*
The 1970 Health Act provided for a major reorganisation of the health services and the subsequent expansion in public expenditure on health. With the new organisation, the cost of the health services was gradually removed from the local rates until, by 1977, the cost of the health services was completely removed from the rates. The change has had enormous implications for local government, not only in the health area but by its extension to the abolition of domestic rates.

Secretary designate for new Department of the Public Service appointed
In effect, pending legislation, the new Department of the Public Service was set up within the Department of Finance.

1973   *Ireland becomes a member of the European Communities*
The implications of this step affect all aspects of national life. As far as the central administration is concerned almost 2,000 additional civil servants are needed to deal with all aspects of EC membership.

Department of the Public Service established

130

The Ministers and Secretaries Act 1973 established the Department of the Public Service (assigned to the same person as Minister as the Department of Finance) and the Public Service Advisory Council.

1977   *Establishment of Department of Fisheries and Forestry*
The Lands functions of the Department of Lands were transferred to the Department of Agriculture and the residual Department was retitled Fisheries and Forestry with the transfer of the Fisheries functions from the Department of Agriculture.

Department of Economic Planning and Development established and other departmental functions redistributed
The establishment of the new Department represented a new departure in that the planning function was assigned to a Minister other than the Minister for Finance. The energy functions were also transferred from the Department of Transport and Power to the retitled Department of Industry, Commerce and Energy.

1979   *First National Understanding for Economic and Social Development*
For the first time, national pay bargaining was conducted on a tripartite basis with the Government involved in relation to matters such as employment, taxation and social policy.

Report of Posts and Telegraphs Review Group
The report recommended the hiving off from the civil service to two commercial state-sponsored bodies of the Postal and Telecommunications Services. The Report has been accepted by Government and implementing legislation is at present before the Oireachtas.

1980   *Major reassignment of departmental functions*
The Department of Economic Planning and Development was abolished and its functions transferred to the Department of Finance. The energy functions were assigned to a new Department of Energy and, with the transfer of tourism functions, the two Departments concerned were retitled the Department of Transport and the Department of Industry, Commerce and Tourism. The Ministers and Secretaries Acts

were amended by the repeal of the provision in the 1973 Act requiring that the Departments of Finance and the Public Service be assigned to the same person as Minister. The Departments of Labour and the Public Service were then assigned to the same member of the Government.

1981 *Reassignment of Industry functions*
With the reassignment of the industry functions, the two Departments concerned were retitled, the Department of Industry and Energy and the Department of Trade, Commerce and Tourism.

Meath County Council

Meath County Council and its County Development Team congratulates the Institute of Public Administration on the occasion of its Silver Jubilee.

We acknowledge the important contribution made by the Institute in fostering education in the public service. The past twenty five years has brought substantial progress generally but particularly in industrial and commercial development in Ireland. County Meath offers excellent facilities for such development and both the County Council and the County Development Team stimulate and assist these projects.

The County has a sound infrastructure and has provided attractive industrial estates at various locations. The County Council involves itself in all areas that will improve the economic and social life of the Community.

Further information can be obtained from The County Development Team, County Hall, Navan, Co. Meath. Tel. 046-21581.

Local Government

DESMOND ROCHE

The general picture of local government in 1957 was one of relative quiet. There were plenty of things to complain about as regards services, but on the point of organisation there was peace. A truce had been declared in the long war between councillors and managers about their respective rights and duties. The City and County Management (Amendment) Act, 1955, product of a ministerial progress round the country and consultations with every local authority, had done the trick. The management structure was preserved with some modifications, mostly cosmetic, but a few significantly moving the balance of power towards the councillors. The year 1955 also saw the last of the general statutes creating a new, post-independence local government: the Local Government (Temporary Provisions) Act, 1923, and the Local Government Acts of 1925, 1927, 1941 and 1946. The 1955 Act was a disappointment – a miscellany of amendments and minor innovations. The creative energy seemed to have been exhausted.

On the services side, the country was emerging from a painful recession produced earlier in the decade by a balance of payments crisis. The acute shortage of investment capital had serious depressive effects on local administration.

In 1957, de Valera regained power with a large majority (78 against a combined FG and Labour total of 53.) Signs of a thaw soon began to appear, as the restraints on capital investment were gradually eased. As the recession lifted, enterprise showed signs of regained self-confidence. The first *Programme of Economic Expansion* appeared in 1958. Sean Lemass took over as Taoiseach in June 1959, and looked round for things to do. Neil T. Blaney, Minister for Local Government since 1957, was first off the mark with a national

133

campaign for rural water supplies and improved urban facilities. Housing, roads and bridges also demonstrated the flexibility of local administration in responding to the call for action.

Health Services
There was also renewed activity in the health services. There were early indications of impatience with the local government boundaries imposed by the 1947 Act on health administration. The Health Authorities Act, 1960 set up four joint authorities combining the cities and counties of Cork, Dublin, Limerick and Waterford. A select Dáil committee on the health services sat from 1962 to 1965 – an index of national concern with their urgent development. Donogh O'Malley, who became Minister in April, 1965, quickly assembled the materials and ideas evoked by the select committee and sketched the lines of future policy in a Government White Paper, published in January 1966. The plan projected the regionalisation of the services and their consequent detachment from the main local government system. A link which had endured for over a century was severed by the Health Act, 1970, under which eight regional health boards took over from local authorities. The boards were a novel form of administrative agency combining local councillors with representatives of the medical, dental, nursing and pharmacological professions, and nominees of the Minister for Health.

Although the rates contribution was less than the state's at the start, and dwindled rapidly to extinction, councillors have retained a small majority on boards. The professional members tend to dominate the boards, despite their minority position. The disappearance of the rates contribution weakens the councillors' position: poor relations at the feast can't very well criticise the repast put before them.

Education
Coolahan (1981) has remarked the 'dramatic increase in government and public interest in education' after 1960, and vocational education shared in the expansion. Vocational schools were raised in status, and offered a comprehensive-type curriculum – in breach of the undertaking given to the Catholic hierarchy by the Minister for Education in 1930, that vocational schools would confine their courses to manual, technical and broadly subjects other than liberal studies. Another manifestation of local education advance was the extension of local authority scholarship schemes under an amending Act of 1961.

Physical planning

The most notable innovation of the decade was the Local Government (Planning and Development) Act, 1963, a move corresponding on the local government level to T. K. Whitaker's *Economic Development* and the Government's *First Programme,* and inspired by the same spirit of rational planning for what seemed to be a golden future. Physical and economic planning would march, shoulder to shoulder, towards the sunlit uplands. The *Second Programme* (1964-70) articulated these hopes: 'The Government's proposals for physical planning and development are designed to ensure that economic and physical planning are properly co-ordinated at both regional and national level and that all major developments will be executed within the framework of a comprehensive physical planning system'. (Part II p. 179). The *Third Programme* (1969-1972) elaborated this proposition and included social development in the grand design. Policies for national prosperity should be 'complemented by regional development policies to ensure that the benefits of economic growth are spread throughout the country'. (p. 160).

The Department of Local Government played a leading role in the early years. The legal framework erected by the 1963 Act gave planning a strong local bias; boroughs and urban districts, together with a long list of 'scheduled' towns were allotted places in the picture along with the larger authorities – county and city councils. But Neil Blaney was already thinking in regional terms. Nine physical planning regions were sketched out on a provisional basis, and a series of regional studies was initiated between 1964 and 1969. They were conducted by experts of international repute: Myles Wright in Dublin, Nathaniel Lichfield in Limerick, and Colin Buchanan in the other regions. The Dublin and Limerick plans were received with passive interest; the Buchanan Report ran into widespread local opposition: it was regarded as threatening too many localities with stagnation and decay.

Neil Blaney left the Department of Local Government for Agriculture in 1966, and with his departure went much of the verve and force behind the physical planning movement. A great deal of the innovation marking the early years may be credited to him – including the establishment of An Foras Forbartha, which he saw as a source of light and guidance in planning matters for both the Department and local authorities. Blaney's successor lacked his fire and determination to transform the planning system into a positive agency for national development on the environmental front. Blaney would certainly have put up a powerful fight against the fate of the Buchanan Report. In the event the report was remitted for further investigation by the network of regional co-ordinating bodies called Regional Development Organisations. They had no executive functions, and little real substance.

Other services

Housing revived rapidly when the Wintry Fifties gave way to the warmth of Spring, not alone in terms of new and reconstructed dwellings, but in major policy statements and legislation. The White Paper of 1964, followed by the Housing Act of 1966, gave a fresh direction and impulse to local housing authorities. The Local Government (Sanitary Services) Act, 1962, provided a statutory basis for the lively group scheme movement – a campaign of co-operative water supplies (and, to a lesser extent, sewerage) which had risen spontaneously, with some encouragement and guidance, from local demands and conditions. Roadworks had already shown signs of post-war recovery: geared to the Road Fund, expansion in car, van, bus and lorry numbers produced cash from motor taxation as well as creating the need for road improvements. The process gathered momentum during the 1960s. A Road Traffic Act of 1961 provided the legal apparatus for coping with increased road use.

Urbanisation

The census of 1966 recorded a population increase of 62,000, the first halt in the decline since the Great Famine of the 1840s. Five years later the census of 1971 reported a small but significant surplus of urban over rural dwellers, using the term urban to mean towns of 1,500 and upwards.

The eastern (mainly Dublin) region exerted an irresistible magnetic force on manufacturing and service industries, and on population. It continues to grow and expand, creating formidable problems of local administration, physical planning, transportation and inner city decay. Problems of urban renewal and inner city regeneration were discerned as early as 1960 and figured in the Planning and Development Act of 1963 and in the *Second Programme of Economic Expansion.*

An Inter-Departmental Committee on Dublin City atrophy reported in 1979 to the then Minister for Economic Planning and Development and some action was put in hands. The job passed to the

Minister for the Environment in 1979. In 1982, however, the opportunity of a half-hung election was seized to apply powerful pressure to accelerate progress in a painfully deprived area in the Northside. An immediate consequence, the Urban Development Areas Bill is at time of writing (June, 1982) making its hazardous way through the Dáil under the aegis of the Minister for the Environment. The Bill proposes to withdraw planning and development powers for certain defined urban areas from the local authorities and vest them in ministerially nominated commissions. These will be exempted from ordinary planning controls. The public will thus be denied participation in their development projects. (*Irish Times,* 28 June, 1982).

This is being interpreted as a criticism of local planning and development, in whose favour it could well be urged that the decisive difference between local authority and the commission is the availability of investment capital. The commissions will operate to a large extent as business concerns – enlightened property developers in the public interest – and will be expected to use their original investment advances as revolving funds.

Apart from the Development Commissions, further legislation is promised for a Dublin Inner City Development Authority. This will give statutory force to the present Inner City Group of central and local officials. Both moves represent a detraction from Dublin's democratically elected city administration.

Local finance

The story of local financing during the past twenty-five years is built round a few well-known themes. These are: the decline of local taxation as an important element in the system; the corresponding growth of state grants; and the disastrous effect of inflation on local costs and resources. These factors were present before the 1950s, but with their increased intensity in recent decades, they have combined to bring local finances to near crisis conditions.

Revenue expenditure by local authorities in 1956-7 amounted to £49.61 million. This comparatively modest sum included £18m for health services, £8m for housing and £12m for roads, but as the tax base on which rates were levied amounted only to £15m, rate poundages were substantial, and steadily rising. With growing activity in local services from 1960 onwards, expenditure doubled between 1957 and 1967, and rates followed the upward trend, but at a slower pace, modified by higher state grants. Rate increases were heavy enough, however, to cause the 1969 mutinies in Dublin city and Bray urban councils against their health services contributions, which led to a four year suspension and replacement by commissioners – the last exercise of this drastic ministerial power.

Some years earlier, however, the agitation against rates had prompted the Minister to modernise the system. An Inter-Departmental Committee on Local Finance and Taxation recommended (1966) that the valuation of rateable properties should be rationalised. It had remained substantially unrevised since 1865. Further reports dealt with essential improvements in the rating system, and the possibility of finding other sources of local revenue. These recommendations formed the basis of a Government White Paper on Local Finance and Taxation (1972) whose main proposals were to retain rates as the major local tax, while pruning it of its numerous defects and making it more productive; to transfer the Valuation Office from Finance to Local Government and reform the valuation system as a matter of urgency.

The White Paper was trampled to death by a proposal to de-rate houses and flats which became a last-minute addition to the 1973 General Election Programme of Fianna Fáil. This idea was so well received that, even though it did not then prove a match winner for Fianna Fáil, the Coalition team which took over in March, 1973, could not dismiss it. It haunted them, threatening electoral misfortune unless they came to terms with it. In a desperate effort to evade the dilemma the new Minister called on the Economic and Social Research Institute to supply (though the terms of reference were couched in more academic terms) arms and ammunition in defence of the rating system. The ESRI Report No 84 (1975) corrected much of the mythology of rates, such as their regressiveness as a tax and their imposition without regard to 'ability to pay'. There is little doubt that if the question of domestic rates had not been prejudged in the popular mind, the proposals in the 1972 White Paper and the 1975 Report would have rescued and rehabilitated the tottering system of local taxation. Myths, however, can only be countered by equally powerful myths: their enormous strength cannot be overcome by rational argument. After a brief pause for thought, the Minister yielded to what he discerned as the will of the people, and commenced a process of phasing-out rates on dwellings over a four year period, supplying the deficiency in local funds from the Exchequer.

While the phasing-out of domestic rates was still going on, the General Election of 1977 returned Fianna Fáil to power, with a mandate to end rates on dwellings and certain other properties including secondary schools and community halls. De-rating became effective from 1 January, 1978 and was given parliamentary cover by the Local Government (Financial Provisions) Act, 1978. The state became, with domestic rate grant, agricultural grant, housing subsidies and various other grants, the largest ratepayer and heaviest contributor to local finance. The government felt justified in assuming powers to control rate levels nominally determined by local councils, and have exercised these controls since 1978 in the form of permitted percentage increases over the previous years' figures. This restraint on rating authorities' former budgetary freedom is also defended in the interests of ratepayers occupying non-domestic properties such as factories, offices, shops, hotels and agricultural land still liable to rates.

The state now shoulders to the the tune of nearly £150m the rates formerly paid by householders. The depressive effect on local government is palpable: the system as a whole has been curtailed of a major part of that freedom of decision, manoeuvre and choice which was cited by the government in their White Paper of 1971 as an essential ingredient of local democracy. This is owing not so much to departmental interference, because the domestic rate grant is distributed, as the agricultural grant has always been, as a bulk payment without poking into details. But the vulnerability of local authorities to inflation, because of the highly labour-intensive character of local services, creates a condition of permanent famine in county and municipal funds. The rate increases authorised each year, ranging from ten to fifteen per cent, have never met local needs in full. Services are beginning to suffer visibly from undernourishment.

It is arguable, but not convincingly, that people who don't pay rates lose interest in local councils and their goings-on. Local democracy would thus be undermined. But ratepayers have always been in a minority. They are now a tiny minority, but that does not seem to diminish popular interest in, say, local elections. A more serious result of domestic de-rating flows from its success in calming the anti-rates agitation, thus taking public attention away from the numerous problems of local taxation, local finance, and State local-financial relations. The question of valuation reform is dormant although it may be revived by whatever decision is handed down in the legal action taken by a group of farmers against rates on land.[1] The White Paper of

1972 promised a further report on the agricultural grant and rating of land; it never came. Nor has anything been heard of the full review of central-local financial relations which was then said to be under way. The ESRI Report of 1975 drew attention (Ch. 8) to the 'marked regional variation in the structure of local finances in Ireland' and suggested a need for some action. Such defects and distortions as existed in 1975 have not been cured – probably aggravated – by the flat percentage increases added to 1977 rates figures in succeeding years. There is a clear need to take up again the task laid down after the 1972 White Paper was put aside, of a full examination of local finances, taxation, and how the burden should be shared between central and local government.

One series of proposals in the White Paper (Ch. 9) has been resurrected recently. A scale of fees for planning applications is to be introduced, and legislation giving local authorities general powers to charge for services is foreshadowed. The purpose is to relieve the chronic cash shortage which afflicts local government; pressure for action on this front has come from local councils and managers. The move will not be popular. Paying for goods and services is a normal feature of society but paying substantial sums for services hitherto 'free' or at virtually nominal costs, tends to rouse old passions. Allegations are already flying of efforts to re-introduce domestic rates under the guise of benefit charges.

A few words about the agricultural grant. In the early 1950's, under the influence of the Minister, Paddy Smith, the employment allowance was increased sharply as a means of keeping workers on the land. It failed in its purpose and subsequent changes in the grant moved gradually through total de-rating of smaller holdings towards the ultimate goal of substituting income tax for rates. That goal is still some distance away, but now well within sight.

A financial innovation towards the close of the period was the revival of the possibility of toll roads and bridges. The Local Government (Toll Roads) Act, 1979 enables local authorities to make agreements with private interests for the construction and maintenance of roads and bridges, and the levy of authorised tolls. Extension of the idea to other public facilities was hinted at, but the suggestion seems unlikely to be taken up.

Organisation and reorganisation
It is sometimes hard to remember, in the welter of assaults on

contemporary local government, that the system was overhauled and re-structured in the 1920s, leaving it very largely neither Victorian nor British. One of the first major reforms undertaken by the new Administration of 1922 was a rigorous trimming of the system; local government was the one sector of government of which ministers had experience and knowledge, especially of its seamier side. They set about the business of reform with confidence and vigour, pruned away most of the smaller bodies, set up the Local Appointments Commission, started a unified local service and began to introduce city and county management. In an excess of reformist zeal they extended to local government generally the dreaded Poor Law apparatus of controls manipulated by the colonialist Local Government Board to keep the boards of guardians in order, and thus the bulk of local administration. This centralist incubus has dominated the system ever since despite vague assumptions that tight controls were necessary only so long as local administration was in disorder, and would wither away when the system had reached the desired level of efficiency.

The 1922 local administration programme was largely completed by 1955, and a pause ensued. A few points in the programme had escaped the net. The aim of the Local Government Act, 1925 to get rid gradually of small urban districts and towns by merging them in the counties, had not been vigorously pursued. And the Greater Dublin question had not been carried to the conclusion marked out for it in 1938 – a combined city and county authority. Attention switched to the local financial problem, which occupied the foreground for the next decade. Structural reform re-entered the picture towards the close of the 1960s, mainly as a result of reorganisation plans for local government in England, Wales, Scotland and Northern Ireland. There the planners of new modernised dispensations found answers on broadly similar lines: fewer and larger units of local government, and the merger of town and county in the enlarged local areas.

It is not surprising that these same ideas were used here, suitably adapted, as the basis for the White (or Green) Paper of 1971 on Local Government Reorganisation. The number of local bodies was cut down, and larger authorities were aimed at. The notion of breaking down the barriers between town and county had not occurred to the system-builders of the 1920s, but as the White Paper pointed out (4.4.2) the same effect is achieved by unifying county administration under county councils. The White Paper proposed therefore to carry the early reorganisation plan a major further step nearer full realisation. All town commissions and most urban district councils were to be absorbed by the county councils; and Dublin City and County Councils, together with Dun Laoghaire Borough Council were to be merged in a Metropolitan Council. These were not, of course, the only changes projected. Both regional and sub-county bodies were discussed: co-ordinating planning bodies for groups of counties; and area committees of county councils for county electoral areas. In addition, non-statutory community councils would be encouraged. But the effective framework of the new local government system would be a single tier of county and (apart from Dublin) county borough councils. Local authorities were not consulted nor advice sought by the commission or otherwise from the public in the drawing up of this paper. The White Paper was compounded from the department's inner resources, with the advice and assistance of other departments concerned.

The White Paper proposals encountered a good deal of political opposition, and drew critical fire from academic and professional commentators. Much of the latter found expression in the IPA document *More Local Government* (The Chubb Report, 1971), which elaborated a plan for massive decentralisation of government to several levels of local administration, regional, county and district.

Local politicians did not concern themselves with new and better structures. Passions were roused at the thought of wholesale abolition of political centres formed by towns and urban districts, and the mere possibility of regional authorities. The realisation dawned that the authors of the White Paper had misjudged the political climate in assuming that measures acceptable in the 1920s would find favour in the 1970s.

The General Election of 1973 brought a new Minister for Local Government who was determined to reject the White Paper and substitute his own ideas. A discussion document was published towards the end of the year, heavily weighted, in consonance with Labour Party ideology, in favour of the elected members. No council or commission was to be abolished, but there was to be a re-arrangement of functions which would leave little significance to urban councils and towns, and raise county councils to a position of almost total dominance. This plan proved unacceptable to the local councillors whom it was meant to placate. They were not hoodwinked.

Little or no progress has been made since 1973. Sporadic attempts have been made to bring the Dublin issue to the point of action but apart from the proposed Inner City agencies, the Government has not signalled that any solution is on the way. Thought and feeling in the Custom House and City Hall (including county and borough councillors) are said to favour a two-tier arrangement – a metropolitan city-council at the top, with borough or district councils handling local issues for populations of about 100,000.

The structure of local government therefore, is much the same as it was twenty-five years ago. There have of course been developments in local administration: the creation of regional health boards of novel composition; county development committees, an innovation monitored by the Department of Finance linking (mainly western) county administration with economic development; regional development organisations which have done some excellent things, but shown inevitably uneven performance; expansion of the concerns of vocational education committees to include community colleges and the supervision of regional technical colleges; and the emergence of ACOT to take over the educational functions of county committees of agriculture.

Local associations

After the abortive central attempts to reorganise the system in the early 1970s there was a mounting consciousness among local authorities of the need to add a strong local input to policy formation. A projected Convention of local bodies led by the General Council of County Councils and spanning the Association of Municipal Authorities and the County and City Managers Association surfaced in 1975 but was frustrated by the then Minister for Local Government. The idea of a single authoritative voice speaking forcefully for local authorities on policy issues languished for some years, but was revived in 1981 in the form of an Irish Branch of the Council of European Municipalities. Establishment of the branch had as its immediate aim supplying a means to intervene effectively in European local government conferences and discussions, but the Irish Council of European Local Authorities will no doubt fill the role of local spokesman in domestic as well as external confrontations. The Institute of Public Administration, which acts as secretariat to the Council has already organised a conference of councillors, managers and others to discuss problems of local finance.

Summing-up

How has local government weathered the vicissitudes of the past twenty-five years? It survived. Local authorities, of course, lost two important social services – health and home assistance; but if a broader view is taken of local administration both these services were merely transferred to another form of local agency. And local government in the narrow sense gained a new range of powers under the local Government (Planning and Development) Acts, 1963 and 1976; the Housing Act 1966 and subsequent Housing Acts; the Roads and Motorways Act, 1974 and the Water Pollution Act, 1977. The most recent addition to its powers is the Fire Services Act, 1981, which has been criticised as inadequate in some respects by the *Stardust* tribunal.

This battery of legal instruments (not a full list, by any means) gave sufficient promise and possibility of action, and indeed much action resulted, most of it good. But the whole scene has been clouded by financial stringency. If one fault more than any other can be imputed to the system of local administration as a whole (and this must include the central authority) it is the failure to grapple in time, and vigorously, with the problem of local finance, which began to loom in threatening proportions during the 1950s.

The rates debacle was a serious setback, but it was not the only failure of the system. Another, in which the Department took a leading role was the vain effort to reorganise local government. After a second abortive attempt in the form of a Discussion Document in 1973, the Department seems to have put the task aside, and given its attention to more pressing affairs. But as the system is far from perfect, the job must be faced sometime. Perhaps there is here another opportunity for the Irish Council to take the initiative; they could at the same time signalise their Continental connections by breaking out of the British way of thinking to which we seem to be indissolubly wedded.

It would be foolish, however, to pretend that, apart from organisation and finance, all is well with local government. There have been other failures. Planning performance has been disappointing. Dublin County Council has been much in the news on its re-zoning decisions, an example of local politics at its worst. One could put this trafficking in land down to a rural bias if planning in Dublin City had not been almost as dismal. Blame can be shifted from one part of the system to others, but the Department, generally the scapegoat in such matters, is not primarily at fault, unless one should censure it for failing to use the current Planning Bill as a means of making dramatic changes in the planning mechanism. NESC Report No. 55 for example,

Urbanisation: Problems of Growth and Decay in Dublin (1981) envisages a two-tier planning system of strategic and local plans, the strategic plan to be prepared by a Greater Dublin Council under the direction of a planning committee representing major public investors – Government Departments, State-sponsored Bodies, Dublin Port and Docks Board and, of course, the Greater Dublin Council. But innovations of such magnitude would require political decisions of major importance. The present Bill, a modest repair measure, is of a different order.

Generalisations are open to all kinds of error, but it is hardly misreading the position to say that Irish local government has done well in work of a positive, constructive, non-ideological character, such as roads, housing, water supply and sewerage, libraries and the like. Their shortcomings in these services can be fairly ascribed to lack of finance, whether capital or revenue. On the other hand local authorities have performed poorly, sometimes deplorably so, in regulatory functions such as planning, control of development, checking water pollution, street cleansing, and coping with litter, graffiti, and bill-posting. Defects in the fire brigade and fire prevention services, exposed sensationally by the report of the *Stardust* tribunal, raise other issues, and neither the Department of the Environment nor local agencies have escaped censure. Much of the local share of the criticism was attributable to inadequate investment in the fire service and sadly, the remedy urged by the tribunal is centralisation of the service under an Inspectorate of Fire Services reporting to the Minister. But take a different problem – that of improving the condition of travelling people – where money had been freely offered by the Government. Here the innate weakness of local bodies, their inability to resist pressure, their populist desire to please the voters, takes over in a craven flight from action.

There is little satisfaction or utility in searching round for instances of local ineffectiveness, but the Wood Quay episode stands out so starkly that it cannot be passed over in silence. It possibly figures in the public mind as a classic case of city hall pig-headedness and philistinism. But if so, the citizenry should, on reflection, see it in a different light. It was in one way an admirable example of local response to public feeling: where the electorate got an opportunity of expressing civic opinion through the ballot box (in 1979) the City Council changed its tune, but by that time it was too late. Things had gone so far that only the Government could have rescued the site, the remains of the Viking town and Christ Church, to say nothing of the civic conscience. They refused to do so, and the Minister for Finance of the time told the Council, in rather brutal terms, that if they were unable to put up the money themselves, they shouldn't strike heroic attitudes. The Government themselves were supported or betrayed (depending on individual feeling) by their archaeological advisors. The City Council acted in the end as whipping boy, in the worst of all possible positions – late converts to a lost cause, sighing for a great opportunity missed, and committed irrevocably to building a lasting monument to their own subordinate condition.

Note to Article
1 The High Court decided (23 July, 1982) that the Valuation Acts and certain valuations of land were not consistent with the Constitution.

References
J. Sharpe Ed. *The Local Fiscal Crisis in Western Europe, Myths and Realities,* London, 1981.

Tom Garvin, *The Evolution of Irish Nationalist Politics,* Dublin, 1981.

John Coolahan. *Irish education: its history and structure,* IPA, 1981.

John Copeland and Brendan Walsh. *Economic aspects of local authority Expenditure and Finance*, ESRI, 1975.

A. J. P. Taylor. 'The failure of the Habsburg monarchy' in *Europe: Grandeur and decline,* Pelican, 1967.

The Health Services and their Administration

BRENDAN HENSEY

Trends before 1957

What happened in the health services in the quarter century since 1957 developed logically from changes in the preceding decade. After much discussion and some controversy, between the state, the medical profession and the Catholic hierarchy, a policy of extending eligibility for services was introduced, mainly under the Health Act of 1953. While the administration of the health services remained in the local government system, there was some consolidation in 1947 when the county councils took over the health functions of the urban district councils and in 1953 when county councils were designated health authorities with comprehensive responsibility for the services.

1947 had also seen the commencement of the trend towards greater state participation in the financing of the services. Up to then, the rates were accepted as the major source of finance for the services and the modest state grants which were paid met only about 16% of the total cost. Under the Health Services (Financial Provisions) Act, 1947, the state undertook to increase its share of the cost up to 50 per cent of the total.

The groundwork preparatory to the introduction of the state-sponsored voluntary health insurance system had also been carried out before 1957. The Voluntary Health Insurance Board was set up early in 1957 and commenced business in October of that year.

The changing health scene, 1957 - 82

Since 1957, and particularly during the 1960s, much was said and written on the health services. A select committee of the Dail sat from 1962-65, a Government White Paper outlining future policy was published in January 1966, and several advisory bodies submitted reports. These included the Commissions on Mental Illness and Mental Handicap, the Consultative Council on the General Hospital Services (the 'Fitzgerald' Council) and other bodies which dealt with such diverse topics as the child care services, the care of the aged, psychiatric nursing services and the restructuring of the Department of Health.

This was a period of scrutiny of existing services, of identification of problems, and of recommendations – sometimes contradictory – for solutions. It was a period of uncertainty for some existing services pending decisions on changes. It was a period of new medical discoveries and of a change in emphasis in the aims of the health services, due to the decline in some former problems, the increase in others and the emergence of some new ones. Heart disease, cancer, psychiatric conditions (including those connected with alcoholism and drug dependence) and diseases associated with ageing and accidents emerged as the main concerns for the health care system. As was the case with tuberculosis in earlier times, these were problems rooted in the way of life of the people, but because this had become so much more complex, solutions were becoming more difficult to find.

These years saw a realisation and acceptance of the fact that advances in medical science would not benefit all who could benefit from them and that, because of the complexity of modern medical organisation, there was a need for change and new involvements in health administration. The extent of the financial problem of the health services became evident and the need for ordered priorities in health expenditure became more apparent. The reports, consultations and proposals of the 1960s resulted in the Health Act of 1970 which is the basis of the present health system. However, there were several significant changes before 1970 which come under the separate headings of administration, finance and service.

Administration
Central Administration
The most noteworthy event in the central administration of the state was the publication in 1969 of the report of the Public Services Organisation Review Group (the Devlin Report), which dealt with the reorganisation of government departments generally. The essential recommendation of this report was that ministers should divest themselves of direct executive responsibility for services, so as to be free to concentrate on the general planning, organisation and review of the services. The report recognised that organisational

developments in the health services had been in accordance with this recommendation and a restructuring of the Department of Health on the principles of the report was accomplished in 1974.

An important Act (the Health (Corporate Bodies) Act) was passed in 1961 to allow the Minister for Health to set up corporate bodies to operate particular health services not suitable for localised operation. Several bodies were set up under this Act, including the Medico-Social Research Board, the National Drugs Advisory Board and the Health Education Bureau. Another Act (the State Lands (Workhouses) Act, 1962) tranferred former workhouse lands to local authorities and, in 1971, the administration of the Central Mental Hospital at Dundrum was transferred from the Department of Health to the newly-established Eastern Health Board. Both moves were in accordance with the general policy of devolving detailed executive work from the Department.

The Minister's powers to set up advisory bodies were widely used during this period. In addition, the National Health Council, a statutory advisory body, continued to exercise its function of examining and reporting on the services until 1968. In 1972, there was an important change for the hospital services in the establishment of Comhairle na nOspidéal, an independent body to govern the creation of new consultant medical posts in hospitals and to advise generally on hospital services.

Local Administration
The local authority system for the health services in the Dublin, Cork, Limerick and Waterford areas was simplified under the Health Authorities Act, 1960, by the establishment of unified health authorities for each of these areas. The number of local authorities responsible for the health services was thus reduced. This was the culmination of the trend towards having fewer and bigger local authorities responsible for health care. This local authority system remained in control of the services until March 1971: new health boards set up under the Health Act, 1970, took over on 1 April 1971.

The idea of taking health administration away from the local authorities was not new. A White Paper published in 1947 tentatively put forward a proposal for special bodies directly responsible to the Minister for Health to administer the health services, with provision for regional co-ordination, but this proposal was not followed up at the time. The idea of special bodies for the administration of the health services surfaced again in the 1966 White Paper, which proposed that legislation should be introduced to transfer health administration from the existing local authorities to regional boards whose membership would 'represent a partnership between local government, central government and the vocational organisations'.

The case for the change in health administration, as stated in the White Paper, had two bases. The first was that, because the state had taken over the major financial interest in the health services and this interest was increasing, it was desirable that a new administrative framework combining national and local interests should be developed for the services. The second reason for change arose from developments in professional techniques and equipment, which meant that better services could be provided on an inter-county basis.

This argument was, of course, of greater relevance in the hospital services. For many of these services, and for the general organisation of hospital services, the county had become too small a unit. In 1966, over half of all in-patients in acute hospitals were being treated in the regional and teaching hospitals in the larger centres, and specialist services at out-patient departments were being organised increasingly on a regional basis. It had become clear that the future efficiency of the hospital services was becoming more and more dependent on full co-ordination of the various units and that a board covering a number of counties could plan and arrange the hospital services for those counties more efficiently. Hundreds of patients were being sent annually from many counties at the expense of the local health authority to hospitals in other areas, but the county concerned had no say in the organisation or operation of these hospitals.

On the basis of these arguments, the case was made for the organisation of the hospital services in larger units, leaving the operation of the other health services, such as the general practitioner service and the preventive service, with the local authorities. However, this option was rejected because of the importance of unitary control and responsibility for all the health services in each area.

The Health Boards

The Health Act, 1970, gave the Minister for Health power to set up health boards with responsibility for the services. Section 4 (2) of the Act specified the constitution of each health board in broad terms. The majority of the members must be appointed by the local county councils and county borough councils (and, in the case of the Eastern

Health Board, the Corporation of Dun Laoghaire) and the remainder of the membership must include persons elected by medical practitioners and members of ancillary professions. Under Section 4 (4), consultations with the county councils and other nominating local authorities were required before regulations could be made under that section.

Each health board set up under the Act is a body corporate, with the usual authority to hold and dispose of land,etc. The Act contains rules relating to the membership and meetings of the boards and provisions allowing them to set up committees (to which functions may be delegated), to act jointly in providing services (including, if necessary, the establishment of a joint body) and to co-operate with local authorities. The board can also enter into arrangements with other bodies, such as voluntary hospitals, to provide services on their behalf.

Eight such boards were set up under the Health Boards Regulations, 1970.

In designing this structure, a number of factors were taken into account. Inter-county arrangements for other services were borne in mind, in particular the regions for local government planning and development (in fact, only counties Roscommon and Meath are in different combinations with other counties for health purposes). Regard was also had to the desirability of not combining too many counties in any one board, of not allowing the population to be served to be much below 200,000 persons and of not having too extensive an area covered by one board. However, it was not by using any exact formula that the decision was taken to have eight boards. This result of the detailed discussions and consideration was necessarily a compromise based on commonsense rather than science.

Membership of the Health Boards
An analysis of the occupations of the first members of the health boards, appointed in 1970, showed that, out of the total of 243 members, there were sixty-one medical practitioners, forty-four farmers, thirty-three shopkeepers, seventeen nurses, ten pharmacists, eight dentists, seven teachers, six solicitors, six trade union officials, six clerks and six company directors. The remaining appointees represent several other occupations. People employed by a health board are not debarred from its membership, with the exception of the chief executive officer, programme manager, finance officer, personnel officer or planning and evaluation officer.

151

Table 1: Health Boards

Title of Board	Functional Area	Population (1979)	Local Authority Members	Medical Practitioners	Dentists	Pharmacists	General Nurses	Psychiatric Nurses	Ministerial Nominees	
Eastern	Dublin City and County, Counties Kildare and Wicklow (1,800 sq. miles)	1,165,000	19	9	1	1	1	1	3	35
Midland	Counties Laois, Longford, Offaly and Westmeath (2,250 sq. miles)	197,000	16	7	1	1	1	1	3	32
Mid-Western	Counties Clare, Limerick City and County, County Tipperary (N.R.) (3,040 sq. miles)	301,000	15	6	1	1	1	1	3	28
North-Eastern	Counties Cavan, Louth, Meath, Monaghan (1,950 sq. miles)	281,000	16	7	1	1	1	1	3	30
North-Western	Counties Donegal, Leitrim and Sligo (2,600 sq. miles)	204,000	14	6	1	1	1	1	3	27
South-Eastern	Counties Carlow, Kilkenny, Tipperary (S.R.), County and City of Waterford and County Wexford (6,630 sq. miles).	367,000	16	8	1	1	1	1	3	31
Southern	County and City of Cork and County Kerry (4,700 sq. miles)	516,000	18	8	1	1	1	1	3	33
Western	Counties Galway, Mayo and Roscommon (5,020 sq. miles)	336,000	15	7	1	1	1	1	3	29

Membership (spanning the Local Authority Members through Ministerial Nominees columns)

152

Local committees
Under Section 7 of the 1970 Act, local committees, whose function is mainly advisory, were established. In the case of most counties, there is one local committee. Local councillors are in a majority in the membership of these committees.

Management in health boards
Each health board is required to have 'a person who shall be called and shall act as the chief executive officer to the board'. The provisions in the 1970 Act with regard to this officer's functions make an interesting departure from the County Management Acts, which governed the management of the services under the former local administration. The Management Acts gave the county manager the statutory responsibility for almost all the functions of the county council, although in performing them he was subject to restrictions and directions by the council. Under the 1970 Act only a limited range of decisions, mainly relating to eligibility of individuals for services and personnel matters, are reserved to the chief executive officer of a health board. Outside these matters he and other officers of the board are specifically required to 'act in accordance with such decisions and directions (whether of a general or a particular nature) as are conveyed to or through the chief executive officer by the board, and in accordance with any such decisions and directions so conveyed of a committee to which functions have been delegated by the board'. When the chief executive officer or another officer acts in accordance with such a direction, he is regarded as acting on behalf of the board. In practice, the health boards have recognised the need for substantial delegation to their chief executive officers of the day-to-day management of the services, while retaining ultimate control in their own hands.

For administrative purposes, the work of the board is divided into three broad programmes covering community care services, general hospital services and 'special' hospital services (mainly the hospital services for the mentally ill and the mentally handicapped). Each of these programmes is in the charge of a 'programme manager'. In addition, there are 'functional' officers in charge of finance, personnel and planning (in the case of the smaller boards, finance and planning were combined under one officer).

The community care programme of a health board covers the preventive health services, the general practitioner services, dental and

153

public health nursing services and the field of activities of social workers. Direct administration of these services from health board headquarters was not recommended; instead, this programme is administered for a number of separate communities under each health board. The services in the community are co-ordinated by the director of community care who is responsible to the programme managers for the operation of this range of services within the community.

An assessment of the changes in administration

When the report of the Public Service Review Group appeared in 1969, it was clear that the administrative changes in the health system which were proposed in the 1966 White Paper and which were then being implemented were consistent with the broad recommendations of the Group's report. The health boards proposed in the Health Bill, 1969 were readily recognisable as executive agencies within the concept of the report and, at the centre, it was clear that the recasting of the role of the Department of Health on the lines proposed by Devlin would be more readily achievable with the new streamlined pattern of the executive agencies for the health services. It was natural, therefore, that the Department of Health should be first to be restructured after the proposals put forward in the PSRG report had been accepted by the government. Indeed, restructuring within the Department of Health was minimal because, for a long time before 1969, the Department had been steered increasingly towards acting on Aireact lines. The establishment of the health boards made it easier to go further with this and to change the nature of the controls on the executive agencies from detailed sanctions to broad directives. As a general assessment therefore, it can be said that if the concepts in the Devlin report are accepted as good, then the principle of the changes made in health administration is also good.

At executive level, the main question is whether events have shown that the decision to depart from the local government system and set up new executive agencies was a correct one. The arguments for this departure were based on the increasing responsibility of the state for financing the health services and on the requirements of an increasingly complex specialised hospital system. If the first of these arguments was valid when the state provided only 50 per cent of the cost of the services, it is all the more valid now when the state is meeting the full cost which has risen dramatically in cash terms, in real terms, or as a percentage of gross national product. The developments in services have confirmed the case for inter-county health administration. In particular, the complexity and cost of staff and equipment for specialised hospital care underlines the need for the system to be effectively linked at regional and national level.

If it is accepted that it was a good decision to remove health administration from the local government system then it must be asked whether the health board system which took over the services was the best choice. At the time the change was being considered, a number of options were looked at. One point of view, derived largely from the Fitzgerald report, was that the organisation of the hospital system required that there should only be three regional boards, based in Dublin, Cork and Galway. On the other hand, some counties, such as Kerry, argued that they were big enough to justify special health boards for their areas. The case for three regions was not accepted – although an intermediate layer of three regional hospital boards with co-ordinating functions was inserted, these boards never worked effectively and no county was given a health board of its own.

It cannot be claimed that the decision to have eight regions and the decisions relating to the areas served by each were indubitably the correct decisions at the time and a study made now might produce different ideas. However, practical considerations dictate that the present structure could only be disrupted with good reason. Changing the structure at this point might not be worth the resulting dislocation – even if some different combinations of counties were arguably better. This might not apply in the case of the Eastern Health Board. The board serves about 1.2 million people and it is much larger than the other health boards. Furthermore, its role in the health system is not as clear-cut as that of the other health boards, as the acute hospital system in the eastern area consists almost entirely of voluntary hospitals, which deal to a great extent directly with the Department of Health. On the other hand, the larger scale of the community health and welfare services in the eastern area might call for special structures for the organisation of the community services. Perhaps some second thoughts on administration in the eastern area are called for, relating more to the working of the system than to splitting or otherwise changing the basic structure of the Eastern Health Board.

Next, it should be asked whether the constitution decided on for the health boards was the right one. The White Paper provided that the membership of the boards would 'represent a partnership between local government, central government and the vocational

155

organisations'. Such a constitution is different from that of the local authorities, and a number of the authorities argued against the departure from the idea that only the elected representatives could be members. In the event, each health board has a membership in which the local authority members are in the majority of one or two, about 10 per cent of the others are ministerial nominees and the remainder are elected by professions, about a quarter of the total membership being doctors. Only the top management of a health board is debarred from membership and indeed most of the professional members on the board are in the employment of the board, or provide services on a contract basis.

An argument against having the professional members on the board is that they form an interested pressure group. However, the professional members are seldom likely to act as a coherent group. Dentists think independently of doctors and the priorities of psychiatric nurses will be different from those of consultant surgeons. Over the years, I have had the opportunity of discussing this issue with many members of health boards and chief executive officers and have formed the opinion that, after some initial suspicion, the participation of the professional members was accepted and, indeed, welcomed by the local authority members.

Discussions at health board meetings have been better informed because of the participation of the professional members and, on the other hand, the professions have perhaps developed a more realistic appreciation of the administrative problems in organising health care. This could be viewed as an example of worker participation which was a forerunner of the ideas since developed for the executive agencies in the public sector generally.

As in any Aireacht – executive agency situation, there is a degree of constructive tension between the centre and the agencies. Health boards desire independence and chafe at the bit of control insisted on by the Department. On the other hand, some ministers sometimes wish to be involved inordinately in local decisions of an executive nature. Department of Health personnel may also become excessively involved in local issues. It is difficult to draw clear lines in many cases of this kind, and to avoid tensions turning into smouldering resentment, intercommunication between the centre and the regions is essential. It has been easier to establish good relations with the eight health boards than with the local authorities and in fact, regular consultations are the practice at all levels, both with the health boards and their officers as a group.

This assessment of administrative change only touches on the broader issues. It should not be inferred that the system is beyond reproach in all its details. However, it is indicative of the acceptability of the system that its role has been extended in some areas (such as the Supplementary Welfare Allowances introduced in 1957 and, more recently, a scheme of repairs of housing accommodation for the aged). It is also of interest that a restructuring of health administration in Northern Ireland a few years later than ours resulted in a basically similar system. There, there are four boards responsible for health and personal welfare services.

Finance

Non-capital public expenditure
The financial arrangements described earlier applied up to 1966. The Health Services Grant from the Exchequer met 50 per cent of the cost of the services provided by the local authorities and the balance was met from local sources. The 1966 White Paper stated that the Government was satisfied that the local rates were not a form of taxation suitable for collecting additional money for the development of the health services. Accordingly, grants supplementary to the statutory 50 per cent were paid to reduce the impact on the rates of the continuing rise in health expenditure. The financial arrangements for the new health boards put these arrangements for supplementary grants on a formal basis. In 1973, the Government decided that the contribution from the rates to the cost of the health service would be phased out entirely. This move was completed by 1977, the culmination of a trend initiated thirty years previously.

In 1971, a scheme of flat-rate health contributions levied on incomes was introduced to meet part of the cost of the services and in 1979 this was converted into an income-related scheme. At present the rate of contribution is 1 per cent of income up to a ceiling of £9,500. In 1973, the Exchequer met 80 per cent of the cost of the service, the rates 14 per cent and the health contributions 4 per cent. In 1980 the Exchequer met about 92 per cent and the health contributions about 6.5 per cent.

These increases in expenditure and in the proportion of the national wealth assigned to the health services progressed through changes in

Table 2: The growth of health expenditure 1957 - 80

Year	Non-capital Health expenditure £m	Percentage of GNP
1957 - 58	16	2.9
1965 - 66	30	3.0
1970 - 71	61	3.7
1975	243	6.5
1980	701	8.2

government and in economic circumstances. The trend pre-dated 1957 (in 1947 - 48, health expenditure was £5.7 million, which was 1.7 per cent of GNP), slowed between 1957 and 1965 and has risen consistently since then. Space does not permit a detailed analysis of the reasons for this trend but it is not insignificant that it paralleled the changes in the economic circumstances of the country. This, indeed, is a common experience in developed countries. In 1960 the United States spent 5.2 per cent of its GNP on health and Sweden spent 3.5 per cent. The present levels in both cases are at about 10 per cent. In one case, reliance has rested mainly on private enterprise and in the other on socialised medicine, so differences in political philosophies do not seem to cause the trend or to affect it materially. Perhaps the cause lies more in the consequences of economic development for health and health services.

Capital expenditure
Prior to 1957, the Hospitals Sweepstakes were the predominant source of finance for capital purposes (between 1947 and 1957, capital expenditure was £27.4 million, of which the Fund met £17 million). This continued into the early 1970s but has now changed. In 1980, total capital expenditure was £35 million. The Exchequer met £34.5 million of that – the Sweepstakes contributed £0.5 million.

Planning public health expenditure
When health was basically a local charge, the determination of the level of expenditure formed part of the local authorities' financial procedures but, as the state became the majority partner in financing the system, central controls increased. This trend was formalised in the Health Act of 1970. Health board spending is limited to what is

approved by the Minister for Health and such limitations can relate to particular purposes as well as to the general level of expenditure.

In practice, the levels of health board expenditure for a year are determined on the basis of discussions aimed at agreeing on the funds needed for continuing services at the level existing at the beginning of the year. There is seldom disagreement about this. Where difficulty does arise is in relation to trends in the services which the local executives may regard as inexorable and in the provision needed for new services or developments introduced by the Minister. The health board system has shown itself capable of controlling expenditure within the limits laid down, as long as those limits were reasonable.

Voluntary health insurance

Since 1957, the activities of the Voluntary Health Insurance Board have expanded greatly – from an initial membership of 23,000 to over 850,000 in 1980. Thus, about a quarter of the population is covered. The Board was set up to deal primarily with the cost of hospital care for the upper income group which was not then covered under the Health Acts. In 1979, when the scheme of compulsory health contributions was extended to that group, the Board's members became eligible for public hospital care (in public wards), without charge, save for consultants' fees. It is a measure of the growing wealth of the community that this did not lead to a reduction in the numbers using the Board's schemes. These schemes are made all the more attractive by the premiums being tax deductible.

An assessment of the financing of health care

The twenty-five years since 1957 have seen the health services changing from being a local service aided by state funds to a service placed fairly and squarely on the shoulders of the state. It is difficult to see how this could have been avoided. Rates as a form of taxation on individuals became discredited as inequitable and no system of local taxation which could replace rates emerged. Hence, if the health services were to be developed, then the money had to be found elsewhere and the exchequer was the obvious choice. The scheme of health contributions introduced in 1971 was designed to relieve the exchequer but it has never met more than a very small percentage of the cost, and these compulsory contributions are now becoming increasingly recognised as being another form of personal taxation.

The health services became a substantial burden on the exchequer but this burden seems not to have been intolerable during a period when a good annual growth rate could be expected in the economy. However, as indicated earlier, economic development seems to bring with it an increasing need, or apparent need, for health care. Medical studies have produced a lengthening list of some fruits of economic development which are thought to impose burdens on the health care system by causing injury or sickness. Tobacco and alcohol are obvious examples, as is the proliferation of mechanical transport. Economic development brings better facilities to meet demands for health care (new drugs, new equipment and new materials etc), thus increasing the ability to meet health needs (for example, the insertion of artificial hip joints). When economic growth ended during the last few years, the demand to maintain the level of health services did not stop. This has produced a financial dilemma which will not be solved easily.

Health services

The 'choice of doctor' scheme
The most fundamental change in the structure of the services during this period was the introduction of the 'choice of doctor' scheme. This replaced the dispensary service, under which salaried doctors appointed for specific districts were available to give general practitioner services to the lower income group (approximately one-third of the population). The new scheme was designed to give a choice of general practitioner who would offer his services in the same manner as to his private patients. The change was an important development in social policy and its introduction was generally welcomed.

Under the scheme, doctors are paid fees in respect of each patient and are given a wide freedom to prescribe treatment and medication. There are restrictions on the entry of general practitioners into the service, but these have been eased in recent years. Drugs and medicine are provided through retail pharmacists, the cost being met by the state. The responsibility for the service rests primarily with the health boards but the payment of doctors and pharmacists is arranged through a joint body, the General Medical Services (Payments) Board. This Board also monitors the visiting and prescribing rates under the scheme, with a view to preventing abuse.

The scheme was introduced in 1972 and for a few years there was an increase in the proportion of the population classified as being in the lower income group, largely because for the first time accurate statistics of that group were compiled and because there was a better take-up of the more acceptable new service. However, since about 1977, the percentage of the population covered by the scheme has dropped back from nearly 40 per cent to under 36 per cent. The number of eligible persons has remained more or less constant since the peak at 1,233,000 in 1977, the decrease in the percentage being due to the rise in total population.

From an administrator's point of view, the design and control of this scheme was an interesting project. It was specified to be a scheme under which those entitled to the public service would get it in the same way as private patients, but this had to be reconciled with public accountability. A computerised system to operate and control the scheme is used by the General Medical Services (Payments) Board to obtain information to enable the Board to monitor individual doctors and pharmacists, and to obtain information from which the Department and the health board can assess the scheme as a whole.

In 1974, the total number of visits to and by doctors under the scheme was 5.35m; the corresponding figure for 1981 was 7.17m. Over the same period the number of pharmaceutical items prescribed by doctors rose from 8.75m to 12.7m. While these figures affect the rise in the total cost of the scheme, they do not represent a comparison of like with like as the number covered by the scheme in 1974 was just over 1m whereas in 1981 it was 1.2m. More significant is the trend in visiting and prescribing rates. The visiting rate was 5.51 in 1974 but it dropped to 5.34 in 1977 and by 1981 had risen to 6.03. It is interesting to note that there seems to be inverse correlation between the visiting rate and the percentage of the population covered by the scheme. Up to 1977, the percentage of the population was increasing and the visiting rate decreasing, whereas since then, both trends have been in the opposite direction. (This correlation, incidentally does not apply to the number of prescription items which increased consistently from 1974). A direct correlation can also be noticed between the rise in the visiting rate and in the number of people covered by the scheme.

These tends raise a number of interesting points. However, the question which should really be asked about the scheme is why it should be necessary for the average person covered by it to see the doctor six times in the year and to get prescriptions covering ten items, while about a quarter of all the persons entitled to the services do not use them at all in a particular year.

Hospital services

In 1980, about 73 per cent of health expenditure was on services in or at hospitals and homes. It is these services, rather than the General Medical Service (which accounts for about 8 per cent of the total cost) which account for most of the rise in health expenditure over the years. The level of activity in the hospital system increased greatly during the twenty-five years since 1957. Statistics over the entire period are not available, but between 1966 and 1979, the number of in-patients in county hospitals rose from 78,000 to 130,000 (not due to the provision of many extra beds but to the reduction of the average length of stay from 11.4 days to 7.8 days). There were similar trends in the voluntary general hospitals. The total number of patients discharged from general hospitals in 1979 was 560,000, about one sixth of the population – a startling figure, even if it does include double-counting of some individuals.

Hospitals and homes accommodated 72,000 births in 1979 as against 48,000 in 1961. (In 1961, 20.4 per cent of births occurred at home: by 1979 this had dropped to 0.7 per cent – a change related to a fall in the infant mortality rate from 30.5 per 1,000 to 12.4).

In psychiatric hospitals, there was a reduction in the number of in-patients (there were 19,801 in 1963 and 16,661 in 1971) and an increase in out-patient care, a trend encouraged since the 1950s by the development of new psychotropic drugs.

A focus for discussion on the development of the general hospital system was provided by the Report of the Consultative Council on the General Hospital Services which was published in 1968. The Council was made up of a representative group of medical consultants under the chairmanship of the late Professor Patrick Fitzgerald. They reported in favour of a new structure involving closer co-ordination between the voluntary hospitals and the then local authority hospitals.

More important and contentious was their recommendation that the number of acute general hospitals outside Dublin, Cork and Galway should be restricted to nine. The principle of this recommendation was accepted at the time by the Minister but it was soon clear that whatever about the medical case for the centralisation proposal, it was not practicable politically to implement it in full. However, in 1975 a hospital plan was worked out with the health boards and accepted by the government under which the number of county hospitals giving full medical and surgical care would, over time, be reduced from twenty-four to fourteen and these fourteen would be expanded and developed. The 'downgrading' of the hospitals not listed for development became a live issue in local and national politics and, after 1977, the decision to restrict the centres for development was reversed so that almost all the county hospitals would be fully retained. The subsequent efforts to improve services by adding staffing and facilities in all these hospitals has contributed in no small way to the financial problems of the health services.

Preventive and welfare services
The Department of Health and the health agencies have developed a greater and more varied role in prevention and health education, extending beyond the control of infectious diseases and the child health examination services which existed in 1957. The Health Education Bureau was set up in 1975 to organise educational programmes and act as a co-ordinating agency for the many voluntary bodies active in this field. Smoking, alcohol abuse, drug-taking and physical fitness are among the items covered by its programmes. The amount of money specifically allocated to the community protection programmes is relatively small (£3 million in 1980) but this does not really reflect the totality of the efforts towards prevention within the health care system.

The health boards have over the years become the agencies for developing a wide range of welfare programmes, including home help services, meals-on-wheels, free milk, child care, welfare homes and cash allowances of various kinds. Health and welfare cannot be neatly separated. This trend recognises this.

The future
To foresee in any detail in 1957 what the health care system would be like in 1982 would have been very difficult. To look ahead now over a similar time span would be even more difficult. These concluding comments therefore relate only to some broad issues.

First, any quick dramatic change in the extent of the problems faced by the system can be ruled out. Genetic factors, environment and personal life-styles are the determinants of health conditions and needs of individuals, and for most of the population. However, during recent years there have been indications that people are becoming more conscious that health is not something that can be ensured by the existence of curative health services. For example, the message about the dangers of smoking seems to be getting through and there is evidence of increasing interest in physical fitness (how many ran marathons in 1957?)

Present economic circumstances impose great strains on the health services. As long as these conditions last, it can be expected that access to many services will become more difficult. Even when the recession ends, financing the health services will cause continuing problems. Economic development above a certain level seems to cause or contribute to health problems, and to increase the demand for health services. So the future of the services will depend to a great extent on whether economic development when resumed is in the pattern of the sixties and seventies or whether a new pattern is evolved.

Administrative structures are not easily changed. While it is to be expected that the structures for health care will be examined and, perhaps, modified, a drastic re-structuring is unlikely. It may be that the greatest change in the future will be the linking to the health boards of the income maintenance services now provided directly by the Department of Social Welfare.

References

1 Hensey, B.: *The Health Services of Ireland,* IPA, Dublin, 1st ed. 1969, 2nd ed. 1972.

2 White Paper: *The Health Services and Their Further Development* (1966) Prl. 8653.

3 *Outline of the Future Hospital System* – Report of the Consultative Council on the General Hospital Services (1958), Prl. 154.

4 Report of the Public Services Organisation Review Group (1966-9), Prl. 792.

5 Restructuring the Department of Health – the Separation of Policy and Execution (1974), Prl. 3621.

6 *Statistical Information relevant to the Health Services,* (vols. up to 1981) – published by the Stationery Office.

7 Annual Reports of the General Medical Services Payments Board – published by the Board, Raven House, Finglas, Dublin 11.

8 Annual Reports of the Voluntary Health Insurance Board – published by the Board, 20/23 Lower Abbey Street, Dublin 1.

State-Sponsored Bodies

JOHN A. BRISTOW

There is no universally accepted definition of 'state-sponsored bodies' but a widely acceptable one is 'autonomous public bodies, neither temporary in character nor purely advisory in their functions, whose staff is not drawn from the civil service, but to whose board or council the governments . . . . appoint . . . . members'[1]. When this definition was coined in 1961, over fifty bodies satisfied it: the tally is now probably nearer a hundred.

State-sponsored bodies are instruments of public policy and the theme of this piece is the political, administrative and financial mechanisms available for monitoring the activities of these bodies in performance of that role. The purpose is not to review the activities of particular bodies, and their experience is used solely to illustrate and exemplify points which are more generally relevant.

This sector can be divided broadly into two parts. First, there are those bodies, usually known internationally as public enterprises, which receive all or most of their revenue from the sale of their products: they carry on activities which, in other countries, may be found in the private sector. Secondly, there are agencies whose income comes totally or mainly in the form of grants and whose function is the implementation of certain aspects of public policy: they perform functions which, in other countries, may be the responsibility of government departments. For the first group, the fundamental question is why these activities are not in the private sector, whereas, for the second, the question is why these activities are not carried out by the civil service. As an economist, I feel more at home with the first question and so my theme will be seen as deriving from that question and the illustrations will be drawn almost entirely from bodies of the first kind.

165

A Synoptic History

The story begins at a time when public enterprises were regarded as one of the successes of Irish public administration; when the accepted opinion was that they had made important positive contributions to economic and social development and had demonstrated the advantages of this form of organisation. It ends at a time when such enterprises are under widespread attack as exhibiting serious symptoms of 'white elephantiasis'. The experience of the past twenty-five years is of some importance now, not only becuase of current concern over the performance of and policy towards long-established bodies, but also because very recent times have seen the creation of new public enterprises, the policies of which exude a remarkable air of *déjà vu*.

From the very beginning, the Irish approach to public enterprise has been pragmatic and opportunistic rather than ideological. To those who are familiar with the economic disasters created around the world by politicians who believe that public ownership is both necessary and sufficient for effective development, the absence of doctrine will be seen as an advantage. However, the obverse of this coin is the absence of coherent policy-making which lies at the root of most of the difficulties now experienced by the state-sponsored sector.

A brief glance at the early history of Irish public enterprise will illustrate the nature of the construction of this sector. The 1930s saw the nearest thing Ireland has experienced to the use of public enterprise in pursuit of an ideology - that is, economic self-sufficiency (which was an ideology rather than merely a development strategy in that it was the reflection of a political philosophy). The Irish Sugar Company was set up in 1933 and the decade saw the beginnings of governmental involvement in peat production (which led to the eventual establishment of Bord na Móna in 1946) and in air transport with the foundation of Aer Rianta in 1937. Import substitution continued to be important in the 1940s with the nationalisation of Irish Steel in 1947 and even after self-sufficiency had ceased to occupy a central position in development policy (Nitrigin Éireann and the British and Irish Steam Packet Company were set up as late as 1961 and 1965 respectively). A variant of it - security of supply of imports in times of international trouble - is still alive today. Not only did this idea provide the rationale for the foundation of Irish Shipping in 1941 but, in 1979, it was the stated justification for the establishment of the Irish National Petroleum Corporation (INPC) and the taking over by that company of the Whitegate refinery in 1982.

166

In other cases, the justification for governmental involvement was unique to each body. Thus, the Electricity Supply Board was established in 1927 in order to provide public financing of an investment project which it was believed could not be privately financed. In the same year, the Agricultural Credit Corporation was set up with the object of promoting the co-operative movement and of providing loans to farmers. The Industrial Credit Company was created in 1933 to remedy a lack of underwriting facilities and to provide a channel of industrial finance. Ceimici Teoranta was established in 1938 to use surplus potatoes to produce industrial alcohol (no such surplus ever materialised and this operation has always had to rely on imported molasses), and Córas Iompair Éireann was set up in its present form in 1950 because the market mechanism was in danger of eliminating the railways.

With hindsight, it is possible to impose a kind of pattern on this hotch-potch.[2] If any common theme existed, it was a belief that economic development would be promoted by certain kinds of activity which were unlikely to be generated by the private sector or which had shown themselves incapable of survival in an unprotected market environment, and which therefore required public support. Or, to quote the most authoritative source (the person generally credited with political responsibility for Ireland's two main phases of industrialisation, as Minister for Industry and Commerce and then as Taoiseach), 'State financed industries have been set up only where considerations of national policy were involved or where the projects were beyond the scope of, or unlikely to be undertaken by, private enterprise'.[3]

The article in which this statement is made is worth pursuing further, both because it presents the opinions and perspectives of an eminent policy-maker in this area and because it is representative of the state of Irish thinking on public enterprise in the late 1950s and early 1960s. The most interesting part of the article is a section entitled 'Problems and Dangers' and what is noteworthy is what Lemass chose to identify as the problems and dangers: the relationship between ministers and boards; the composition of boards; the distinction between state-sponsored bodies and civil service departments; the limits of parliamentary power in regard to these bodies, etc. It was all very sensible (with the possible exception of his opposition to the establishment of a parliamentary committee) but it now seems rather complacent: the system was seen to be working well and the main danger was that politicians might endanger that system by getting too interested in the activities of these bodies. Even the financial comments now read like descriptions of

Edwardian summers. The main worry was that certain bodies would earn excess profits in an effort to minimise the need for external capital: 'Meeting the capital needs of State organisations is not ordinarily a problem for the Government'.[4]

Looking back after nearly a quarter of a century, what strikes one about this article is what is left out. In all the discussion of organisational relationships, whose leitmotiv was the need to preserve flexibility of action whilst ensuring that these bodies served government policy, no questions were asked as to what government policy was or how it would be known if a state body was following it. He says that 'In competitive private enterprise the making of profits is the acid test of economic merit, but in the case of state enterprise different considerations and tests apply'[5] but he does not discuss what these considerations and tests might be. The over-riding concern was with structures, with little or no attention given to the policies which those structures might generate.

Nor is there any evidence that other minds were exercised over these matters. An early manifestation of academic interest in state-sponsored bodies was published in 1961[6] - coincidentally, by another future Taoiseach but one who at that stage was still an outsider politically. Again, this was almost totally concerned with structures rather than policies. To be fair, there is some reference to issues of efficiency, but these issues were not explored at anything like the length devoted to organisational matters.

This was the situation into the 1960s, and there are two possible reasons for the lack of attention to criteria of performance. Firstly, there was the lack of any overall policy objectives which could be given operational significance. Each body was set up for reasons which seemed good at the time and which were more or less peculiar to that body. No adequate mechanisms were established, even on a body-by-body basis, to monitor performance in relation to the original objectives or to review the continuing relevance of those objectives. Nor could such a mechanism be derived from a general political, economic or administrative strategy in relation to public enterprise, because no such general strategy existed. This was one legacy of the non-doctrinaire ad-hoc approach which characterised the establishment of this sector.

Secondly, the general lack of concern for fundamental issues was probably encouraged by the fact that state-sponsored bodies did not usually create financial difficulties for the government. When Lemass was writing, the ESB was receiving a small subvention for rural electrification and the need for a subsidy to CIE had only just been recognised. All other enterprises at least broke even. The financial health of the semi-state sector gave the political and administrative machinery an excuse for its lack of concern with the way in which resources were used in that sector and was a major contributory factor to the prevailing view that efficiency required the minimum interference with the operations of these enterprises.

Unfortunately, however, this apparent health was an illusion and it is worth spending a little time describing how this illusion was created.[7]

All public enterprises in Ireland have, at one time or another and to a greater or lesser degree, taken advantage of the power of government to protect them from the rigours of the market. Three forms of assistance can be distinguished.

First, the regulatory power of government has been used to distort demand or costs so as to produce a higher degree of profitability than there would have been otherwise. Thus, a licence is required for the importation of sugar and, as the sole holder of such a licence, the Irish Sugar Company had a monopoly of the home market. The carriage of passengers and freight for hire by road has been subject to licencing, the effect being to restrict the degree of competition faced by CIE. Ceimici Teoranta produces industrial alcohol for which there is no real market: petroleum distributors have been required to purchase this product as an additive, in quantities and at prices determined by the Minister for Agriculture. A similar market was created for Bord na Móna by the fact that the ESB was obliged to generate a high proportion of its power from peat over a period of twenty-five years when this fuel was more expensive than oil. Changes in relative fuel prices have of course eliminated this example (peat now being cheaper than oil) but the exercise is being repeated in that the ESB is now required to buy oil from the INPC, although cheaper oil is available from other sources. Irish Steel Holdings was protected in an unusual way: its main raw material is scrap steel, but there has been an embargo on the export of this material and the company has not had to compete with foreign buyers in the market for Irish scrap. Nitrigin Éireann would have made even larger losses than it has but for the fact that the Gas Board has been required to sell natural gas to it at prices below those charged to other consumers. Similarly artificial prices are charged to the ESB.

The second source of assistance has been the ability of certain bodies to exploit their state-supported monopoly position to cross-subsidise activities which make losses. Classic examples of this would be the subsidisation of rural by urban consumers of electricity, of train by bus passengers and of trans-Atlantic routes by European routes within Aer Lingus.

These devices all involve the subsidisation of the activities of state-sponsored bodies other than by taxation. Sugar consumers subsidise the Sugar Company; transport users subsidise CIE; petrol consumers subsi-. dise Ceimici Teoranta; electricity consumers subsidise Bord na Móna and now subsidise the INPC although they in turn receive a subsidy from future gas consumers who also subsidise Nitrigin Eireann; sellers of scrap steel subsidise Irish Steel; and so on. These means of supporting state-sponsored bodies disguised underlying weaknesses which became more apparent with the increasing hostility of the economic environment of the 1970s and, because they did not involve disbursements from the Exchequer, they enabled the political and administrative systems to escape the responsibility of monitoring performance in this sector. No operational criteria had been developed for judging whether public enterprises were in fact acting according to the objectives of national policy, and the lack of continuing financial involvement meant that the need for such criteria was not forced upon politicians, civil servants or the general public.

Two opportunities did present themselves but they were not grasped. The first was related to the third way in which these enterprises were assisted: through the government's role in supplying capital. This role was exercised by means of a general requirement that major capital projects obtain governmental approval, regardless of the way in which they were to be financed and by means of the provision of government capital either in the form of loans or equity or government guarantees for both the interest on and the redemption of loans which the enterprises might raise themselves on the market. The guarantee means that regardless of a project's prospects it is seen by the market as riskless (or, at least, no more risky than lending to the government). The price of capital is thereby lower than would otherwise be the case because it is the taxpayer, and not the purchaser of the loan stock, who bears the risk. Other possibilities for assistance arise when the government is the direct provider of capital - most obviously in the case of equity injections which, if made with no prospect of dividends, are in effect capital grants.

Clearly, whenever an enterprise presents proposals for a capital project - and particularly when government finance is required - an opportunity exists for the application of efficiency criteria. However, the political and administrative systems have been rather ineffective in this regard, and this is a matter to which I shall return later.

The other opportunity for increased concentration on policies was presented by the forms of economic planning which were in vogue from the late 1950s to the late 1960s. This is not the place for an analysis of Irish planning experience, but one must wonder why it could have been said that the Second Programme - technically the most sophisticated of these exercises - 'hardly affected the role of the public sector at all'[8] or, more generally, that 'For all (public enterprises) contribute to Irish planning, they could just as well be in the private sector'.[9]

The construction of a plan involves the definition of objectives, decisions as to how conflicts of objectives will be resolved, a consideration of whether those objectives can be effectively achieved under existing policies, and the development of new policies more in accord with the achievement of objectives. Such a planning environment would have been ideal for an assessment of the role of public enterprise as an instrument of policy. The problem was that the programming activities of the 1960s bore little resemblance to this conception of planning. Above all, they were not seen as vehicles for the appraisal and development of government policy. There was far more discussion of distinctions between indicative and directive planning and of the inability of governments to force actions upon the private sector than of the function of the programmes in relation to the power of governments to alter their own policies.

This failure to understand that the main value of planning in a mixed economy is that it can provide a coherent framework for the appraisal of government policy, and the obsession with questions such as 'how can we get the private sector involved in plan construction to the extent that it will actually do what the plan sets out for it?' explains why, at a time when institutional innovation was probably more acceptable than it had been for a long time, an opportunity for a fundamental review of the objectives and policies of state-sponsored bodies was not seized upon. In an era which had seen a complete change in the strategic foundations of Irish economic policy, attitudes to public enterprise remained as complacent as they had been in the 1950s.

The first real signs of change appeared in the late 1960s. In 1968, the Department of Finance instituted a series of studies as part of an appraisal of the public capital programme which covered, along with programmes administered by government departments, certain state-sponsored bodies. The intellectual background to these activities was the growing interest among academics and administrators around the world in cost-benefit analysis as a tool of policy analysis, and in Planning-Programming-Budgeting Systems (PPBS) as a structure for public budgeting and decision-making. Experiments in PPBS were actually conducted on a number of public expenditure programmes in Ireland in the 1970s, and the earlier appraisal studies paved the way for these experiments.

It is worth noting that some public enterprises themselves responded to this new interest in policy appraisal by commissioning cost-benefit studies.[10] This in itself is a revealing indication that a more critical and analytical approach had become the order of the day for policymakers.

These developments ushered in the present era and there is no longer any need to talk historically. Aside from the increased acceptability of ways of thinking derived from microeconomics, two major factors have dramatically altered public discussion of and attitudes towards state-sponsored bodies as instruments of public policy. The first was the establishment of the Joint Oireachtas Committee on State-Sponsored Bodies and the second has been the very recent recognition of the urgency of the need to control public expenditure more effectively.

The Joint Committee was set up in 1976, but did not get into its stride before it lapsed on the dissolution of the Oireachtas in May 1977. It was reconstituted in May 1978 and then began its most fruitful period to date, publishing eighteen reports, covering twenty bodies, between February 1979 and May 1981. (A full list of these reports can be found in the Appendix). The Committee lapsed again with the dissolution of the Oireachtas, and was reconstituted in July 1982.

The significance of this Committee does not lie in its being part of the formal policy-making process because it is not part of that process. The main roles in policy making continue to be filled by the management and boards of the bodies themselves, the officials and ministers of the sponsoring departments (and sometimes the Department of Finance) and the Cabinet. None of these has any obligation to refer any recommendation or decision to the Committee, even for its advice, let alone its approval. Nor has the establishment of the Committee changed traditional legislative procedures: its terms of reference give it no part to play in the framing or parliamentary consideration of new bills concerning state-sponsored bodies. None of its reports has yet been the subject of debate in either the Dáil or the Seanad. Its functions are to examine the performance of public enterprises and to report its findings, together with any recommendations it wishes to make, to both houses of the Oireachtas.

172

Its significance lies in the way it has exercised these functions, and three features of its activities may be given particular emphasis. Firstly, it has made very effective use of sources of expertise outside the traditional departmental structures - and especially of economists, of whom there are few in the departments responsible for state-sponsored bodies. Secondly, it has subjected members of boards to public, oral cross-examination - a new experience for most of them. This cross-examination was frequently tenacious and of considerable analytical quality. Regrettably, the Committee has not yet subjected either ministers or civil servants to this treatment. Thirdly, service on the Committee has been a valuable educational experience for the members (seven TDs and three senators) who, perhaps in most cases for the first time, have been obliged to confront policy issues in an analytical and non-partisan way. In general, therefore, the value of the Committee has been that it has broken free of the traditional framework which was dominated by the mutually supportive - indeed cosy and complacent - relationship developed over the years between a state-sponsored body and the department responsible for it.

Chronologically, the most recent development has been the realisation that tighter control must be exercised over the public finances. A general concern to control the growth of public expenditure has encouraged a more critical eye to be cast on those aspects of the activities of state-sponsored bodies which have implication for the Exchequer on either current or capital account. The rapid growth of CIE's deficit to be covered by government subvention; the realisation that bodies such as Nitrigin Eireann will need either continuing support or a capital injection if they are not to be crushed by borrowing incurred when losses were expected to be temporary, and the substantial capital needs of the airlines for fleet-renewal are all examples of mounting claims on the Exchequer at a time when a reduction in the ratio of government borrowing to national income is a primary objective of financial policy. Although the sceptic may question the intentions of a government which, despite its pleas for stringency, can find the funds for a public enterprise to purchase and refit an obsolete oil refinery whose continued existence is difficult to justify, there can be no doubt that the general financial environment has generated - in political and official circles and in the public media - an increased questioning as to whether Irish society is getting value for money from its state-sponsored sector.

Policy Objectives and Criteria of Performance

In a society which, in general, is prepared to allow the market to determine how resources are used, the justification for the establishment of a public enterprise is based upon the belief that the market mechanism has failed (or would fail) to promote the objectives of society in a particular area and the criteria of performance should then reflect the nature of that market failure.

The sources of market failure of most relevance to public enterprise are, firstly, monopoly, secondly, externalities and, thirdly, distributional considerations.

A number of control devices have been proposed for monopolies which are nationalised, or which are otherwise subject to public control. The most widespread (and probably the most practicable) has been the definition of a maximum rate of profit combined with price control and periodic investigations of technical efficiency. In no case was nationalisation used in Ireland as a means of controlling an existing monopoly, but these matters have been relevant to the ESB and will become relevant to the Gas Board. The Electricity Supply Act, 1927 - under which the ESB was established - clearly intended (in Section 21(2)) that the Board should not have the power to earn monopoly profits, but this of course is insufficient to promote efficiency since monopoly power enables high profits to be made even in the face of grave inefficiency. It needs to be supplemented by price control and by the occasional, externally conducted, technical review. In recent years price control has often been exercised more to delay price increases which would otherwise have ocurred at electorally sensitive times than in the interests of efficiency. The device of technical review has been used quite frequently, most notably in relation to the ESB and CIE.[11]

If the control of monopoly is based on a belief that profitability may not be sufficient for efficiency, then the argument for public intervention based on externalities - the second source of market failure - is based on a belief that profitability may not even be a necessary condition for efficiency. The appeal to externalities in one form or another explains the existence of every Irish public enterprise and so the possibility of deriving performance criteria from these externalities is of considerable importance.

A market mechanism works on the basis of a network of signals in the form of prices and, for the outcome to represent an efficient use of the nation's resources, it is necessary (though not sufficient) that two conditions be satisfied. Firstly, everything to which the members of society assign a value must be assigned a price by the market (i.e. must be traded); and secondly, the price assigned by the market must reflect the value assigned by the members of society. Externalities - sometimes called external economies or diseconomies - arise when either of these conditions is not satisfied.

In the establishment of public enterprises in Ireland, employment creation and the balance of payments have been particularly favoured arguments (they have also been used to justify grants to the private sector, an alternative way of dealing with external economies). In relation to particular activities, probably the best way to approach the idea that employment is an external economy is to argue that the market assigns too high a price to labour and therefore that, in one way or another (for example, by the use of public enterprises excused from the profitability criterion), employers need to be induced to take on more labour than they would in a free market environment. The most obvious source of this 'excess price' of labour is the use of the monopoly power of the trade unions to produce wage levels above what are necessary to clear labour markets. Whether this is a good or bad thing is irrelevant: the price thrown up by the labour market is distorted and the way is open for policies, such as the creation of public enterprises, designed to counteract that distortion.

The argument relating to the balance of payments is similar. Presumably, a preference for exports over domestic sales and for domestic purchases over imports reflects a belief that the market price of exports understates their value, and that of imports understates their cost, which in turn implies that the currency is overvalued. One policy response to this situation might be devaluation; another might be to subsidise (perhaps through public enterprises) activities which earn foreign exchange.

There are of course other types of externality but they all have the same fundamental characteristic: that a benefit or a cost is either not priced or is subject to a distorted price such that the market mechanism would lead to an undesirable pattern of activities. The objectives of public enterprise can then be described in terms of counteracting the effects of the externalities.

The point of this discussion is that it is all too easy to resort to vague appeals to 'social benefit' in order to justify losses or to support the use of governmental power to distort the environment within which public enterprise operates. Ideally, one wants to derive performance criteria from the objectives of the enterprises, those objectives themselves being derived from the identification of some defect in the market system. Only if that defect is defined precisely can any progress be made along this path.

But this is not enough. If an enterprise is making a loss it could be claimed that the continuation of the activity is justified on the grounds that the loss results from the need to take account of an externality. But how large a loss can be justified by such a claim? Some knowledge of the magnitude as well as the nature of the externality is required.

It can now be seen, in principle, how a criterion of performance may be derived for an enterprise whose objectives are based upon the existence of externalities. A target is set, perhaps in the form of a rate of return on capital. It is then arranged for the enterprise to receive, in one form or another, an amount equal to the value of the external economy it creates or of the external diseconomy from which it suffers. If it meets its target rate of return there is satisfaction; otherwise there is not.

This approach is in very clear contrast to that adopted towards Irish state-sponsored bodies during most of their history. That approach was characterised by: a lack of precision as to the nature of the externalities which these bodies were supposed to deal with (indeed, a failure to think in these terms at all, resort being made to vague references to things which sounded impressive like 'import-saving' or 'employment-creation'); a failure to consider the magnitude, and therefore the quantitative implications, of these externalities, and a consequent willingness to pursue whatever policies were necessary to ensure that an enterprise, once set up, could survive, regardless of the cost (especially if that cost were not borne by the Exchequer).

Similar analysis can be employed when the objectives of an enterprise are influenced by the third type of defect in the market mechanism: that the market may generate an unacceptable distribution of real living standards.

The first question which arises concerns the merits of redistribution in kind rather than in money, but as there is nothing peculiar about public enterprises in this respect (after all, it could be argued that public support for education and health care is based on the belief that what makes people poor is lack of education or health care rather than lack of money) I shall not pursue this point. However, any agency responsible for monitoring the performance of these enterprises should consider the question.

Related to this is the matter of defining the beneficiaries of this redistribution. Societies usually want to arrange redistribution so that it is the poorest who benefit most, but this does not happen in many cases. Firstly, the amount of electricity or transport required by an individual is largely a matter of personal taste, so two people with the same incomes can differ greatly in the extent to which they benefit from the redistributive actions (through cross-subsidisation) of CIE or the ESB. For example, simply by switching from bottled gas to electricity for cooking or increasing the frequency with which he visits his friends, a rural dweller or train traveller can increase the benefit he receives from these policies. Secondly, over a wide income range in the case of electricity and a narrower income range in the case of public transport, consumption of these items - and therefore the benefit from the subsidy - tends to increase with income.

Even when it has been decided who should receive this type of assistance, there remains the question of the level of assistance. Historically, this has tended to be answered in a way which, for a redistributive policy, is arbitrary - i.e. which has nothing to do with the degree of disparity between the rich and poor. Thus, the level of subsidisation under the rural electrification scheme is determined by the decision that urban and rural tariffs will be as near equal as makes no difference. Why just this amount of redistribution, no more and no less?

Finally, there is the question of how redistributive policies operated by public enterprises are to be financed. In most cases, the source of finance is a mixture of Exchequer grant and internal cross-subsidisation, with the mix varying from case to case. So, for example, most of the burden of financing below-cost rural electricity supply has fallen on urban consumers, with some Exchequer contribution towards the capital costs of the distribution system. The case of CIE is complex and has been changing over the years in that the Dublin buses at one time offset the losses on other parts of the system - that no longer happens and the burden is now borne by the Exchequer with a little help from certain long-distance provincial buses. Since it can be assumed that society not only wants redistribution to benefit the poor but also wants the rich to pay, the main argument against using cross-subsidisation in this area is the converse of the argument against benefits in kind: there is no guarantee that it is the rich who suffer. Just as in the case of externalities, there is a strong argument in favour of the costs of non-commercial practices which are carried on for redistributive reasons being financed from the exchequer.

The theme of this section has been an acceptance that markets may not produce results which accord with the objectives of society and that the purposes of state-sponsored bodies may be characterised as the generation of a pattern of production and distribution more in accord with those objectives, but that those purposes will not be achieved unless they are specified with more precision than has been typical heretofore. This is what was meant in the previous section by the lack of an analytical approach to policy in this area.

Some Organisation Issues

A simplified, but not seriously distorted, description of the theory of semi-state organisation is as follows: the government is responsible for determining the general objectives to be served by an enterprise and for laying down the broad guidelines within which an enterprise's policies are to be constrained. The enterprise itself is responsible to the government for the construction and implementation of technically efficient and financially sound policies to achieve those objectives within those constraints. The corollary of this is that it is not the job of an enterprise to make strategic decisions (though it may, through its sponsoring department, give advice on such matters) and it is not the function of politicians or their officials to get involved in day-to-day decisions concerning the operations of enterprises.

The theoretical ideal that ministers and their officials should leave detailed matters to the enterprises is vulnerable to attack primarily because many of the day-to-day decisions of state-sponsored bodies inevitably have 'political' implications. For example, although the pricing policies of these bodies do not have noticeable effects upon the rate of inflation, things like bus fares and electricity charges are visible, and for governments who claim an ability to influence the general price level, and part of whose appeal to the electorate is based upon such a claim, the temptation to interfere with public sector prices is often irresistible. Also, operational decisions of public enterprises frequently have different effects upon particular groups - sectoral or local - and political pressures may then impel ministers to respond to the pleas of those groups by intervening in the decisions.

These actions produce a lack of clarity as to who - the minister or the enterprise - is responsible for any decision. This can have harmful effects upon the morale of the board and staff of a public enterprise, especially - as is usually the case - if the ministerial decisions in question cause a deterioration in the financial position of the enterprise. Not infrequently, a proposal aimed at improving the financial health of an enterprise (e.g. an increase in prices or the closure of plant) is rejected or delayed by a minister. No compensation is paid to the enterprise, and the enterprise, rather than the minister, bears the odium of the failure to improve profitability).[12] The prevalence of ad hoc, uncompensated interference by ministers also makes the application of rational performance criteria more difficult and, in particular, reduces the value of financial accounts as indicators of performance.

The converse of this has been a tendency for ministers and the Oireachtas to abdicate responsibility for the development of policy at the strategic level. The reason that certain activities are in the public rather than the private sector is that the market, in relation to those activities, will not produce the results required by the objectives of society. Those objectives, while they may be investigated and elucidated through various kinds of analytical processes of an essentially technical nature, can only be determined through a political mechanism. A political system such as exists in Ireland may not be ideal for this purpose, but it is even less desirable to give the enterprises themselves a dominant role in determining their own general objectives. They have no responsibility to society at large and are above all else quite properly concerned with the maintenance of their organisations. Also, by having excessive power to influence the definition of their objectives, enterprises are in effect determining the criteria according to which they will be judged - hardly a state of affairs conducive to social efficiency.

Of course, this discussion of who should be responsible for what should not overlook the fact that, whatever the formal hierarchy of responsibility, there is bound to be a set of informal relationships involving ministers, members of the Oireachtas, departmental officials, and the boards and the management of the enterprises. Such informal relationships are essential for the working of any system, and simply reflect the reality that any organisational decision-making requires multidirectional flows of information, analysis, proposal and counter-proposal. However, informal systems can become less efficient than they might be if the balance of power within them is markedly different from what the formal system prescribes. This has happened in the case of Irish state-sponsored bodies because, until recently, the Oireachtas and departmental officials have not had the technical competence required for the effective definition of objectives and monitoring of the performance of public enterprises. As a result, the departments (and their ministers) have tended to act more as lobbyists on behalf of 'their' enterprises than as critical exponents of a partial replacement for market disciplines, which is allegedly their true role.

It has already been pointed out that recent years have seen decided improvements in these matters. The value of the Joint Oireachtas Committee appears to have been accepted by the political system, and departments with a key role in these matters have taken steps to improve their analytical capability (for example, the Department of Energy - responsible for the ESB, Bord na Móna, the Gas Board and the INPC and the Department of Transport - responsible for CIE and the air transport companies - have recruited economists of proven skill and independence of mind). But there is no cause for complacency and perhaps two areas of continuing organisational weakness can be identified.

Firstly, as in other areas of government, confidence in the system would be improved if major decisions were made more openly, perhaps by giving the Joint Oireachtas Committee a role in making such decisions. For example, there is evidence that the decision to purchase the Whitegate refinery was not obviously reconcilable with the findings of specialist consultants[13] and the kind of open investigation conducted by the Committee would have forced the government to reveal publicly the way in which the various considerations were balanced.

Secondly, although they may work somewhat ineffectively, there are well-established parliamentary procedures and official mechanisms for dealing with decisions which involve disbursements by the Exchequer, but those procedures and mechanisms can rarely be used in this context because, as was noted earlier, direct financial support for public enterprises is a rarity. This is the point of the suggestion made in the previous section that the social benefits produced by state-sponsored bodies be expressed in monetary terms and 'purchased' by the government in the form of a direct grant and the implied suggestion earlier in this section that enterprises receive financial compensation when ministerial intervention operates against their financial interests. The whole panoply of established parliamentary and official procedures would then be available for use in overseeing the performance of these bodies as instruments of policy.

This is a counsel of perfection in that no-one believes that analytical techniques exist which could place an exact monetary value on all aspects of the activities of these bodies which reflect their public nature. All that can be claimed is that a movement in this direction would facilitate the operation of effective criteria of performance and would expose more clearly to public view the issues at stake.

Reports of the Joint Oireachtas Committee on State-Sponsored Bodies

Irish National Stud Co. Ltd., Feb. 1979, Prl. 7869

British and Irish Steam Packet Co. Ltd., Mar. 1979, Prl. 8063

Min Fheir (1959) Teo., Jul. 1979, Prl. 8242

Córas Iompair Eireann, Oct. 1979, Prl. 8438

Ceimici Teo., Oct. 1979, Prl. 8475

Aer Rianta Teo., Nov. 1979, Prl. 8582

Arramara Teo., Jan. 1980, Prl. 8686

Bord na Móna, Mar. 1980, Prl. 8808

Voluntary Health Insurance Board, Mar. 1980, Prl. 8899

Agricultural Credit Corporation Ltd., Apr. 1980, Prl. 8944

Industrial Credit Co. Ltd., Sep. 1980, Prl. 9261

National Building Agency Ltd., Oct. 1980, Prl. 9480

Comhlucht Siúicre Eireann Teo., Dec. 1980, Prl. 9555

Aer Lingus Teo. and Aerlinte Teo., Dec. 1980, Prl. 9584

Irish Shipping Ltd., Mar. 1981, Prl. 9663

Nitrigin Eireann Teo., Apr. 1981, Prl. 9752

Foir Teo., Apr. 1981, Prl. 9944

Radio Telefís Eireann, May 1981, Prl. 9945

References

1 Fitzgerald, G.: 'State-Sponsored Bodies', Dublin, IPA, 1961, 2nd ed., p.5.

2 See Fitzgerald, op. cit. Chap III, and Bristow, J.A.: 'Public Enterprise,' 'Economic Policy in Ireland,' Dublin, IPA, 1968, pp.175-180.

3 Lemass, S.F.: 'The Role of State-Sponsored Bodies in the Economy', Administration, Vol. 7, No. 4, p. 278.

4 See Lemass, op. cit., p.288.

5 See Lemass, op. cit., p. 287.

6 See Fitzgerald, op. cit.

7 For more detailed discussion of this question, see Bristow, op. cit.

8 Bristow, J.A.: 'State Enterprise and Economic Planning in the Irish Republic', Journal of the Statistical and Social Inquiry Society of Ireland, Vol. XXI, Pt. III, 1964-65, p. 92.

9 Bristow, J.A.: 'The Public and Co-Operative Sectors in Ireland', Annals of Public and Co-operative Economy, 1969, Vol. 40, No. 3, p. 304.

10 See, for example, Bristow, J.A. and Fell, C.F.: 'Bord na Mona: A Cost-Benefit Study', Dublin, IPA, 1971; Mulvey, C.: 'An Application of Cost-Benefit Analysis to the Strategic Shipping Sector', Journal of the Statistical and Social Inquiry Society of Ireland, Vol. XXII, Pt. III, 1970-71, and O'Donoghue, M.: 'A Cost-Benefit Evaluation of Irish Airlines', Journal of the Statistical and Social Inquiry Society of Ireland, Vol. XXII, Pt. I, 1968-69.

11 See, for example, Report of the ESB Investigation Committee, Dublin, Stationery Office, 1972, and McKinsey International Inc.: 'The Transport Challenge: The Opportunity in the 1980s', Dublin, Stationery Office, Prl. 9433, 1980.

12 For further discussion of this issue see

National Economic and Social Council: *Enterprise in the Public Sector,* Report No. 49, Dublin, Stationery Office, Prl. 8499, 1979.

13 See *Irish Times,* 1 September, 1982, p. 12.

182

A Generation of Public Expenditure Growth: Leviathan Unchained

MOORE McDOWELL

'. . . the nature of men being as it is, the setting forth of Publique Land, or of any certaine Revenue for the Commonwealth is in vaine; and tendeth to the condition of mere Nature, and War, as soon as ever the Sovereign Power falleth into the hands of a Monarch, or of an Assembly, that are either too negligent of mony, or too hazardous in engaging the publique stock . . .'

Hobbes: Leviathan, Ch. XXIV

One consequence of the recession of the 1970s was the destruction of the prospect of unending economic expansion. A return to public awareness of the economist's idea of scarcity and a re-appraisal of the size, role and efficiency of the public sector were inevitable. These have been reinforced by growing doubts about the need for a high level of public spending in order to maintain aggregate demand. Attempts at demand management by fiscal policy in Ireland have not been successful.[1]

Attitudes to the public sector, hitherto regarded as heretical, have enjoyed greater respectability with the accession to power of President Reagan and Mrs Thatcher. 'Supply siders' and 'Monetarists' have not only launched successful assaults on the 'Keynesian' theoretical orthodoxy, but, pace press commentaries to the contrary, are seeing their counter-revolution justified – even if the costs are higher than anticipated.

As a result, the 1960s liberal consensus view of public spending as a desirable complement to the private sector is being replaced by the view that it is a costly substitute. This change in attitude has been slow to percolate into public discussion in Ireland.

True, the implication of run-away government spending on the public finances is widely understood, as is the need to cut spending and/or raise taxation. But this has not been translated into action. The difficulty lies in a widespread view that public expenditure has attained its present level in fulfilling generally accepted social goals. To cut it would not only threaten the livelihoods of those dependent on the exchequer, but would represent a retreat from a set of socially agreed policy targets. Cuts, therefore, run into opposition from a formidable alliance of three separate lobbies: Keynesians, who believe public spending is necessary to maintain employment; those committed ideologically to socialisation of the economy, and those who see their individual living standards under threat.

Unfortunately, this demand for a large public sector is only weakly associated with a willingness to pay the necessary taxes, or to see that they are paid.

Herein lies the essence of the fiscal crisis besetting Ireland after twenty-five years of steady growth in public spending. In the context of rapid economic growth, an expanding tax base makes growing public spending easy to accommodate politically. However, a stagnant, or declining level of real income per head means sharper political opposition to funding increased public sector activity.

Given the degree of recent publicity to the level of public spending, it will be sufficient to present a highly summarised version of developments here, and to confine detailed discussion of figures to certain key areas.

Table 1:

Year	GNP £m	Cg £m	Kg £m	G £m
1958	600.9	145.4	37.4	182.8
1962	783.8	196.2	58.8	255.0
1966	1073.9	303.6	83.1	386.7
1970	1648.5	546.1	157.7	703.8
1974	2968.5	1091.1	411.9	1503.1
1978	6403.4	2667.6	943.1	3610.7

GNP = Gross National Product at Market Prices
Cg = Public Authorities Current Spending
Kg = Public Authorities Capital Spending

Source: National Income and Expenditure issues

Total government spending has exceeded 50 per cent of GNP since the early 1970s. In contrast, at the beginning of the period under review, combined government spending amounted to only 30 per cent of GNP.

While GNP rose (in nominal terms) by a multiple of just under 10.5, and total government spending by a multiple of 20, the fastest growth in the latter came not from current spending (a multiple of 18) but from capital spending (a multiple of 25). The latter rose from 25 per cent of government spending in 1958 to approximately 35 per cent in 1982.

This clearly implies that restoring a balance to the current budget is not sufficient to get the public finances back into order. In future the capital side of the budget is going to need even tougher scrutiny. Indeed, the impact of past borrowing for both capital and current purposes has been to reduce the degree to which current spending can be cut, since an increasing amount of it is pre-empted by debt-service charges.

Public sector capital spending shows other disturbing trends. Between 1958 and 1978, annual Gross Domestic Physical Capital Formation (GDPCF), which includes the investment activity of the semi-states, rose by a multiple of 20. Within that, capital grants to industry (dominated by the IDA) multiplied by 12, and direct capital formation by government (mainly infrastructure) by 18. Thus, private and semi-state investment are becoming increasingly important.

But while GDPCF rose from 12 per cent of GNP in 1958 to 20 per cent in 1966 and 27 per cent in 1978, the performance of the economy has not kept pace. Despite the higher level of investment in the 1970s than in the 1960s, growth in output per head was lower in the more recent period. It appears that the social return to investment has been falling. At the same time, the net social cost of investment - in terms of the net factor payments leaving the economy to fund the foreign borrowing which has financed an increasing proportion of this investment – has risen.

Part of the blame for the apparent fall in the social return to investment may be laid at the door of the private sector. For example, over the last decade much investment in the private sector was aimed at moving from relatively expensive labour and energy intensive modes of production to a relatively cheap capital intensive one. That is, it aimed at producing the same level of output with less labour and energy. If real wage growth is not halted, this inevitably means higher unemployment and lower growth in output per head of the population. Complementary to this type of effect is the impact of two unexpected recessions - investment was planned to meet higher levels of demand, and showed a

185

Table 2:

Year	GDPCF £M	GDCPG £m	%	KGR £m	%	PCP £m	%
1958	72.3	16.9	20.3	6.7	9.3	37.8	52.3
1962	143.3	25.6	17.9	5.5	3.8	65.1	45.4
1966	207.8	42.4	20.4	11.1	5.5	99.3	48.0
1970	396.5	69.2	17.4	28.1	7.1	173.4	43.7
1974	870.8	72.0	8.3	35.5	4.1	362.0	41.5
1978	1848.5	155.6	8.5	81.2	4.9	765.0	41.3
1980	2568.0	n/a	n/a	n/a	n/a	1305.0	50.8

GDPCF = Gross Domestic Physical Capital Formation
PCP = Public Capital Programme

Source: National Income and Expenditure, Economic Review and Outlook

lower than anticipated real return when that demand did not materialise.

There is, however, much evidence of appalling public sector investment decisions, which points to a catastrophic fall in the productivity of public sector investment. The rate of return to private sector investment may well have fallen over the years since 1958, but while its contribution to growth in output per head may have declined, no one has suggested that it has in general failed to increase total employed factor productivity. The same could hardly be said of the public sector.

At least some of the responsibility for the steady rise in the incremental capital-output ratio (the inverse of the overall return to capital formation) must be borne by the extremely suspect performance of public sector investment, which cannot be explained away by asserting that there is no measurable direct return to infrastructural investment. If the latter is indeed 'productive', this will show up sooner or later in a general increase in output per head. The onus of proof, therefore, seems to lie with those who claim for public sector investment the returns often claimed for it.

In the context of an increase in current government spending since 1958 to the 1982 level of about 45 per cent of GNP, much attention has been paid to the growth in public sector pay. There are reasons, however, for believing that while pay in the public sector is a major source of our problems, the data on which much public comment has been based do not properly reflect the underlying reality.

Recent work by Michael Ross of the ESRI on public sector pay has drawn attention to the difficulties in measuring this elusive entity.[2] The National Income and Expenditure Tables figures for employee incomes in Public Administration and Defence (PAD) account only for earnings of those in the 'core' of the public sector, producing the 'public' goods of administration, policing, security and regulation. They do not, for example, include the wage element in post office spending, nor the earnings of secondary teachers. Quite clearly, they do not include all those items which most people would include as public sector pay. This brings the question as to what exactly is included, or ought to be - to which there is no easy answer.

Beyond the core of PAD it is very hard to define exactly where the public sector ends and the private sector begins. There are also difficulties involved in defining how much of 'transfer' spending by the government is in fact expenditure on pay in subsidised enterprise – CIE being the most obvious case in point.

Legally, public sector pay might be defined by the legal status of the employing agency. Economically, however, it means budget spending on wages, directly or indirectly, in the sense that the numbers employed and rates of pay are determined by government receipts rather than by market sales. The matter doesn't even end there. If we adopt the economic definition, and use sophisticated accounting to sort out how much of a university lecturer's pay should be counted in public sector pay we are faced with a further problem: much of the 'market' element may in fact be determined by the government rather than by the market - for example, RTE licence income.

Granted these reservations about the statistical adequacy of discussions of public sector pay, the figures nevertheless show some interesting trends. First, the ratio of PAD to total current spending has fallen over the last twenty-five years from 18 per cent in 1958 to just over 13 per cent in 1978. It did increase as a percentage of GNP – from 4.7 per cent to 5.5 per cent, reflecting increased spending mainly on security. The big increase in the more widely (if arbitrarily) defined public sector wage bill is due to non-administrative incomes at local and central government level, including the health services, P&T, and secondary teachers.

It is doubtful, however, if much is to be gained from further concentration on pay. John O'Hagan[3] has recently pointed out in a

Table 3:

Year	Cg £m	PAD £m	GW £m	GW* £m
1958	145.4	28.0	56.4	61.7
1962	196.2	36.4	70.1	82.8
1966	303.6	53.9	104.1	123.4
1970	546.1	84.2	168.2	206.0
1974	1091.1	168.9	316.8	370.5
1978	2667.6	353.4	746.7	909.5

CG = Current Public Spending
PAD = Public Administration and Defence
GW = Public expenditure on wages, salaries and superannuation
GW* = GW + wage etc, in P&T and secondary teachers' salaries

Source: National Income and Expenditure, Appropriation Account

similar context the arbitrary nature of distinctions between public spending on goods and services and on transfers. Similarly, the line between public sector pay and other spending heads is of doubtful value.

For this reason, the approach taken by Frank Gould in an article in a recent issue of this journal[4] may well be preferable. Gould concentrates on examining public spending by programme spending area (Defence, Agriculture . . .) rather than on divisions between purchases, transfers and pay.

Gould's purpose was to examine the behaviour of the component parts of public expenditure in order to detect relative shifts between areas of concentration, and possible party political biases. There was some inter-temporal and inter-programme variability of growth rates - but it is noteworthy that these were relatively small. Between the early 1960s and the late 1970s virtually all programme areas showed a rate of expenditure growth in the range of between 1.2 and 1.8 that of GNP (all in current money values).

Drawing these strands together, the following picture of public spending growth emerges. Public spending, current and capital, has grown much more rapidly than GNP over the period since 1958. Within this total, the ratio of current spending to direct capital spending has also increased steadily (direct capital spending fell as a proportion of the Public Capital Programme). Within current spending PAD fell, while

Table 4: Ratios of programme growth rates to GNP growth selected periods, 1960 – 77

	Greater than 2	Between 1 & 2	Between 0 & 1	Negative
1960 – 69	None	Education 1.6 Other Economic Services 1.6 Housing 1.5 Agriculture etc. 1.5 Transport etc 1.4 Health 1.4 Other Community & Social Services 1.3 Mining etc. 1.2 Social Security & Welfare 1.2 Public Debt 1.2	Other General Governmental Services 0.9 Defence 0.8	None
1970 – 77	None	Other Economic Services 1.8 Public Debt 1.8 Social Security & Welfare 1.4 Defence 1.4 Health 1.4 Other Community & Social Services 1.3 Mining etc. 1.3 Other General Governmental Services 1.3 Education 1.2	Housing 0.9 Transport etc. 0.9 Agriculture etc. 0.6	None

Source: Frank Gould (1981): 'The Growth of Public Expenditure in Ireland 1944-77', *Administration*, Vol. 29, 2.

189

expenditure on goods, services, transfers and subsidies has increased. In so far as one can distinguish between direct payments to employees and other forms of government spending, the large increases are apparently due to increased payments outside the administrative sub-sector.

When government spending is described in these terms, and an explanation is sought for its growth, conventional approaches to the analysis of public expenditure growth are less than satisfactory.

John O'Hagan's recent study on public expenditure in Ireland offers an econometric investigation of the determinants of its growth. With more than the usual caution of a hypothesis tester, he suggests that '. . . the evidence for Ireland . . . is not incompatible with the hypothesis of a demonstration effect, nor with Wagner's Law. . . (nor is it) compatible with the hypothesis that the recession of 1974-5 caused an upward shift in the public sector share . . .'[5].

The hypotheses to which he refers may be summarised in three propositions:

1 a rising real income per head is associated with a growing public sector for a variety of reasons based on income elasticity of demand for the output of government;
2 growth in the size of the public sector in a large country will induce a political demand for a similar expansion in a small neighbouring one;
3 social disturbances lead to once-and-for-all shifts in the share of public spending;

O'Hagan draws attention to the difficulties and limitations inherent to the type of data he uses, and also to the strong evidence of autocorrelation in his results. He indicated the possibility of specification errors.

Gould's paper does not use econometric techniques, but provides strong associative evidence to support both the Wagner's Law and displacement effect hypotheses. Moving from a purely conventional economic analysis he examines the possibility of party political influence on public sector growth. His conclusion was 'that with the exception of the first Fine Gael - Labour interparty government, there is little to distinguish interparty government from Fianna Fail'.[6]

Gould also briefly discusses the possibility of a 'Relative Price Effect'. This refers to the possible impact on public expenditure growth of a lower than average (for the economy) rate of increase of labour productivity in the services sector. Briefly, if manufacturing industry determines wages, and if labour captures productivity growth in industry, then wage costs will rise in the services sector - including the public sector. Since there is relatively little productivity growth in this sector, by assumption, unit wage costs must rise, and the maintenance of any given volume of public sector output will require expenditure on that output to rise more rapidly than GNP as a whole.

In discussing this issue, however, Gould implicitly raises a basic question to which neither he nor O'Hagan gives explicit consideration. He indicates that the unit cost of supply of public sector output has risen in relative terms - yet assumes volume demand remains unchanged. In conventional microeconomic terms, this requires some further explanatory variable. What he has in fact touched on is the issue of the role of the public sector in determining spending on its own output – an issue which, while overtly discussed by political scientists, has been ignored by mainstream economic analysis.

Basic to the approach of Gould and O'Hagan (in a long tradition) is the implied hypothesis that the volume of public sector output is demand determined. Resources are shifted from the market sector by a political process reflecting the wishes of the body politic as a consumer of the 'output' of the public sector. This 'output' can be income redistribution, more jobs or hospital beds, or more guards on the beat.

Alternatively, an increased level of economic activity requires an increased supply of public sector 'output' as an input to final production.[7] Whichever view of the public sector - or combination of views - is used, the clear implication is that the observed level of expenditure, and changes in expenditure, are to be explained in terms of a relatively passive response of output to an exogenous demand function.

This raises a basic econometric problem - identification. O'Hagan mentions the possibility of specification errors, of which the identification problem is a major source. If, as real income grows over time we observe increased spending on public sector output, is this in fact due to a shifting demand function or to a shift in the supply function, or both? Until the supply side of a market is specified the demand side cannot be measured by ordinary least squares regression analysis, and vice versa.

The conventional approach, measuring levels of spending, and deriving estimates of income elasticity of demand implicitly assumes a constant supply function and a demand function which shift with real incomes. The observed increase in expenditure, however, could in principle be the result of a shifting supply function with a given and relatively price inelastic demand function.

On the supply side, my central proposition is, that whatever the income elasticities of demand for the output of the public sector, there is every reason in principle to expect that the supply function can and does shift. Analysis of public expenditure growth cannot, therefore, be divorced from the economics and institutions of public sector supply. This is seen to be due to three factors – the economic and political analysis of the state, the analysis of property rights and public sector supply, and the micro-economic impact of conventional fiscal policy.

It is in connection with the first of these that the title of this paper, and the introductory quotation from Hobbes, were chosen. The key is the contrast between the Hobbesian view of the state as an economic entity with its own goals and the view of the state common to nineteenth and twentieth century liberals – an essentially benign contractual arrangement.

A modern Hobbesian approach replaces the king with the state apparatus of the public sector which has goals it seeks to achieve, subject to political and economic constraints. The state, in other words, can be viewed as a 'very large firm'.

The second factor mentioned above helps tie the Hobbesian view of the state into an explanation of a continuously growing public sector. The problem is to explain why Leviathan should seek an increasing share of GNP. If the public sector is treated as a firm, why should it seek to maximise sales rather than some profit analogue? In the theory of the firm profit maximising monopolies (and Leviathan usually eliminates competition by law) do not seek to maximise sales, unless other restrictions are placed on their activities.

A possible motivation for the modern version of Leviathan seeking continued expansion is to be found in the literature flowing from a book published by William Niskanen[9] in 1971. Niskanen offered an analysis of the behaviour of 'a utility maximising bureaucrat' (a producer who cannot effectively appropriate any net wealth he creates at the margin) who faces a totally different set of incentives from those facing a contracting agent in the market economy. On the basis of these institutional constraints on his behaviour, Niskanen concludes that the bureaucrat will seek to maximise the budget under his control. This in turn leads 'bureaux' (i.e. public sector firms or agencies) which have some degree of monopoly power vis-a-vis the legislature (representing the public) to seek not to produce the 'optimal' amount of a public or merit good but to maximise total revenues subject to total cost being equal to total revenues. In general this means 'over-production'. It also, under certain circumstances, gives the bureau an incentive both to

192

produce at inflated costs and to seek, via political manipulation, to increase the legislature's willingness to pay (or reduce its willingness to cut back spending).

Niskanen's original work has been subjected to criticism, and he has amended it in some respects himself.[10] But the criticism has not shaken the underlying hypothesis: that utility maximising behaviour by public sector employees *can* lead to overlarge and rapidly expanding public expenditure.

The third factor mentioned offers a supply side explanation of evidence of displacement effects during recessions - especially that noted by O'Hagan for 1974-6. The interesting question here is why, once the peril had passed, public expenditure did not drop back as a percentage of GNP.

In a different context, two Oxford economists examined this phenomenon in relation to the low growth rate of the UK economy. Robert Bacon and Walter Eltis[11] offered a physiocratic analysis of Britain's poor growth record which they blamed on the shift of resources away from the production of marketed goods towards the public sector. During economic downturns, state agencies 'solved' the unemployment problem by responding to public demand to create jobs. For Niskanen-type reasons, they did not release this labour when the economy entered an upturn - with a resulting ratchet effect decline in the capacity of the marketed goods sector.

On the demand side, a further weakness in the conventional approach is to treat the demand for expenditure on public sector output as being determined by the usual and independent-of-supply income and price type variables. Taking price as given, demand is described as being determined by changes in the level of GNP – which can be either due to an income elasticity of consumption for the output of the public sector, or due to a GNP elasticity of demand for that output as an input into the aggregate production function.

This approach ignores the possibility that, *ceteris paribus,* the composition of output (private and public sector production) may not be simply the result of the demand for consumer and producer goods - but may itself influence the level of demand for public spending.

Put another way, the growth of public spending may depend on the existing level of public spending. What is envisaged here is that political activity and pressure by public sector employees can be - and is - directed towards shifting the demand function for public sector output to the right at any given level of income. This implies that the rate of growth of demand for public spending is a positive function of the level of public spending.

There are two possible rationales for this hypothesis. The first pertains to the possible differential voting behaviour of bureaucrats, a matter of some academic controversy. The second pertains to a sort of 'snow-ball' effect whereby public sector employees -like other employees - will lobby to increase expenditure on their output, and, over time will cause public expenditure to rise at an exponential rate. Neither is fully satisfactory, but both do offer some basis for hypothesising a demand function shift related to the existing level of public spending.

There are, therefore, reasons to believe, a priori, that the economic self-interest of those employed in the public sector can help explain its growth. Casual observation certainly supports this belief - the explosion of expenditure on health and education, for example. Apart from demographic changes, institutional changes since the mid 1960s have substantially altered the bargaining power of the employees concerned. These are the 'free' secondary education scheme and the extension of non-selective health care.[12]

On the capital side, surely the budget-maximising bureaucrat is a better explanation than public demand for the growing, economically unjustifiable direct public sector investment in such concerns as Irish Steel, NET, Aer Lingus, and the INPC.

It is hard to believe that public demand as expressed by the median voter (if he exists) or any other variant on the Downsian analysis of voter preferences for public spending is the basis for the continued pumping of public monies via TV licences into RTE; or via subsidies into CIE. We accept willingly that it is self -interested pressure from the building industry that determines the level of public spending on construction - so it seems reasonable to apply the same logic to semi-state bodies. This analysis also makes it clear that the system of semi-state organisation of responsibility, hailed as a paragon of enlightened delegation, has consequences for legislative supremacy which are of doubtful value. It reduces the flow of information to legislators on which they may base judgements on the performance of those enterprises. The experience of the Government in dealing with NET over Marino Point is a glaring example of this problem.

The 'liberal' economists' approach to the phenomenon of public spending ultimately comes up against the following intellectual obstacle. It is presumed that the level and mix of public sector activity is in some sense determined by the political expression of a consumers' demand system. Yet it is obvious that most members of the public (even some inside the state sector) are grossly dissatisfied with that level and mix. It is also widely believed that even if the level of public spending were acceptable, the public sector as a producer is seriously inefficient in conventional economic terms, being a high cost and non-innovative means of supplying goods or services which the private sector could produce much more cheaply – *vide* the comparative cost of courier services and P&T, the costs of pirate radios and so on[13]. Economists believe that markets - even political ones - generally perform fairly efficiently. If this is so, why does the body politic not demand the reforms everyone agrees are necessary?

It may be suggested that a sort of 'prisoner's dilemma' is responsible: behaviour which if undertaken and enforced collectively is Pareto optimal is rejected at the individual level as not maximising individual self-interest. For example, if it is agreed that public spending on 'free' drugs is too high, collective action to limit the scheme's application is sensible. But if an individual were to reduce his own consumption of free drugs, this would be irrational. However, the economic analysis of the state insists that it is precisely in such instances that an efficiently operating political system will generate a collectively enforced policy to secure the desired end.

For neo-Hobbesians, armed with Niskanen's model of bureaucratic behaviour, no such difficulties arise. The political and economic market power of the interest groups we lump together as Leviathan determines the outcome. It is, therefore, to the advancement of the interests of those groups that one should look for an explanation of public expenditure growth since 1957, not to self-defeating exercises in distinguishing between income and demonstration effects.

I will now consider the implications of the foregoing for economic policy. There are two basic approaches to public policy on government and other public sector spending. The first of these accepts the institutions as they are, and seeks to find economic and institutional means to channel their activities into socially desirable channels. Using this approach involves wrestling with such problems as what rate of discount to require state agencies to employ in evaluating projects, whether public investment should ignore risk-aversion; when and in what circumstances to require public sector agencies to use marginal cost pricing, and so on. It has proved a highly profitable vein of exploitation for academic economists, and one singularly lacking in realistic concrete results. It has also bred a school of economic practitioners versed in the

195

esoterica of cost-benefit analysis. This technique is increasingly widely felt to be, to paraphrase Dr. Johnson, the last refuge of many economic scoundrels. When has a cost-benefit study undertaken in Ireland shown that the object of the investigation has not yielded a handsome social surplus?[14]

Politically, this approach has led to internal efficiency criteria being imposed – such as the ill-fated Planning – Programming – Budgeting Systems (PPBS) – and the attempt of the legislature to exercise control through select committees (such as the Joint Houses of the Oireachtas Committee on Semi-State Bodies). By and large, these efforts are unlikely to have much effect in curbing the growth of public spending. Parliamentary committees are at the mercy of the agencies they investigate for information; they have very imperfect information on true production costs – being presented mainly with agencies' own cost schedules. Their concern is in general with whether agencies carry out assigned functions efficiently; the question of whether the function ought to have been assigned in the first place is rarely raised.

Internal attempts at controls, such as PPBS, or zero-base budgeting, offer some hope superficially. However, experience has shown that PPBS has led only to further complications of bureaucratic procedures without any obvious gains in economic efficiency. Zero-base budgeting has simply not been adopted - and, if adopted, it can always be neutralised by suitable value judgements on the ends of the bureaucratic activity.

The second approach is to adopt a new-institutional analysis of the public sector. At one level, this requires public recognition of the existence of what has become known as 'collective failure'. This refers to the old tradition in economics that public sector production of goods and services is necessitated by the existence of 'market failure'. The assumption is that public sector activity is a simple corrective device.

Collective failure, however, refers mainly to the kind of misallocation of resources inferred by Niskanen; it also, and more generally, means the possibility 'that government action to correct market failure may not only lead to non-market failure within the public sector, but to the active encouragement to the private sector to protect its interests through methods which produce further market failure'.[15] This implies an equal (or even greater) willingness to submit the activities of the public sector to the kind of critical scrutiny traditionally reserved for firms in the market sector. It means, too, being willing to reverse the procedure of socialisation of decision-making where circumstances indicate. Above all, it means being willing to apply the discipline of the market place, or some close analogue, to public sector agencies - including the possibility of closing them down. It is, however, administratively tedious, raises the problems of 'quis custodiet . . .', and involves the political decision-makers in prolonged public battles with agencies skilled in manipulating public opinion.

Far better, then, to adopt a root and branch reform based on a Hobbesian recognition of the need for some system of checks on the power and expansion of Leviathan.

In recent years, on the fringe of mainstream political economy, suggestions have emerged on how to deal with this problem. Three of them will be discussed here, and of those three, two are worthy of serious consideration at a time when reform of the tax system is already on the political agenda. We will deal with the third first.

This idea is based on recognition of the bilateral monopoly nature of the relationship between the people (via the legislature and/or the Department of Finance) and public sector agencies – the outcome depends on a bargaining process in which most of the cards are held by the agencies. If full information on costs and objectives were available to the 'purchasers' of the agencies' activities, then an optimal outcome could be hoped for. But it is not.

There is, however, an alternative to the costly acquisition of information by the legislature: competition for available funds by agencies leads to volunteering of information. Further, if competition existed in the area at present under the control of a single agency, information about time costs of production etc., would emerge through a public sector equivalent of tendering in the market sector. The implication is that a competitive structure of supply can obviate the information and control problems associated with monopoly state agencies.[16] This suggests that the policy of 'rationalisation' which reduces competitive tendering in the UK's ITV system has lessons for us where RTE is concerned; in another area, industrialistion policy might benefit if two or three IDA type organisations were competing for funds - giving them an inducement to keep costs to a minimum, and to use those funds to the best possible effect.

The other two suggestions are concerned with controlling the rate of growth of Leviathan in general, and providing an incentive system for public sector institutions to maximise output rather than labour cost.

Firstly, it is obvious that expansion of the public sector requires an ability to appropriate a greater volume of resources - which in the end means raising taxes (or using an inflation tax). Establishment of restrictions on tax revenues simulataneously restricts the activities of the public sector. Such thinking lies behind the well-publicised moves in the US to curb the growth of property taxes, starting with 'Proposition 13' in California in 1978. If this logic is followed to its conclusion, one of the cherished aims of liberal tax reform has to be jettisoned. That aim is the securing of a 'comprehensive' tax base - a widening of the tax net to cover as many activities as possible, with a corresponding reduction in the rate applied to each activity.[17] Instead, a narrow tax base, because of the possibility of avoiding tax payments if the rate rises, effectively limits the revenue which can be raised. Viewed in this light, the present calls for restoration of rates and more comprehensive definitions of taxable income assume a less desirable appearance. Indeed, the general consensus seems to be that a more comprehensive tax base is necessary in order to finance existing (and foreseen?) levels of public sector expenditure.

The second proposed reform is the reintroduction of earmarking of tax revenues.[18] For the last fifty years earmarking has been reject on two grounds:

1 it reduced the flexibility of response of macro-economic fiscal policy;
2 it reduced the government's ability to redistribute income through taxation.

Earmarking, however, can be used to 'build into the very structure of Leviathan's coercive power an automatic interest in yielding that power for the common good'. [19] The principle is that Leviathan 'rips off' part of tax revenue for the benefit of the public sector. To get him to produce a desired output rather than pad the payroll, the tax base must be made a commodity the consumption of which is highly complementary to the availability and consumption of the desired product. For example, all revenues raised from petrol would be earmarked for physical road improvement. Of course, even this will not guarantee the limitation of road improvements to those the marginal value of which equals the marginal cost to the motoring public. But the incentive to raise petrol tax simply to increase the public sector payroll is sharply reduced.

A first step towards such a 'constitutional' control on public spending - albeit much more general and less restrictive than those just described - was the proposal which emerged in 1980 and 1981 on the expenditure implications of legislation. In its report for the year ending 31 October 1980, the Public Service Advisory Council (PSAC) discussed problems of

Public Expenditure

costs, efficiency and disclosure of relevant information in relation to
public sector expenditure programmes. Amongst the many improvements in
reporting and control procedures which the PSAC recommended was
one which called for explicit costing of all legislative or programme
proposals being made in the Oireachtas, with a subsequent monitoring
of actual costs.[20]
Administration - Public Expenditure Growth - 9

This proposal was subsequently adopted by the then Minister for
Finance, John Bruton, in his 1981 White Paper on budgetary
procedures. In addition to many interesting suggestions on longer term
planning in the budgetary process, the White Paper called for full
financial disclosure in legislative action.[21]

Bruton submitted that *all* legislation which had *any* financial
implication would require a clause setting out the expenditure
commitment involved – on which the Oireachtas would vote. This
would implicitly limit the spending to the amount set out in the bill,
thus depriving Leviathan of access to the taxpayers' pockets via the
blank cheque. It's not clear that Bruton's proposal will not be
implemented – but if it is not, the declared interest of his successor in
putting the public finances into order by controlling public spending
will lack credibility.

Notes to Article

1 cf. M. McDowell: 'Irish Budgetary
Policies', *National Westminster Quarterly
Review*, August 1981, for a brief outline
of the problems of Irish fiscal policy
and their consequences since the
middle 1970's.

2 Michael Ross: 'Central Government
Expenditure: Outlays on salaries,
wages, pensions and allowances, and
their geographic distribution in
selected years since 1960', Dublin,
ESRI, forthcoming

3 John O'Hagan (1980): 'Demonstration, Income and Displacement Effects
as Determinants of Public Sector
Expenditure Shares in the Republic
of Ireland', *Public Finance/Finances
Publiques*, Vol. XXV, No. 3.

4 Frank Gould (1981): 'The Growth of
Public Expenditure in Ireland 1947 -

1977', *Administration*, Vol. 29, No. 2.

5 O'Hagan, op. cit.

6 Gould, op. cit. p. 128.

7 This raises the further possibility that
the convention of treating the output
of much public sector activity as a final
'consumer' good involves a substantial
degree of double counting leading to
an inflated estimate of the value of
GNP. Even more disturbing is the
possibility that much public sector
(and private sector) services output is
in fact merely the process of trans-
ferring resources from one use or
group in society to another. Not only
does this imply double counting in
conventional measures of aggregate
economic output, but points to the
possibility that this transfer activity,
coupled to attempts to counter it,
results in a reduction in the level of

output below its theoretical maximum. On this, see: J. L. Anderson and P. J. Hill (1981): 'Economic Growth in a Transfer Society – the United States Experience', *Journal of Economic History*, Vol. XLI.

8 This supply side emphasis is to be distinguished from a recent approach adopted in analysing US public sector growth. The latter attempted to explain the growth in public spending as being the result in a shift in the supply curve of tax revenues – the consequence of increased market sector efficiency and the increase in female labour participation. The statistical fit offered is strong, but the analysis leaves a basic question unanswered: if indeed the supply of tax revenue has shifted, why has this not resulted in a decision to reduce tax rates rather than to increase public spending? cf. J. B. Kaw and P. H. Rubin (1981): 'The Size of Government', *Public Choice*, Vol. 37, No. 2.

9 William Niskanen (1971): 'Bureaucracy and the Theory of Representative Government'.

10 cf. Albert Breton and Ronald Wintrobe, (1975) 'The Equilibrium Size of a Budget Maximising Bureau', *Journal of Political Economy*, Vol. 83, William Niskanen (1976): 'Bureaucrats and Politicians', *Journal of Law and Economics*, 1976.

11 Robert Bacon and Walter Eltis (1976): 'Britain's Economic Problem: Too Few Producers', London, Macmillan.

12 Health Board employees, according to Devlin, increased in number from 24,000 in 1971 to 38,000 by the end of the decade.

14 The only honourable exception of which I am aware is Sean Barrett of TCD, whose cost-benefit analysis of CIE's rail operations suggest a negative return (S. D. Barrett (1982): 'Transport Policy in Ireland', Dublin IMI.)

15 Alan Peacock (1976): 'On the Anatomy of Collective Failure', *Public Finance/ Finances Publiques*, Vol. XXXV, No. 1.

16 cf. Thomas McGuire, Michael Coiner and Larry Spancake (1979): 'Budget Maximising Agencies and Efficiency in Government', *Public Choice* Vol. 34.

17 cf. Geoffrey Brennan and James M. Buchanan (1977): 'Towards a Tax Constitution for Leviathan', *Journal of Public Economics*, Vol. 8.

18 Geoffrey Brennan and James M. Buchanan (1978): 'Tax Instruments as Constraints on the Disposition of Public Revenues', *Journal of Public Economics* Vol. 9.

20 Public Service Advisory Council Report for Year ending 31 October, 1980, PRL 9786, p. 6.

21 'A Better Way to Plan the Nation's Finances', Stationery Office, Dublin, October 1981.

13 There is an economic rationale for conventionally inefficient public sector production being genuinely socially acceptable, which is based on problems of contract policing under competitive tender (cf. Thomas Borcherding (1980): 'Towards an Economic Theory of Public Sector Supply', Sinnon Frazer Discussion Papers in Economics, 1980). Borcherding, however, abstracts from the monopoly element in public sector supply.

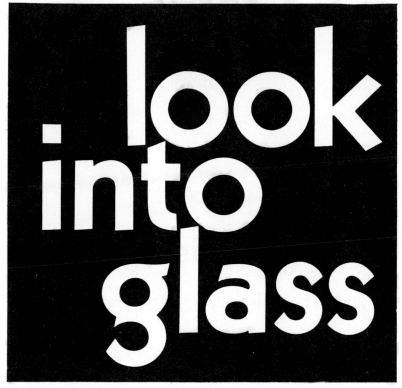

Clear thinkers go for glass, because they know
that their customers do. Glass dresses a product
as nothing else can; shows it off beautifully too.
So think clearly. And let the world see your
product.

THE IRISH GLASS BOTTLE COMPANY LIMITED

DIARIES
& Analysis Books

Quality Irish made products

*Available from all leading
Stationers.*

BROWNES DIARIES & ANALYSIS BOOKS ARE
PUBLISHED & PRINTED BY IONA PRINT LTD.,
33 BOTANIC RD., DUBLIN 9.   Tel.: 303911.

a member of the Jefferson Smurfit Group

Social Policy: 1957-82

TONY McCASHIN

Historical background

Prior to the mid-nineteen sixties the rate of development of social services was slight – the most significant legislative development was the 1952 Social Welfare Act which laid the foundations for the social insurance and social assistance services.[1] Historical observation and economic analysis suggests that the growth of Irish social services awaited a period of economic growth. But to attribute the emergence of a rapidly-developing welfare sector solely to economic growth is to posit too mechanistic a link between the economy and the welfare services. The rapid economic growth we experienced during the late fifties and sixties was *necessary* to the development of welfare services but it was not sufficient.

The specific economic policy orientation during the sixties and seventies linked economic growth and the development of welfare services. It bore witness to Keynesianism – the economic paradigm which provides the rationale, both theoretical and political, for government intervention in the economy. Kennedy and Dowling have described the fiscal policies of the post-war era but more particularly have designated the policies in 1959-68 as 'fiscal policy for sustained growth'.[2] This fiscal policy determined high levels of expenditure on roads, schools, industrial development, hospitals and so on.

A vigorous anti-interventionist philosophy of government prevailed prior to the sixties. It was only with the dilution and disappearance of this anti-state, anti-interventionist ethos that substantial state intervention could emerge. John Whyte, in his classic study of church-state relations, documents the profound anti-interventionist stance of the Catholic Church and he describes the theological and secular versions of this perspective in terms of 'subsidiarity' and 'vocationalism' respectively:[3]

By the forties a rift had emerged in Ireland between two philosophies of government. One could be called 'vocationalist', and called for the diffusion of responsibility among vocationalist groups. The other could be called 'bureaucratic', and defended the centralisation of authority in government departments.[4]

The widely-supported vocationalist philosophy waned and was replaced by a perception of government which not alone tolerated but demanded state intervention in social matters:

The divergence between bureaucratic and vocational viewpoints died away. Churchmen became strikingly more relaxed in their attitude to the State. They ceased to utter warnings against the encroachments of State power: indeed, they were more likely to criticise the State for doing too little than too much.[5]

In the absence of the philosophical shift documented by Whyte it is difficult to accept that economic growth alone led to the extensive social policies developed in the sixties and seventies.

Increasingly the public was beginning to recognise the vast needs in Irish society and the necessity of systematic effort to meet them. Journalists noted a change in the national psyche in the early sixties towards a new commitment to economic and social goals. Irish society now sought the fruits of political independence: the material and social requirements of citizenship in the form of adequate incomes, decent housing and equal social and economic opportunities for all. The factors leading to this transformation are a worthy subject of historical research: Connery, Brown and McCarthy have referred to the impact of television (inaugurated in the early 1960s); the revelations of social inequality contained in the OECD analysis of Irish education *Investment in Education;* the public horror at the housing deprivations of Dublin city articulated by the Dublin Housing Action Committee in the early and mid-sixties; rising expectations engendered by economic growth from 1959 onwards; increased confidence and sense of purpose arising from participation in the UN and contact with the United States and the advanced British welfare state.[6] Even among the professional analysts the calls for economic growth and social development were urgent and shrill. 'Unless the Republic can maintain an annual rate of economic growth of about four per cent on average over the next decade, we are likely to wilt and vanish as a viable economic community'.[7]

These were some of the important factors in the development of the welfare state in Ireland. They need to be integrated into the wider theoretical debate on the development of the welfare state to provide a comprehensive explanation of the Irish experience. Within the theoretical debate, the traditional explanation for the growth of the welfare state – in the British case at least – is the gradual growth of a sense of social obligation and the increasing knowledge of social need. This explanation, labelled the 'social conscience thesis' by Baker, has recently given way to a variety of other arguments.[8] Some writers have concentrated on political causality, arguing that welfare states have developed by virtue of the influence of social-democratic politics or the exertions of organised trade unionism, or both.[9] Another argument is that demographic factors and economic growth are the true causal forces – independently of the political history and culture of a society.[10] A third viewpoint has been called the 'convergence thesis'; this asserts that industrialisation is the important explanatory factor, as industrialisation forces a convergence towards welfare state provisions among all industrialised societies whatever their political regime.[11] A fourth argument is that the welfare state emerges and develops as it does because of the political needs of the capitalist state; welfare, it is argued, is used as a mechanism of political control whereby mild reforms are used to defuse revolutionary analysis and action.[12]

The paucity of historical research in the Irish context forces us to ignore this tantalising debate as it might apply to Ireland, but we can report on one recent contribution to this discussion. Gould, in his study of the growth of public and social expenditure in post-war Ireland offered this conclusion: 'It is probable therefore that the biggest single factor responsible for the relatively faster growth rate of public expenditure relative to GNP in Ireland during the 1960s and 1970s was the need for Ireland to catch up industrially and economically and in social welfare standards with her neighbours and trading partners and the subsequent faster growth rate that this need simply and directly generated'.[13] This finding offers tentative support for a 'convergence'-type explanation, although it is not formulated in these terms, and seems to discount hypotheses of a 'political' nature, with the possible qualification that in the immediate post-war years there seemed to be consistent party political differences on the issue of social expenditure.

Ireland is a virtual laboratory for the testing of hypotheses about social, political and economic determinants of the growth of welfare. If any versions of these hypotheses were applicable to Ireland they would need to take account of the specific cultural and historical circumstances of Ireland which we referred to earlier, i.e. the dilution of the anti-interventionist notions of the role of government, the emergence of a national, popular commitment to economic growth and social development and the adoption of Keynesian economic policies.

Social policy developments
Writing this when there is more public controversy than ever about the distribution of incomes and public expenditure and services, it would seem provocative to argue that there have been enormous strides in social policy in the last two decades, but this is the case. The crucial test of a society's changing commitments and achievements in the social area is the extent of development of its income maintenance services, administered in Ireland by the Department of Social Welfare. The extent of development of these areas of social policy can be looked at in three ways. First, have new services and benefits been introduced? The answer to this question is a resounding Yes. From the mid-sixties onwards we can trace, year by year, the continual initiation of new services and benefits. In 1966 the children's allowance scheme was redrawn; in 1967 an occupational insurance scheme was introduced and free travel was initiated for recipients of social welfare old-age pensions; in 1970 invalidity pensions for the long-term ill, and deserted wives' allowances, were introduced, as were also retirement pensions; unmarried mothers' and deserted wives' benefits were introduced in 1973, and pensioners' wives' allowances in 1974.

Second, the evidence is heartening concerning the living standards of recipients of welfare payments. As the data in Table 1 shows, the real value of social welfare payments has grown considerably over the years. The real value of contributory old-age pensions increased by 89 per cent from 1966 to 1981; the comparable figures for unemployment assistance and children's allowances payments are 98 per cent and 59 per cent respectively. In line with the overall increases in living standards, therefore, the real living standards of the poor have increased significantly in the past two decades.

Social Policy

Table 1: Trends in the real value of welfare payments
(May 1966 = 100)

Payment	1971	1976	1981
Unemployment benefit (single man)	106	114	149
Unemployment benefit (man & wife + 4 children)	109	133	168
Old age pension (couple, aged 70-80) contributory	116	130	189
Children's allowances (4 children)	121	121	159
Unemployment Assistance (single man)	135	149	198
Widow's pension (4 children), non-contributory	122	193	263
Unemployment assistance (man & wife + 4 children)	127	160	205

Third, the benefits and services in the income maintenance system have been gradually improved and extended. The most important improvement is the continual growth in the coverage of the social insurance system. In 1966 the total insured population was 774,877, and by 1979 this figure had grown to 986,037; as percentages of the labour force the respective figures are 69 per cent and 85 per cent. These figures quantify the fact that most of the citizens are now somewhat protected against the vicissitudes of the market economy. That protection takes the form of an entitlement 'earned' by way of insurance contribution. Insurance benefits have two significant superiorities over their means-tested counterparts: they have higher levels of payment, and they are an entitlement, rather than a stigmatised service incorporating elements of administrative discretion. The relative growth of the insurance sector of social welfare has been paralleled by a significant change within the social assistance means-tested sector; the means tests themselves are gradually being made less stringent. In successive budgets, governments have lowered the amounts by which means-tested assistance payments are reduced by virtue of the assessed income of recipients. For instance, the actual threshold of assessed income above which assistance payments are reduced was relaxed by £1 (weekly) in

207

1974 and this was repeated in 1975. More recently the amount of the deduction per £1 above the threshold has been decreased to £1.30 and to £1.40 in turn.

Table 2: Recipients of social insurance and social assistance* payments plus adult and child dependants

	1966	1971	1976	1981
Social insurance	322,918	392,750	532,237	587,130
Social assistance*	213,794	321,474	344,461	449,218
TOTAL	536,712	714,224	876,698	1,036,348
Payments in respect of Children's Allowances*	944,455	990,472	1,152,618	1,199,652

*Children's Allowances are given separately, being non-contributory payments but outside the social assistance category since they are non-means-tested.

Source: *Dept. of Social Welfare Annual Reports.*

A whole host of other extensions and improvements have been made across a wide range of benefits and services. During the mid-seventies the eligibility age for old-age pensions was reduced from 70 to 69 (1973), from 69 to 68 (1974), and from 68 to 67 (1975); free travel, first introduced in 1967 for recipients of social welfare pensions, was extended in 1971 to include spouses when accompanying pensioners, and in 1972 to all persons over pension age; the age limit for children's allowance payments was extended, in 1973, to 18 years for children in education or apprenticeships (or who are handicapped); pay-related benefit, started in 1974, was extended in 1975 and again in 1976. These are only examples. The consequences of these developments are vividly shown in Tables 2 and 3, which present details on the numbers of recipients and amounts of expenditure. The total number of recipients and their dependents now stands at 1,036,348, compared with 536,712 in 1966. The expenditure data in Table 3 is self-explanatory. In real terms, and allowing also for population, there has been a threefold growth in aggregate social welfare expenditure.

Table 3: Expenditure on all social welfare services

Year	Total current expenditure all social welfare payments (£,000)	Total current expenditure per 1,000 population (£,000)	Index of real expenditure per 1,000 population in 1966 = 100
	(1)	(2)	(3)
1966-67	59,910	20.8	100
67-68	64,823	22.4	104
68-69	73,362	25.2	112
69-70	88,447	30.2	125
70-71	108,740	36.9	141
71-72	126,111	42.3	149
72-73	143,556	47.5	155
73-74	194,927	63.4	185
December 31			
75	350,485	110.3	223
76	428,054	132.6	209
77	488,231	149.2	228
78	556,881	168.0	242
79	638,432	189.5	292
80	853,597	250.7	267
81	1,133,654	329.6	300
1981 ÷ 1966/7	18.9	15.8	3.0

Note: The first eight rows of the Table use financial years to end March; subsequent rows use calendar years. In column (3) the data of (2) were deflated by the CPI for May in each year. The 1981 expenditure figure is the second supplementary estimate as provided by the Dept. of Social Welfare.

Other policy areas reflect a similar pattern of development – new services, increased real benefits and extensions and improvements onto the foundations of the system. Space precludes a full account of changes in these other areas of health, housing and education; details can be ascertained in the relevant sections of recent publications.[14] These wide-ranging developments can be described for the purposes of this discussion as inputs and outputs, and some summary indicators of these are given in Table 4. Under inputs we include the 'hardware' of social provision – teachers, schools, hospitals, houses, nurses, doctors and so on. The figures document the long-run improvements. Ratios of doctors, teachers, schools, houses and so on have all considerably improved. On the 'outputs' side, children are staying on longer at school, life expectancy and infant mortality have improved considerably, overcrowding and bad housing have declined and housing standards are now considerably higher. These 'inputs' and 'outputs' are not causally related in any simplistic fashion; policy changes resulting in more and different inputs have not been the only cause of changes on the outputs side. For example, improved participation rates in second-level education cannot be attributed solely to legislative and institutional changes such as the free education scheme or the raising of the minimum school-leaving age.

Table 4: Selected social indicators

Year	Health Expenditure		Local authorities dwellings built	% Participation in school, 16-year-olds
	Current £m	Constant (1970 prices) £m		
1966/7	41.0	51.5	2,989	41.2
67/8	44.9	54.8	4,079	45.5
68/9	50.6	58.7	4,045	50.4
69/70	59.2	64.1	4,613	54.2
70/71	76.2	76.2	4,706	55.7
71/72	86.6	80.8	3,875	58.0
72/73	108.1	91.3	5,902	58.3
73/74	142.8	108.3	6,072	60.2
74	179.6	116.5	6,746	66.6
75	242.6	130.2	8,794	68.6
76	274.6	124.9	7,263	71.4
77	328.0	131.3	6,333	na
78	400.0	148.7	6,073	na
79	458.0	154.0	6,214	na

What have been the general directions of policies common to all the areas of social service provisions? We can identify firstly a pattern of 'universalism', the practice of extending social provisions to wide or universal categories in the population irrespective of income. In 1967 a scheme of free second-level education was introduced, which subsidised all schools waiving fee income; the health services have been made available to the point where *all* persons are now entitled to free public hospital care; in 1977 a cash grant was introduced for all first time purchases of new homes, irrespective of income, and rate payments on all private residences were abolished.

A second general trend is *professionalisation*, the increasing reliance on paid, professional workers in various social service areas. This has happened most notably in education where the decline in numbers of voluntary religious teachers has led to their substitution by paid professional teachers, but also to a considerable extent in the personal social services field and in health services. Increasingly, voluntary social work organisations, local and national, are staffed by lay persons professionally trained and working in social services as a career. Third, as the population structure and the economy have changed the provisions of social services have become more *centralised*. In education, a policy of closing small village one- and two-teacher schools has been pursued and facilities have become more concentrated in larger centres; the county-based health services have given way to regional health boards which administer centrally-determined services and policies; in social welfare even the old local, discretionary home assistance service has been changed to supplementary welfare which is shaped by a central piece of legislation incorporating minimum payments, uniform means tests and so on. Fourth, obviously, all the social service areas have been subject to enormous 'demand' pressures arising from the rapidly-growing population.

Social policy – an overview and evaluation
The foregoing analysis, reading as it does like a litany of achievement, invites complacency. It is important, then, to contrast the account with some responses to two crucial questions: does poverty still persist in Irish society, and has equality been brought about as a result of these policy developments? Taking the poverty issue first, Table 5 collates and summarises key results from recent studies on this subject which have in common the use of the 1973 Household Budget Inquiry as their basic data source, but the studies vary considerably on points of definition and methodology, most notably on the issue of a defined

211

'poverty line'. There is still considerable poverty in Irish society; the IPA publication[15] reported an overall risk of poverty at 23 per cent (at poverty line C) and the ESRI study,[16] basing the poverty line on unemployment benefit payments + 140 per cent, gave an overall figure of 19 per cent. While the 'one million poor'[17] title of a recent publication may be rhetorical, the available studies consistently record a high level of poverty in Ireland.

Table 5: Compilation of results of recent studies on financial poverty

	Poverty line	Per cent in poverty	Other results
1. Chapter 2 *Poverty and Social Policy*	Poverty line 'C' equals official poverty line plus 40%	23%	43% of poor outside labour force. 21% of poor in farm households.
2. Chapter 5 of ESRI Report No. 109	140% of Unemployment Benefit entitlements.	19.9% with Disposable Income below poverty line.	38.7% of poor are in working-class households. 26.8% of poor are in farm households.
3. Chapter 1, Part 1 of *One Million Poor.*	Social Welfare Benefit Payments.	20%	One-third of poor households had children. 26% of poor households retired.

We must also acknowledge high levels of poverty in other dimensions, e.g. housing. A NESC Report (1977) estimated 2,000-3,000 people as homeless[18] while the 1971 census yielded a figure of almost 15,000 persons residing in mobile homes. Homelessness is extensive, but we lack sufficient basic, contemporary figures to be definitive. This ignorance also affects our knowledge of other aspects of poverty and severe deprivation; we have no data on illiteracy or the extent of poverty-related illness.

Table 6: Percentage of direct, gross and disposable income (unweighted) going to x% of households, 1973

Gross income range	% of households	% of direct income	% of gross income	% of disposable income
Under £7	6.8	0.20	0.87	0.96
£7-£10	4.3	0.39	0.90	0.98
£10-£15	8.3	1.18	2.52	2.78
£15-£20	6.4	2.04	2.77	2.99
£20-£25	7.7	3.77	4.29	4.45
£25-£30	10.0	6.55	6.85	7.10
£30-£40	16.2	13.94	13.99	14.23
£40-£50	12.7	14.42	14.05	14.10
£50-£60	8.8	12.51	11.99	11.89
£60-£70	5.6	9.62	9.10	8.86
£70-£80	4.4	8.73	8.22	7.86
£80 and over	8.8	26.66	24.46	23.80
Gini		0.439	0.380	0.364

Source: Nolan (1977) Table 6

The issue of equality throws up far more complex issues which are rendered still more complex by the paucity of data. There are two ways in which we can develop this analysis; the first is to look at available studies on income distribution – some of these data are given in Tables 6, 7 and 8.[19] These statistics show that in 1973 at the lower income ranges, households with weekly incomes of less than £7 – comprising 6.8 per cent of all households- had a mere 0.2 per cent of all direct income; at the other extreme those households with incomes in excess of £80 – 8.8 per cent of all households – commanded 26.66 per cent of direct income. As the further two columns in Table 6 show this income inequality is somewhat diminished when gross income (direct income + transfer payments) is considered and diminished further when disposable income is considered (gross income minus taxes and social insurance). From a social policy perspective the central point to be noted is that the gini co-efficient measure of income inequality is reduced by the state interventions in the form of transfer payments and taxation.

Table 7: Average weekly income, taxes and benefits of all households in state in 1973, classified by direct income

Direct weekly household income	Direct income £ (1)	Cash benefits £ (2)	Direct taxes £ (3)	Non-cash benefits £ (4)	Indirect taxes £ (5)	Final income £ (1)+(2)−(3)+(4)−(5)	Ratio of final to direct income
Under £7	1.55	8.44	0.03	4.00	2.79	11.17	7.22
£7 and under £15	10.90	6.07	0.45	4.18	4.28	16.42	1.51
£15 and under £20	17.52	4.72	1.20	4.31	5.00	20.35	1.16
£20 and under £25	22.50	3.70	1.95	5.48	5.62	24.11	1.07
£25 and under £30	27.40	3.24	2.41	5.82	6.67	27.38	0.99
£30 and under £35	32.26	2.75	3.18	6.40	7.69	30.54	0.95
£35 and under £40	37.37	3.02	3.74	6.10	8.69	34.06	0.91
£40 and under £50	44.61	2.77	5.00	6.81	8.94	40.26	0.90
£50 and under £60	54.64	2.62	6.43	6.50	10.44	46.90	0.86
£60 and under £80	68.85	2.57	9.07	7.03	11.73	57.65	0.84
£80 and over	112.61	1.94	13.50	7.24	14.75	93.54	0.83
All households	36.00	4.22	3.94	5.69	7.45	34.51	0.96

Source: Central Statistics Office, Redistributive Effects of State Taxes and Benefits on Household Incomes in 1973. (Table B and C)

The gini co-efficient is the most commonly used summary measure of income inequality. It ranges between 0-1: the lower the figure the less the inequality. Turning to Table 7, the picture is complicated by the introduction into the analysis of non-cash transfers to households and payments by households of indirect taxes. The overall result as given in the 'final income' column is one of modest redistribution between income groups – the lower income groups being net beneficiaries and the higher income groups net contributors. But this general assessment ignores the fact that those on the lower incomes pay considerably higher percentages of income in indirect taxes than their higher income counterparts, and that higher income households also gain considerable non-cash benefits – an average of £7.24 weekly for the highest income range compared to £4.00 for the lowest income range. The last column in Table 7 gives the ratio of final to direct income. It is a measure therefore, of the proportion of income which comes from, or goes to, transfers. Those with a ratio higher than 1 are net beneficiaries of transfers, those with a ratio less than 1 are contributors. Examination of the column reveals that although the net impact of taxes, transfers and non-cash benefits is overall redistributive the point at which redistribution ends and begins is disappointing; the ratio in this column ranges very high – as expected – at the lowest income ranges, but quickly approaches unity and at modest levels of direct income households become net contributors.

The data of Table 8 report gross income figures (urban households only) for certain years and the trend revealed is one of diminishing inequality. The gini co-efficient declined from .359 in 1965/66 to .352 in 1973 to .344 in 1974, and rose slightly thereafter. Case study analysed elsewhere confirms the impression of narrowing income disparities. From the mid-sixties to the mid-seventies the net incomes of unskilled workers and welfare recipients, for instance, have increased relative to the incomes of white collar employees and senior administrators – although considerable inequalities persist.[20]

Moving from the specific issue of distribution between income groups to the wider impact of social policies on the social structure our analysis must be more pessimistic. The income/taxes/transfers data is indicative of a very modest redistribution and quoting a recent study, 'it is possible that redistribution is not merely following the course mandates by class divisions; perhaps in levelling tax and distributional

215

Table 8: Decile shares of gross income for urban households, 1965/6, 1973, 1974 (nine months), 1975 and 1976

Decile	Percentage of gross income				
	1965/66	1973	1974	1975	1976
1	1.7	1.7	1.7	1.7	1.7
2	3.5	3.4	3.6	3.4	3.3
3	5.6	5.5	5.6	5.2	5.2
4	6.5	6.8	7.0	7.0	6.6
5	7.9	8.0	8.2	8.0	7.8
6	9.0	9.4	9.5	9.3	9.2
7	10.7	10.9	10.9	10.9	11.0
8	12.8	13.0	12.9	13.0	13.2
9	16.4 ⎤ 42.4	16.2 ⎤ 41.4	*40.7	*41.7	16.6 ⎤ 42.0
10	26.0 ⎦	25.2 ⎦			25.4 ⎦
Gini co-efficient	0.359	0.352	0.344	0.352	0.362

Source: Nolan (1977) Table 15

*Because the top income range contains more than the top decile in the 1974 and 1975 surveys, the share of the top decile has not been interpolated logarithmically.

transfers the state is unintentionally shaping class boundaries, and, once formed, perpetuating them'.[21] Analysis of our education and housing systems supports this perspective; again and again analyses of these sectors make the indictment that social class structures are being perpetuated by the pattern of social policies which has evolved in recent years.

Tussing, on the education system, says: 'The system of finance for education in Ireland runs against the interests of the poor, the working class and the large majority of Irish people. It is essentially a regressive system, in which the many support the few, and there are demands that the few who benefit must be given more.'[22] Baker and O'Brien, Blackwell and others have pointed to the grossly regressive impact of the housing subsidies (purchase grants, tax allowances, stamp duty exemptions, non-taxation of imputed income) to the owner-occupied sector – subsidies which in effect reinforce consumption differentiation between social class groups.[23] The IPA compilation on social policy concluded: 'it seems fair to argue that a significant social services sector exists along with persistent social class inequalities and that some identifiable public expenditures (in education and housing) and policies (absence of certain forms of taxation) actually contribute directly and significantly to this inequality'.[24]

Our assessment of social policy is that, despite considerable development, widespread financial poverty and social deprivation exist, and that our network of taxes and transfers is only modestly redistributive and coexists with many inegalitarian state social policies.

The future

As we write, the obsessive preoccupation of economists and politicians is with the state of the economy in general and public finances in particular. The implication for social policy seems clear and unambiguous: the years of development and initiative are over, and social advancement must now yield to economic prudence. These arguments have been so extensively reported that they are not documented here. Rather, an argument is advanced that present economic circumstances offer a renewed opportunity for a sustained implementation of redistributive social policies and not an excuse for a dismantling of social service achievements to date. However, two other arguments must first be faced – both of a structural and ideological nature. One is the neo-liberal position as expounded by Friedman in the US or the IEA in Britain.[25] This argument sees the current crisis as the logical consequence of social expenditures which have monopolised social provisions, reduced individual initiative, lessened economic growth through punitively high levels of taxation and resulted in ineffective, regressive social provisions overseen by excessive bureaucracies. Compound these tendencies with the peculiar Irish diseases of a small tax base, unproductive public capital spending and a rapid growth of public sector pay expenditures, financed partly by foreign borrowing, and this scenario is complete. The argument is then developed that economic growth requires the drastic abandonment of welfare state policies, i.e. the re-privatisation of social and public services which will result in lower taxation, greater freedom of choice and a re-allocation of economic activity back to the market sector and away from the state. This neo-liberal assault on the welfare state has a long pedigree, theoretically and politically, in the US and Britain but its influence is only now gradually developing in Ireland, whose economic circumstances have proved a fertile ground.

An equally sweeping attack on the welfare state in today's stagnant capitalist economics comes from the neo-marxist camp. This view of the immediate financial crux of welfare is most cogently argued in O'Connors' 'Fiscal Crisis of the State'. He argues that it is a mistake to see the problem as one of imbalance between government income and expenditure.[26] He directs our attention to the forces which create this imbalance. In capitalist economies, state expenditure serves two functions. One relates to the economic needs of capital. The state has an important role in easing the way for capital accumulation. The other function is political. The state must sustain the support of its citizens. It has to maintain its legitimacy.

Legitimacy is secured through the provision of services and benefits to the population and capital accumulation is secured through state-supported or state-undertaken activities (research and development, infrastructural provisions, transportation and so on). Fiscal crisis emerges when the available revenue can no longer sustain both the legitimation and accumulation functions. Revenue could of course be raised through social service cut-backs, solving the budgetary problem, but this leaves the legitimacy problem unsolved. Conversely, the accumulation problem would be unsolved if the strategy was to reduce services to capital or impose inflationary tax increases. The present fiscal problems of the Irish economy could be formulated in the above terms with the Irish feature that borrowing, in the short term, evaded the legitimacy-accumulation trap. This brand of neo-marxist analysis has gained increasing ground and O'Connor's seminal study has spawned similar British analyses[27] and an initial application of the 'fiscal crisis' notion to Ireland.[28]

Both the neo-liberal and neo-marxist analyses of the present difficulties have an air of wishful thinking about them. Professor Hirschman would accuse both these approaches of the 'structuralist fallacy', the tendency to diagnose fundamental problems when the disorder is mild and only temporary: 'Structuralist thinking about a problem or crisis comes easily to those who dislike the institution that experiences the problem or finds itself in crisis. For example, right wing and conservative people dislike the welfare state and oppose its expansion: they are naturally prone to interpret any difficulties it encounters as symptoms of a deep-seated malady and as signals that radical retrenchment is in order. For similar reasons left wing and liberal opinion has traditionally opted for structuralist explanations

Table 9: Exchequer and social insurance expenditure on the social services, 1976 to 1980

	Expenditure (current prices)					As % of Government Expenditure				
	1976	1977	1978	1979 provisional	1980 estimates	1976	1977	1978	1979	1980
Current Expenditure										
Education	223.6	260.1	302.1	380.1	462.9	13.4	13.3	12.6	13.1	13.1
Health	254.0	309.8	375.0	469.0	650.0	15.2	15.8	15.6	16.1	18.5
Housing	29.7	30.7	45.0	53.0	63.0	1.8	1.6	1.9	1.8	1.8
Social Welfare										
(i) social insurance fund	198.5	234.6	265.7	295.2(d)	382.0	—	—	—	—	—
(ii) exchequer	246.9	274.5	314.4	373.9	444.0	14.8	14.0	13.0	12.9	12.6
Total (excluding social insurance fund)	754.2	875.1	1,036.5	1,276.0	1,619.9	45.2	44.7	43.1	43.9	46.0
						As % Public Capital Programme				
Capital Expenditure										
Education	28.0	37.4	46.9	53.1	49.1	5.1	5.7	5.9	5.3	4.3
Health	11.2	16.0	21.5	27.5	28.0	2.0	2.4	2.7	2.8	2.4
Housing	107.1	100.7	135.5	159.3	182.5	19.5	15.3	17.0	15.9	15.8
Total	146.3	154.1	203.9	239.9	259.6	26.6	23.4	25.6	24.0	22.5

Source: NESC Report no. 53, Table 41

219

when it came to account for difficulties experienced by capitalism.'[29] A similar line of argument has been bluntly propounded by Katznelson: 'it is far from clear that the welfare state is in greater difficulty today than, say, a quarter century ago'.[30]

There is a middle way between the extremes of left and right. Their monolithic analyses provide no help in the development of social policies which will make our society fairer. Further advances in social policy terms in Ireland's present economic position are both possible and necessary. At present the thrust of policy-making is towards retrenchment and cutback, the argument being that public expenditure and social expenditure has risen enormously, that its share of total GNP has become unacceptably high, and that social expenditure must be curbed if sufficient resources are to remain for private consumption and employment-creating investment. The political additive is that tax resistance has set in. The figures in Table 9 show the amounts and shares of relevant expenditures in recent years. I would argue that the goals of economic efficiency and financial rectitude are served by a strategy of greater redistribution and more effective social policies.

First, one of the reasons for the inadequate state revenues is that the tax base has been eroded through regressive tax expenditures. An immediate reduction in these would render the tax system more equitable and generate additional tax revenue; as NESC Report No. 21 pointed out, 'tax reliefs within any given tax structure may be regarded as "implicit" public expenditures'.[31] Principal candidates for review here must be the mortgage interest tax relief, the child dependant tax relief which compounds the effects of the cash paid children's allowance payments, and interest relief for personal borrowings.

Second, and as a development of the point about mortgage interest tax relief, public expenditure on housing requires critical reappraisal. At present, the state generously subsidises the purchase of private houses (via tax reliefs, purchase grants, stamp duty exemptions) which are more accessible to higher income groups and which rapidly inflate in relative value. Moreover the imputed income of owner-occupation is no longer taxed, and rates on domestic property were abolished in 1977. An immediate change here would be the reintroduction of rates on domestic property – NESC Report on Social Policy priorities noted that 'the revenue foregone from domestic rates, without taking account of factors which might have made for particular buoyancy in this area, is equivalent to almost one-fifth of the 1981 budgeted current deficit.'[32]

Third, a little-discussed aspect of the limited tax base in Ireland is that as the ESRI Director recently argued, 'there is a good case for making public sector employees contribute to the social insurance fund'.[33] This group of employees are guaranteed by the community against the hazards of unemployment and sickness and receive income-related, inflation-proofed pensions.

Fourth, taxation on capital and wealth is now virtually non-existent. In 1980 taxes of this nature yielded less than 1 per cent of total tax revenue. In the interests of economy and of equity, therefore, this imbalance in the tax structure needs correction. Rottman, Hannan and their co-workers put the point as follows; 'as taxation in capital and on inherited wealth drifted towards the inconsequential, an awareness of social class would have alerted policy makers to the possibility that Ireland may enter the twenty-first century with an upper middle class so privileged and so securely entrenched as to harken back to its nineteenth century predecessors'.[34]

Fifth, some areas of public expenditure contribute to economic and social inequality and they should be curbed. In particular the education system is still used overwhelmingly by the upper middle class – subsidised at considerable public expense. The critical analyses by Tussing and Barlow[35] of educational financing suggest ways in which public expenditure and education can be restricted to make them more equitable and more economical.

The history of our developments to date as we have seen has been a history of constantly rising expenditure to meet the costs of more and more services being provided to ever widening groups in the population. Demographic pressures and the foreseeable economic circumstances make a continuation of this past trend impossible. Nor does the solution lie in resurrected liberalism or neo-marxism. The way forward is to pursue a strategy of equality in the financing and redistribution of welfare.

References

1 See John Curry, *Social Services in Ireland,* Institute of Public Administration, Dublin 1979. On specific policy areas see Brendan Hensey, *The Health Services of Ireland,* 3rd edition, IPA, Dublin 1979, Chapters 1-4; John Coolahan, *Irish Education – History and Structure,* IPA, Dublin 1981, Chapters

1-5; Desmond Farley, *Social Insurance and Social Assistance in Ireland,* IPA, Dublin 1964; P.A. Pfretzschner, *The Dynamics of Irish Housing,* Dublin, IPA 1965. For a statistical compilation and a brief account of main policy changes up to the mid-seventies, see *Towards Social Report,* National Economic and Social Council, Dublin, 1976, Report

No. 25.

2 Kiern A. Kennedy and Brendan R. Dowling, *Economic Growth in Ireland: The Experience Since 1947*, Gill and Macmillan, Dublin 1975, especially chapter 15.

3 J. H. Whyte, *Church and State in Modern Ireland, 1923-70*, Gill and Macmillan, Dublin 1971.

4 Ibid, p. 117.

5 Ibid, p. 352.

6 Brown describes this psychic change as 'renewed national self confidence', see Terence Brown, *Ireland: A Social and Cultural History, 1922-1979*, Fontana 1981, p. 241. See also Donald S. Connery, *The Irish*, London, Eyre and Spottiswood, 1968; Charles McCarthy, *Decade of Upheaval*, IPA, Dublin 1968.

7 Patrick Lynch, 'Escape from Stagnation'. *Studies*, Summer 1963 p. 162.

8 John Baker, 'Social Conscience and Social Policy' *Journal of Social Policy*, Vol. 8, no. 2, 1979, pp. 177-206.

9 See Ramesh Mishra, *Society and Social Policy*, Macmillan Press, London 1977, especially pp. 100-109.

10 Harold Wilensky, *The Welfare State and Equality*, University of California Press, 1975.

11 Clarke Kerr et al, *Industrialism and Industrial Man*, British Second Edition, Pelican Books, 1973.

12 For an overview of this Marxist perspective see John Higgins, 'Social Control Theories of Social Policy', *Journal of Social Policy*, Vol. 9, no. 1, January 1980, pp. 1-23. Two of the classic expositions of this perspective are John Saville, 'The Welfare State: An Historical Approach', *New Reasoner, 3, 1957-58* and Frances Fox River and Richard Cloward, *Regulating the Poor*, London, Tavistock, 1972.

13 Frank Gould, 'The Growth of Irish Public Expenditure, 1947-77',

Administration, Vol. 29, no. 2 1981, pp. 130-131.

14 See especially *NESC Report 25* op. cit.

15 L. Joyce and A. McCashin (eds.) *Poverty and Social Policy in Ireland*, IPA, Dublin 1982, Chapter 2.

16 Rottman, Hannan, Wiley, Hardeman, *The Distribution of Income in the Republic of Ireland: A Study in Social Class and Family Cycle Inequalities* ESRI Report no. 109, Dublin 1982, Chapter 5.

17 Eithne Fitzgerald, 'The Extent of Poverty in Ireland', Chapter 1, Part 1, Sister S. Kennedy (ed) *One Million Poor*, Turoe Press, Dublin 1981.

18 *NESC Report no. 25* op. cit.

19 The income distribution data are taken from Brian Nolan, 'The Personal Distribution of Income in the Republic of Ireland' *Journal of the Social and Statistical Inquiry of Ireland*, 1977-8, pp. 91-161, and *The Redistributive Effects of State Taxes and Benefits on Household Incomes in 1973*, Central Statistics Office 1975.

20 See NESC Report no. 11, *Income Distribution: A Pilot Study* 1975, and Joyce and McCashin op. cit., pp. 23-24.

21 ESRI Report 109, op. cit., pp. 87-88.

22 A. Dale Tussing, 'Equity and the Financing of Education', *One Million Poor*, op. cit., page 201.

23 T. J. Baker and L. O'Brien, *The Irish Housing System: A Critical Overview*, ESRI Broadsheet no. 17, Dublin 1979; J. Blackwell, 'Do Housing Policies Show a Redistribution to the Poor?', Kilkenny Poverty Conference Paper, 1981.

24 Joyce and McCashin, *op. cit*, p. 90.

25 Milton Friedman, *Free to Choose*, Penguin Books 1980; Arthur Seldon, *Whither the Welfare State?*, Institute of Economic Affairs, paper no. 60, London 1981.

26 James O'Connor, *Fiscal Crisis of the State*, St. Martin's Press, New York,

1973.

27 Ian Gough, 'State Expenditure in Advanced Capitalism,' *New Left Review*, 1975.

28 Philip O'Connell, 'A Sociology of Fiscal Crisis', Paper to Sociological Association of Ireland Conference, 1982.

29 A. O. Hirschman, 'The Welfare State in Trouble; Systemic Crisis or Growing Pains', *American Economic Review*, Vol. 70, no. 2, p. 116.

30 Ira Katznelson, 'Accounts of the Welfare State and the New Mood', *American Economic Review*, Vol. 70, no.

2, p. 119.

31 NESC Report no. 21, *Report on Public Expenditure*, Dublin 1975, p. 11.

32 NESC Report no. 61, *Irish Social Policies, Priorities for Future Development*, Dublin 1981, page 23.

33 Kieran A. Kennedy, 'The State of the Dublin Finances', *Administration*, Vol. 29, no. 2 1981, p. 146.

34 ESRI Report no. 109, p. 182.

35 A. Dale Tussing, *Irish Educational Expenditures: Past, Present and Future*, ESRI Report No. 92; A. C. Barlow, *The Financing of Third Level Education*, ESRI Report No. 106.

Siúcra

... agus cupán deas tae.

Ireland and The World 1957–82

PATRICK KEATINGE

1957 was an unusually eventful year for Irish foreign policy, with even the Dáil lifting its head more than once from the parish pump in contemplation of the outside world. The autumn session saw parliamentary controversy over positions adopted in the United Nations General Assembly, while earlier there had been a rather sudden awakening of interest in current developments in European integration, which included the signing of the Treaties of Rome. Throughout the year the IRA border campaign, which had led to formal recriminations from London the previous December, impinged on parliamentary as well as electoral politics.

These matters contained much that was novel then, but which twenty-five years later resound with familiar echoes. They serve to illustrate the continuing major themes in the state's involvement with the outside world, or perhaps we should say worlds, for a small country's external environment can rarely be seen as an undifferentiated whole. Global issues are confronted in the universal inter-governmental organisations such as the United Nations, but dealings between particular groups of states – 'regional' international politics-have their own distinctive multilateral networks, while a third mode of diplomacy is the time-honoured bilateral relationship between one government and another, without the intervention of third parties. A state's foreign policy may be seen as the government's response to matters arising in each of these types of external environment. For quite long periods these responses may be formulated and implemented on separate tracks, but there will occur, usually in quite random fashion, particular circumstances which draw the threads together.

One such turning point serves to divide the last twenty-five years into two periods of almost equal length. Up to 1969, the state was drawn increasingly into international issues going beyond the traditional emphasis of bilateral relations with the United Kingdom, but the experience was in important respects rather disjointed, and the period may be labelled one of 'tentative internationalisation'. After 1969, the move towards and experience of membership of the EEC led to involvement in a unique form of regional collaboration – 'intensive multilateralism' – the implications of which are perhaps still not fully grasped.

Tentative internationalisation (1957–69)

Irish participation in the United Nations was still a novelty in 1957, the main lines of policy emerging in only the most general terms before Frank Aiken was appointed Minister for External Affairs in March 1957.[1] His predecessor, Liam Cosgrave, had enunciated three basic principles: support for the position and authority of the UN itself, on the grounds that a 'rule of law' was necessary for weak states; independence of concerted bloc voting in the Assembly; and support for those states upholding the values of the 'free world'.

There was something for everyone here, but the new government controversially emphasised the second principle, especially when the Irish delegation at the General Assembly voted to discuss the question of Chinese representation in that body. Thus in the autumn of 1957 Ireland had already acquired the identity of an 'activist' small state and, given the policy of military neutrality, as manifested in the refusal to join NATO in 1949, some observers referred to Ireland's position at this period as 'neutralist'. There was a lasting general impact on Irish attitudes towards world affairs. The novelty and visibility of these positions in the late fifties came to represent a golden age of Irish foreign policy in which a myth of courageous independence would serve as a yardstick against which subsequent Irish positions were to be measured.

In retrospect we can see that this yardstick was a superficial one, and the characterisation of Irish policy as neutralist was not wholly accurate. Supporting the United Nations itself was to support a body which at that time was still fundamentally pro-Western in its orientation. Irish activism within the General Assembly did not threaten that orientation, and in the sixties it became less evident. One explanation is that in response to dependence on the United States as a source of direct foreign investment the Irish government felt less inclined to take diplomatic positions critical of that country.[2] At the same time, with the prospect of EEC membership, there was a greater

226

sensitivity to the assumed susceptibilities of our new European partners. These suggestions of a deliberate change in the emphasis of policy by the Irish government are plausible up to a point: certainly in the later sixties the deafening silence on the part of the government over one of the major global issues of that period, the Vietnam War, cast a pall over the image of Irish independence in the General Assembly.[3]

But there is also substance to the official line that it was not that Irish policy changed, rather that the international system, and the nature of the United Nations in particular, changed significantly during the sixties. The polarisation of Cold War politics weakened and questions of decolonisation became less those of political status (with which Ireland could sympathise totally) than questions of economic equity (in which Ireland's position as a rapidly industrialising western economy was much more equivocal). The General Assembly grew from 81 members in December 1957, in which a pro-Western majority prevailed, to 136 in December 1969, in which the Afro-Asian voting predominance was the central diplomatic reality. In effect, Ireland started the decade at the liberal end of the diplomatic spectrum modelling herself on other European neutrals such as Sweden, and ended the decade – still with a voting pattern very close to that of Sweden – in the centre of a spectrum in which the avant garde of diplomatic radicalism was to be found in the economic and political demands of the Third World.

Nevertheless, given these qualifications, three persistent themes could be seen in Irish policy on global issues. First, there was a concern with decolonisation questions, albeit with moderate and gradualist responses, consistently eschewing the ever more popular demands for significant economic pressures on the colonial powers (mainly in Southern Africa) and for the Non-Aligned Movement's commitment to support for the use of force in national liberation. A second continuing interest was disarmament, the high point being the adoption in 1961 of an Irish draft resolution on nuclear nonproliferation – the first formal stage leading to the Non-Proliferation Treaty of 1968. Policy on both decolonisation and disarmament was mainly declaratory, but in the third sort of activity, peace-keeping, more was demanded. Ireland entered the UN at a time when there was a novel demand for 'middle powers' to perform the type of peacekeeping role which evolved after the Suez Crisis of 1956. The state's first large-scale participation was in the Congo between 1960 and 1964, an experience which brought home the costs, both human and material, of being involved in international politics beyond the level of declaratory policy. Nevertheless, the commitment to this type of activity persisted both in the Cyprus force from 1964 and in an ultimately unsuccessful attempt to resolve the central political issue of peacekeeping which, like so many central political issues, was expressed in financial terms.

Foreign policy in the United Nations context through the fifties and sixties was in the most literal sense of the term a question of 'external affairs'. The declaratory nature of most of these activities made few demands on the exchequer or on sectional interests, and there were few votes to be gained by trying to relate global concerns to a constituency-oriented electoral system. There was remarkable ministerial continuity in the person of Frank Aiken: never an enthusiastic parliamentary performer, his commitment to the General Assembly rather than to the Dáil did not escape notice. As a very senior member of his party, he held External Affairs almost as his personal fief. One general consequence of his department's close association with United Nations policies, to the near exclusion of other areas of Ireland's external relations, was that it remained a very small department on the outer margins of a rapidly developing administrative system.

The Minister for External Affairs' predilection for global politics should not be allowed to obscure the important developments occurring at the regional level. Up to 1957 Ireland had only one foot rather gingerly placed on the path towards European integration.[4] A founder member of the Organisation for European Economic Co-operation (OEEC) and of the Council of Europe, she had nonetheless refused to join the North Atlantic Treaty Organisation (NATO) in 1949 and, more significantly, was not a member of the vanguard of European integration, the six states which had formed the Coal and Steel Community in the early fifties. It was the latter group's move to create a European Economic Community which opened up the options for Ireland's economic foreign policy in 1956 and 1957; in response to this project, the other west European states, under the leadership of the United Kingdom, tried to create a comprehensive free trade arrangment for all the west European states – the Maudling Plan. This attempt to restructure Ireland's immediate external economic environment coincided with the advent of the Fianna Fáil Government early in 1957, and with the change of attitudes within the Department of Finance towards the role of government in the economy – the 'Whitaker revolution'.

Initially, the government's preferred outcome was participation in a comprehensive but rather loosely organised free trading arrangement with special consideration for agricultural produce and with a very long transitional period for the weaker economies. This minimalist strategy, however, ran against the mainstream of the free trade negotiations; when Maudling's comprehensive arrangements collapsed and were replaced by the more restricted European Free Trade Association (EFTA) in 1959, Ireland found herself in a position of isolation. The options were reconsidered in the subsequent eighteen months and by the summer of 1961, full membership of the EEC, with its potential for agriculture, became the main goal of government policy. This choice was seen primarily in economic terms; although the EEC's political aspirations were quite marked and were in general paid more attention in the early sixties than they were to be ten years later, Seán Lemass managed to play down the difficulties which would arise in terms of sovereignty and neutrality. The latter issue was raised during 1962, but no clear lines were drawn as to what pressures it might face within the EEC and President de Gaulle's rejection of British membership early in 1963 made it an academic question. Between 1963 and 1969 membership of the EEC remained a primary objective but the political consequences were not discussed extensively.

One consequence of this sequence of events was that Ireland's European policy was 'internalised', rather than being seen as a matter of foreign policy as such. The diplomatic aspects – the negotiation of inter-state agreements – were thwarted; 'Europe' remained an internal debate between sectional interests and the government about hypothetical options. The political costs, in terms of constitutional questions or neutrality, were not teased out. Substantive policies in the major economic sectors were redirected through broader networks (the General Agreement on Tariffs and Trade and the Organisation for Economic Co-operation and Development), or through the bilateral regime which emerged in the form of the Anglo-Irish Free Trade Agreement of 1965. Actual economic interactions with the outside world were also mediated, with a high degree of autonomy, by semi-state bodies, in particular the Industrial Development Authority. The Minister for External Affairs took very little interest in all of this; the authority of Seán Lemass on such matters rested not merely on his position as Taoiseach, but on his reputation as economic innovator. Thus the administrative consequences of not getting into the EEC the first time around can be seen in the tentative internationalisation of some of the major home departments (Finance, Agriculture, Industry & Commerce) and in the role of the head of the home civil service, Dr. Whitaker, as a major diplomatic actor with regard to economic foreign policy.

With the novelty of UN membership and the potential novelty of the EEC it is easy to lose sight of Anglo-Irish relations during the late fifties. Up to 1949 this bilateral relationship had been the *alpha* and *omega* of Irish foreign policy; it was reflected in constitutional issues and the dispute over partition, and could be seen in the government's attempt to maintain a proper distance from the great power politics of imperial Britain – especially marked in the support for Irish neutrality. To some extent participation in international organisations offered Ireland escape routes from the constraints of this unbalanced bilateral relationship. UN policy could be seen as a manifestation of psychological independence, and Europe as a possible means of reduced material dependence, but neither escape route could be anything more than a temporary and partial relief.

Anglo-Irish relations through the late fifties and sixties took two main forms. Dublin was on the defensive with regard to partition so long as the IRA took it upon themselves to lead the pace in the border campaign of the mid-fifties. Eamon de Valera not only took firm action against the IRA on his return to office in 1957; he set his face against trying to internationalise the Northern Ireland problem, in spite of demands to take partition to the United Nations. From the moment he became Taoiseach in 1959 Seán Lemass showed his intention of defusing the symbols of antagonism and of seeing reunification as a matter of gradual economic convergence, on the assumption that this would eventually transform traditional attitudes which had prevented reconciliation between nationalists and unionists. This policy could best be seen in the meeting between Lemass and Captain Terence O'Neill in 1965, with its follow-through in the form of the committee to consider revision of the Constitution.

The economic theme was also seen in the creation of the Anglo-Irish Free Trade Agreement in 1965, at that time regarded as an interim context for increasing industrial free trade with a view to eventual EEC membership. But this agreement followed previous bilateral economic negotiations in excluding any special consideration for the problems of Irish agriculture, and thus illustrated what had always been the essential weakness of Ireland's negotiating stance in this bilateral framework.

Anglo-Irish relations, like European policy, were also 'internalised' to a large extent during this period. The strictly diplomatic aspects were not often visible; Lemass saw Stormont rather than Whitehall as his stage and the Anglo-Irish Free Trade Agreement was generally presented as a matter of 'low politics', with economic rather than political consequences. By this time London had placed Dublin in a peculiar diplomatic limbo, in which Anglo-Irish relations were treated together with those of Commonwealth states, in spite of the fact that Ireland since 1949 had no longer been a member of that body. A British Ambassador, recalling that period, referred to the 'Isle of Wight syndrome' – a habit of mind which induces a tendency to 'forget entirely that Ireland is independent'.[5] The tradition was also firmly established in Dublin that the North was 'Taoiseach's business', and all those concerned, from de Valera to Lynch by way of Lemass, encouraged a low profile on partition. The major administrative consequence was that there seemed to be no administrative consequence. Policy innovations took the form of a series of *ad hoc* measures involving relatively few individuals, particularly Lemass himself and Dr. Whitaker, while substantive measures were merely dimensions of the normal activity of the major home departments. There was no particular administrative unit with the responsibility 'for looking North', a deficiency of Whitehall also, which had the unhappy consequence that when the political stability of Northern Ireland collapsed both administrations had to improvise from scratch.

1969 and All That: the development of 'Intensive Multi-lateralism'

The patterns of policy responses and processes were to be altered quite significantly by external developments occurring in 1969. Globally, the general trend towards East/West détente was a favourable background for innovation at the regional and bilateral levels; in particular the relative 'demilitarisation' of international politics in western Europe was to permit a studied vagueness about Irish neutrality. Regionally, the resignation of President de Gaulle in 1969 allowed a new French government to reopen the door to enlargement of the EEC. Bilaterally, increasing instability in Northern Ireland led to the direct involvement of the Dublin and London governments in Northern affairs in August 1969. Of these developments, the opening of the European door was to represent the central element in Irish foreign policy for the following decade, first during entry negotiations (1970–72), and then in the experience of membership.

Membership of the EEC represented a qualitative change in the way in which Ireland interacted with the world. In general, interdependence between industrialising states demonstrates the connections between internal and external influences; negotiating in a diplomatic coalition like the EEC makes it impossible to distinguish clearly between foreign and domestic policies. The context of policy covered in the international framework is broad, and this is not the place to assess the European dimension of the major sectoral policies.[6] However, one consequence of European involvement deserves a brief comment. The first major energy-induced economic recession of the seventies, associated with the October 1973 Middle East War, coincided with Irish accession and some of the damage caused was mitigated by the beneficial effects of the transitional stage of EEC membership.

The process of policy-making has been considerably affected, involving most home departments and their respective constituents, and sectional interests in the Brussels system. This raises important questions, particularly at parliamentary level, which is in any case generally assumed to be lagging behind the needs of policy-making in an industrialised society. It also raises questions about the traditional role of diplomacy as the centralised expression of the state's interests with regard to the external environment. Insofar as membership of the Community both internationalises interests and fragments them within national societies, it can threaten to circumvent the function of the orthodox diplomat.

Nevertheless, it can be seen in a general sense that EEC membership implies an important role for national diplomacy. There is an underlying need for coherence in overall political strategy and a need for co-ordination of the activities of the major agencies of the central administration. In response to these needs Irish governments have varied their approach between two broad strategies. The first is the 'Communautaire' emphasis; based on the assumption that the state is in the long term a net beneficiary of EEC membership and that a domestic consensus recognises this, it sees advantages for weak member-states of adherence to the 'rules of the game'. This approach, coloured by a fair measure of integrationist rhetoric, was the predominant strategy during Garret FitzGerald's term of office as Minister for Foreign Affairs between 1973 and 1977.

An alternative approach – or, more accurately, a persistent temptation – places more stress on immediate national advantage. It assumes that Community policy-making is not necessarily evolving along integrationist lines, that short term conflicts demand a dismissive attitude towards the 'rules of the game', and that the inter-governmental policy-making process is fair game for electoral or party political manipulation. The domestic consensus on membership may reflect dissillusionment with the actual performance of the Community, which could partly account for a readiness to resort to this 'green gaullism' towards the later seventies. The Community was undergoing increasing difficulties, and when the second major recession began in 1979 its effects could not be mitigated by the once-off measures of the transitional stages of membership. Even before this several important aspects of Ireland's participation in EEC policy-making reflect this approach. Although Dr. FitzGerald encouraged a gradual move towards majority voting in the Council of Ministers, as early as 1974 his government did not hesitate to threaten a veto, nor did his or succeeding governments show in the manner of their nomination of Commissioners that they were placing European considerations above those of party. Though not reflecting the principled minimalism of Denmark or the unprincipled obstruction of the United Kingdom or France, Irish attitudes towards European integration did become less enthusiastic with the experiences of membership.

This ambivalent diplomatic stance has also been reflected in uncertainties about administrative co-ordination. The Devlin Report of 1969 may generally be regarded as the base line for administrative reform, but as it gave little guidance as to how the national administration might be expected to fit into the Brussels network the question of co-ordination has remained open. The major economic departments – Finance through its overall budget control, or Agriculture (given that the Common Agricultural Policy is a world of its own) – often seem either to go their own way or to exert their own measure of co-ordination. The Department of Foreign Affairs, through its supervision of negotiating structures such as the Permanent Representation in Brussels, and with its tradition of negotiating skills, has at least a foot in the door of policy co-ordination. With the tendency to regular summit diplomacy, institutionalised in the European Council from 1975 onwards, the contribution of the Department of the Taoiseach has become more obvious. Where then is the regular focus of administrative co-ordination concerning Ireland's participation in the EEC? Arguably, it all depends on the issue, and perhaps on the particular emphasis given to his role by the Taoiseach of the day. In any event, the supervision of the state's external relations in the seventies is a far cry from the simple

233

Lemass/Aiken division of labour in the sixties.

The way in which global diplomatic issues were now approached within the regional network – the process of European Political Co-operation (EPC) – went largely unnoticed throughout the seventies. This consultation between foreign ministries with a view to taking concerted action where consensus prevailed, evolved slowly outside the normal Community framework and with limited effects on the foreign policies of individual member states.[7] EPC first acquired significance at the Conference on Security and Co-operation in Europe (CSCE), which culminated in the Helsinki Agreements of 1975. Solidarity was also evident on the political aspects of Mediterranean policy and particularly on the 'southern enlargement' of the Community, and by the late seventies there was solidarity on the perennial problems of the Middle East. While voting within the UN General Assembly reflected this solidarity it also reflected its limitations and a member-state like Ireland could maintain its traditional stances in General Assembly politics. In particular, the Irish position on decolonisation and disarmament was only marginally influenced by EPC disarmament especially is an issue in which there is little agreement between the member-states. Moreover, Ireland proved to be acceptable as a peacekeeping state, with the continuing involvement in Cyprus and subsequently in the Lebanon.

Participation in EPC has had important effects on the expansion of the state's diplomatic machinery. Within the Department of Foreign Affairs itself it has necessitated the creation of a Political Division with, for the first time, a degree of geographical and issue-orientated specialisation.[8] Overseas representation also expanded in response to the exigencies of EPC though compared with other smaller member-states Irish diplomatic representation overseas is still very thin.[9]

Most of this passed unnoticed by political elites and interests within Ireland. In 1981, however, suggestions in some other member-states that EPC might be expanded to include military security, caused apprehension about Irish participation. In particular, it was held that this would impinge on Ireland's unique neutrality and in the autumn of 1981 Irish diplomats succeeded in maintaining recognition of the principle that EPC was to cover only the 'political aspects of security', such as disarmament and confidence-building measures in the CSCE.[10]

Another new area of foreign policy during the last ten years has been development co-operation, usually referred to as 'aid', in the sixties. This was a feature of international relations long before Ireland joined the EEC, but her contribution had then been largely a matter for non-governmental organisations, and in particular for missionary orders – an exception proving the rule being the participation of the Institute of Public Administration in offering training courses to Zambian officials in the mid-sixties. Membership of the EEC gave this policy area a considerable boost; it was widely argued that Ireland should at least try to approach the level of official development aid given by other member-states. Policy development was gradual, from the creation of the Agency for Personal Service Overseas (APSO) in 1974, through the establishment of an Advisory Committee on Development Co-operation in 1979, and the creation of a joint committee of the Dáil and Seanad in 1982.

Meanwhile, multilateral and bilateral official aid policies and contributions were developed and particular recipient states were identified. However, repeated demands that all these activities should be integrated within a comprehensive policy framework have not yet been met. Development co-operation is significant as being an extension of pro-Third World declaratory policy into a type of activity with visible financial and potential political costs. This has brought it into the policy-making arena in a more structured way than many other foreign policy issues; budgetary targets and limitations, regular lobbying structures and processes and even electoral promises have been in evidence since the mid-seventies. But there are signs that development co-operation has reached a plateau of achievement beyond which it will become increasingly difficult to move. Budgetary contributions have been vulnerable to increasing economic pressures, while the ability of governments to implement their initial commitments has been doubtful.[11]

Bilateralism: Anglo-Irish relations and the North (1969–82)

1969 was a turning point in Anglo-Irish relations, with the break-down of the provincial political system based on Stormont bringing conflict within the North onto the diplomatic level between Dublin and London. The participation of both sovereign governments in the EEC, though not leading to any significant ameliorative action, has at least had the effect of moderating the extent of bilateral antagonism. One accommodation to this difficult situation, for example, has been the deliberate insulation of European matters from bilateral matters, as occurs within EPC where the dispute has been a taboo subject. EEC membership also moderates Anglo-Irish relations by precluding the imposition of formal sanctions by either side, and in allowing for a small measure of co-operation in border areas.

The major developments in Anglo-Irish relations since 1969 have been eventful and cannot readily be encompassed here.[12] There have been very low points, particularly the period between the imposition of internment in Northern Ireland in 1971 and the burning of the British Embassy in Dublin at the beginning of 1972. There have been high points, such as the attempt to reach a long-term solution through power sharing and a modest Council of Ireland, as proposed in the Sunningdale Agreements in 1973. The greater part of the process however, has been characterised by stalemate within the North and between Dublin and London, though there has also been an awareness by both governments of a common long-term security interest in rescuing the dispute from the politics of the last atrocity.

Anglo-Irish relations in the seventies, in contrast to those of the sixties, have been 'externalised', and have thereby emerged much more clearly in the context of foreign policy. The diplomatic issues have often been visible, both on a day-to-day basis, with repeated security incidents, and in the attempts to find long-term solutions. The diplomatic processes have also been visible in the quest for support from third parties, especially the United States and the EEC member-states, and in bilateral interactions at all levels. A tendency to hold summit meetings at critical stages was rationalised in 1980 with the establishment of regular Anglo-Irish Intergovernmental Council meetings between the heads of the governments, supplemented by ministerial and official meetings.

Anglo-Irish relations have also been more evident in terms of administrative structures. At its most obvious this is seen within a specialised unit in the Department of Foreign Affairs, but it has been noticeable that the Department of the Taoiseach has been closely (and sometimes controversially) involved. The sensitive nature of Anglo-Irish relations and the attention of the media have also served to politicise the activities of some senior officials to a degree unusual in Irish administrative tradition. Ambassadors and diplomats in significant missions, such as Washington, have occasionally found themselves to be the target of political criticism from within their own governments.

Anglo-Irish relations have also become increasingly politicised at the parliamentary level. At the beginning of the seventies differences in approach were by and large contained within the parties, the most obvious strain being seen in Fianna Fáil during the Arms Crisis of 1970. The Coalition government between 1973 and 1977 at least started to think aloud about the wider ramifications of Northern policy, but with the collapse of the Sunningdale Agreement in 1974 attitudes towards Irish unity were subsumed under the heading of 'law and order' or 'security policy'. In 1981 an uneasy bipartisanship over Northern Ireland became more difficult to sustain, and basic differences emerged between the major parties. The North was not a critical electoral issue, but the divergence between Fine Gael's long-term comprehensive approach, seen in Garret FitzGerald's 'constitutional crusade' in 1981, contrasted with Fianna Fáil's claims of an imminent deal with London, leading to a 'final solution.'

Irish foreign policy on the defensive (1979–82)

1979 saw the onset of serious economic recession, out of which the industrialised world has yet to move. East/West relations deteriorated significantly; détente had lost impetus and credibility, uncertainties about strategic doctrines were increasing, and the Soviet intervention in Afghanistan at the end of the year served only as a catalyst for new perceptions of diplomatic instability. Regional responses to these pressures have tended to put Ireland on the defensive diplomatically. With regard to economic issues, this defensiveness was seen in the general failure of the EEC to cope with recession and, in particular, in the increasing onslaught against the Common Agricultural Policy – the corner stone of Ireland's material benefits from membership. With regard to diplomatic issues, the suggestions that the Community was an appropriate vehicle for new security measures raised questions about Ireland's military neutrality. Bilateral relations remained confused. Charles Haughey's emphasis on inter-governmental processes and 'solutions' reached their apotheosis in his summit meeting with Margaret Thatcher in December 1980, but inflated expectations were dashed by mutual recriminations over the hunger strikes in Northern Ireland in the summer of 1981, and the apparent irrelevance of the Anglo-Irish process with regard to the question of reunification.

Against this background of deteriorating external circumstances, and of governmental and electoral instability at home, there was an international crisis in the spring of 1982 which demonstrated the unpredictability and complexity of international politics, actual and potential connections between what were generally regarded as separate issues, and the narow limits on Ireland's room to manoeuvre. The Falkland Islands crisis was a further instance of a disturbing readiness to resort to force. The initial solidarity within the framework of EPC was transformed by the dissent of Ireland and Italy – the former on the ground that support for Britain's attempt to regain control of the islands by military means was inconsistent with the maintenance of Irish neutrality. It remains to be seen whether EPC in general has reached its limits in this particular unexpected test, but it does seem that Irish neutrality has become a more visible and potentially contentious issue between the EEC member-states. The crisis also demonstrated the complex linkages between disparate economic and political considerations within the Community, particularly in the way in which British tactical obstruction of the annual farm price review was overriden by a majority vote of the Council of Ministers, causing a constitutional crisis within the Community political system, with mixed implications for a small country like Ireland. More immediately, the Falkland Islands crisis threw Anglo-Irish relations into disarray and neutrality became a divisive matter not merely between Dublin and London but between nationalist and unionist elites within Northern Ireland. A wholly unforeseen and in some respects anachronistic and distant crisis had served to place Ireland in a position of vulnerability within its immediate diplomatic environment.

Conclusions

During the last twenty-five years Ireland's involvement with the outside world has changed quite dramatically. In 1957 the state had diplomatic relations with twenty other countries; by 1982 the number had risen to fifty seven. The 'tentative internationalisation' of the late fifties and sixties has been replaced by the continuous and intensive multilateral negotiations characterisic of industrialised west European states, particularly structured within the European Community. The complexity and significance of the state's external relations are amply illustrated by the multi-faceted crisis in the spring of 1982.

Whatever the consequences of this sequence of events, it raises the question of the way in which our political system responds to this type of external stimulus. One remarkable feature throughout the last quarter century is that in spite of the significant transformations described above parliamentary structures and procedures have seemed to carry on as if very little new had occurred. The one institutional innovation, the Joint Committee of the Dáil and Seanad to review the secondary legislation of the European Communities, serves to emphasise the lack of any serious attempt to equip our parliamentary institutions for dealing with foreign affairs in general. The Joint

Foreign Affairs

Committee has problems enough in its own field – it was unable to meet for twelve months in 1981/82 – but much, including European Political Co-operation, lies outside its competence. There has been no serious attempt to bring parliamentary politics into the formulation of policy towards Northern Ireland and in the endless struggle for limited parliamentary time foreign policy issues fight a losing battle against the tidal wave of constituency business. There are signs that the new generation of party activists are more aware of external pressures than their predecessors but they too come up against the local orientation of Irish party politics.

The administration, by virtue of its direct involvement in intensive multilateralism, has had to do better than that but whether it does as well as it might remains an open question. In general the layperson is left with the uneasy impression that the relatively informal patterns of policy-making which eventually coped with the transitional stages of EEC membership and with the settled routine of the late seventies may be over-stretched in circumstances of persistent instability. Other small member-states have responded to similar problems with a more self-consciously structured and tightly controlled approach to policy-making. Even allowing for differences in political culture and administrative tradition, there may be important lessons to learn.[13] Self-examination, however, is ultimately the responsibility of political leadership.

Notes to Article

1 By far the most comprehensive account of Irish policy at the UN is Norman J.D. MacQueen, (1981) 'Irish neutrality: the United Nations and the peacekeeping experience, 1945–1969', unpublished D.Phil., New University of Ulster.

2 James Wickham (1980) 'The Politics of Dependent Capitalism: International Capital and the Nation State', in A. Morgan and B. Purdie (eds.), *Ireland: Divided Nation, Divided Class* Ink Links, p. 58.

3 The personnel of the Irish delegation at New York was also changed, a factor given some prominence by one of those involved: see Conor Cruise O'Brien (1969), 'Ireland in International Affairs', in Owen

Dudley Edwards (ed.), *Conor Cruise O'Brien Introduces Ireland*, Deutsch, p. 132.

4 See Miriam Hederman, 'Irish attitudes to European integration, 1948–1961', unpublished Ph.D., Trinity College Dublin, 1981.

5 John Peck, (1978) *Dublin from Downing Street*, Gill and Macmillan, p. 18.

6 For a general survey, see Trevor C. Salmon, 'Ireland' (1981) in Carol and Kenneth J. Twitchett (eds.), *Building Europe: Britain's Partners in the EEC*, Europa.

7 See Padraic MacKernan (1982), 'Ireland and European Political Co-operation', *Ireland Today: Bulletin of the Department of Foreign Affairs*, No. 984, January 1982; and Patrick

239

Keatinge, 1982 'Ireland' in Christopher Hill (ed.), *National Perspectives on European Political Cooperation*, Allen and Unwin.

8 See Patrick Keatinge, (1978) *A Place among the Nations: Issues of Irish Foreign Policy*, Institute of Public Administration, pp. 212, 269; Dermot Keogh, (1982) 'Ireland' in Zara Steiner (ed.), *Foreign Ministries of the World*, Times Books.

9 See Christopher Hill and William Wallace (1979), 'Diplomatic Trends in the European Community', *International Affairs*, Vol. 55, No. 1, Table 1, p. 58.

10 For details of the emergence of this issue see Trevor C. Salmon (1982), 'Ireland: a Neutral in the Community?', *Journal of Common Market Sudies*, XX, No. 3.

11 See Mary Sutton (1977), *Irish Government Aid to the Third World – Review and Assessment*, Trocaire/Irish Commission for Justice and Peace, 1977; Declan O'Brien (1980), *Ireland and the Third World – a study of government aid*, Irish Commission for Justice and Peace; Richard F. Quinn (1980), *The Missionary Factor in Irish Aid Overseas*, Dominican Publications.

12 See Patrick Keating (1982), 'An Odd Couple? Obstacles and Opportunities in Inter-State Political Co-operation between the Republic of Ireland and the United Kingdom' in Desmond Rea (ed.), *Political Co-operation in Divided Societies: a series of papers relevant to the conflict in Northern Ireland*, Gill and Macmillan.

13 See Brigid Laffan (1981), 'Ireland and Denmark in the European Community – Political and Administrative Aspects', *Administration*, Vol. 29, No. 1.

CORK
COUNTY COUNCIL

congratulates the Institute of Public Administration on its Silver Jubilee.

The fledgling Institute of the late 50's and early 60's has grown in stature and importance with the years. Its contribution to public affairs and in the development of staff organisations to meet the changing needs of the Public Service has been immense.

The Council extends its best wishes to the Institute for its continuing success in these challenging times.

IRELAND'S
LEADING CURRENT
AFFAIRS MAGAZINE

Covering Politics, Current Affairs, The Law,
Business, Personal Investment, Sport and the Arts and
many areas of importance in Irish life.

———————At all Good Newsagents————————

The Physical Environment

FRANK CONVERY

It is convenient to divide actions which influence environmental quality into those which involve major direct investment by the state and those where the private sector is predominant. This can be highly simplistic as the influence of government – through taxes, subsidies and regulations – is pervasive, and in some sectors such as housing and factory construction both the state and the private sector are major investors. My purpose is to provide the reader with a qualitative sense of some major actions and trends affecting the quality of Ireland's physical environment since 1957. Where it is germane, some aspects of the economic development are touched on.

Direct state investment and environmental quality
Before the second world war, the only major impact made by the state on the environment was through the Electricity Supply Board's hydro-electric projects on the Shannon. In 1945, the passage of the Turf Development Act, the Minerals Act, the Forestry Act and the Arterial Drainage Act presaged a much more active state role in resource development. By the mid 1950s these legislative initiatives were beginning to find expression in action on the ground and they reached full flower in the 1960s. Table 1 shows the areas involved in state afforestation, arterial drainage and turf development projects in 1957 and then in 1980. Together, they comprise 8.9 per cent of the state's total land area.

Relatively quickly, therefore, the state has made a significant direct impact on the physical environment through the medium of resource development.

State forestry
The state afforestation programme has concentrated on upland areas

243

Map 1 FOREST AREAS

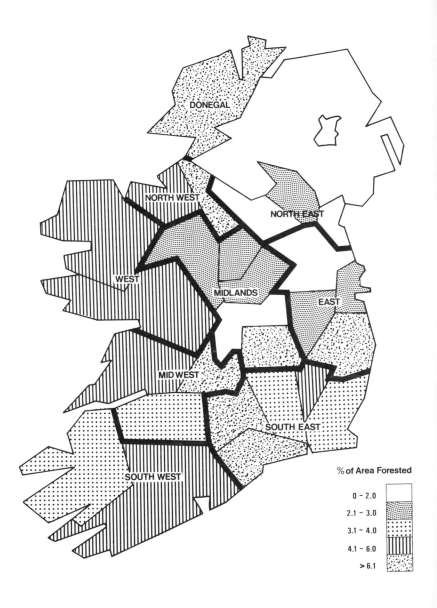

% of Area Forested

0 - 2.0	
2.1 - 3.0	
3.1 - 4.0	
4.1 - 6.0	
> 6.1	

Table 1: Total area of state forest, arterial drainage and bog development by Bord na Móna, 1957 and 1980 (000s acres)

	State forest area	Arterial drainage[a]	Bog area in production	Total
1957[b]	286	211	49	546
1982[b]	825	573	116	1514
1957-82	539	362	67	968

[a] Area drained under provisions of the Arterial Drainage Act, 1945.

[b] Or closest year for which data are available.

[c] There are in addition 69,000 acres which are being developed for future production under the provisions of the Third World Development Programme.

Source: Forest and Wildlife Service, Office of Public Works and Bord na Móna.

unsuitable for agriculture. On such sites, coniferous species native to North America – mainly Sitka Spruce and Lodgepole Pine – have been planted. In recent years much of this planting has taken place on peatlands in Western counties (Map 1). The Forest and Wildlife Service is now the biggest landowner in the state. Young forests are a pervasive feature of the rural landscape and economic, social and environmental consequences follow from the creation of this resource.

The state forestry capital stock was conservatively estimated in 1977 to be worth £275 million (adjusted to 1982£) and to be capable of yielding a real rate of return on investment in the range of 2-4 per cent (Convery 1979). Achievement of this return depends on advances in forest product development and marketing, which are parsimoniously funded at present. In addition, major institutional changes are required: the timber management functions of the Forest and Wildlife Service are run with civil service administrative procedures and need to be organised in a commercial, business-oriented manner.

If these changes take place, the outlook is exciting. Wood output is expected to increase from 0.317 million cubic metres (M^3) in 1979 to 1.623 million M^3 in 1990 and 3.026 million M^3 in the year 200. Ireland will progress from being a major timber importer to being self-sufficient for wood and possibly becoming an exporter. Forest-based employment should increase from 6,300 in 1981 to 8,800 in the year 2000. Most of this employment will be provided in rural areas. The net returns of the forestry programme to the Exchequer should be positive within 15 years and increase to about £20 million (adjusted to 1980£) annually to the year 2000. While the potential contribution of state forestry in the economic and social domain is positive, what impact has it had on the physical environment?

The most obvious change has been in the upland landscape. Some have seen this as adding a vertical dimension and variety of colour to a stark and barren landscape while to others it is an unimaginative intrusion into harmonious and familiar vistas.

The expanses of even-aged, single species forests provide a homogenous habitat which cannot sustain the variety and quantity of wildlife maintained by a forest comprised of different species and ages. By providing cover and shelter, even this can help to sustain particular species, for example, the pine marten, although particular forms of heath and heather-loving bird life can be adversely affected.

Forests have a high rate of evapo-transpiration – they pump large volumes of water into the atmosphere. As a result, the flow in water-courses in highly afforested areas is reduced after afforestation. In heavily populated areas with relatively low rainfall such as the South of England, this can be a significant cost, since additional water storage capacity must be installed in order to compensate for the reduction in flow-rate. In areas with surplus water and therefore flooding problems, the reduction of the run-off rate is a benefit. Unfortunately, although this is an impact of some potential significance in Ireland, there is no empirical basis on which to judge its magnitude or implications. To complicate matters further, because of the convention of ploughing up and down the hillside to facilitate drainage during planting, the initial effect of afforestation can be to increase and to concentrate water run-off.

Extensive outdoor recreation – hill-walking, orienteering, hiking – has been encouraged and facilitated by the large areas acquired by the state for afforestation in upland areas. From 1970, the forests have been open to the public, and this comprises a major benefit of the forest investment.

While the bulk of afforestation has taken place on previously treeless areas, some has involved the prior clearance of existing 'scrub' woodland. This has given rise to conflict, especially when the woodland in question was one of the few remaining areas of 'semi-natural' native forest. However, over the past decade, and particularly since passage of the Wildlife Act in 1977, the Forest and Wildlife Service has been careful to protect the remainder of such areas under its control. Conflict between development and conservation still occurs in relation to undisturbed natural areas such as 'virgin' raised and blanket bogs. Organisations with a development ethos find it difficult to recognise the value of maintaining the integrity of a particular eco-type.

Most countries have developed a system of National Parks to protect areas of unique ecological interest and distinction and/or beauty. The Forest and Wildlife Service perform some of these functions in Ireland and a unit in the National Parks and Monuments Branch of the Office of Public Works is also developing a role in this area. The National Heritage Bill, introduced in the Senate on July 1st, 1982, proposes the designation of areas in Killarney, Connemara, Donegal and the Burren as National Parks to be administered by a newly established National Heritage Council. The Council is to amalgamate functions at present carried out by the National Parks and Monuments Branch of the Office of Public Works, the National Museum and other parts of the Civil Service.

Arterial drainage
Because of the saucer-shaped physiography of Ireland, rivers flow slowly through poor channels, so that much of the land suffers from periodic or prolonged flood damage. Arterial drainage consists of deepening and widening river channels so as to remove surplus water and reduce the level of the water-table.

The capital cost of arterial drainage is born entirely by the Exchequer, and projects are carried out by the Office of Public Works. Maintenance of schemes is charged to the county, so that the benefitting landowners bear none of the costs directly.

The Office of Public Works initiates proposals on the basis of a priority list developed pursuant to the passage of the Arterial Drainage Act 1945. Since 1945, thirty-four schemes have been completed, and three are in progress. Over 600,000 acres will have been influenced by drainage when those schemes are complete (compared with a total area of 450,000 acres drained under provisions of the Acts of 1842, 1863 and 1925). The regional distribution of farm-land affected is shown in Map 2. Almost all the arterial drainage investment has been made above a line joining Dublin and Killarney, with the Midlands, Galway

247

Map 2 ARTERIAL DRAINAGE

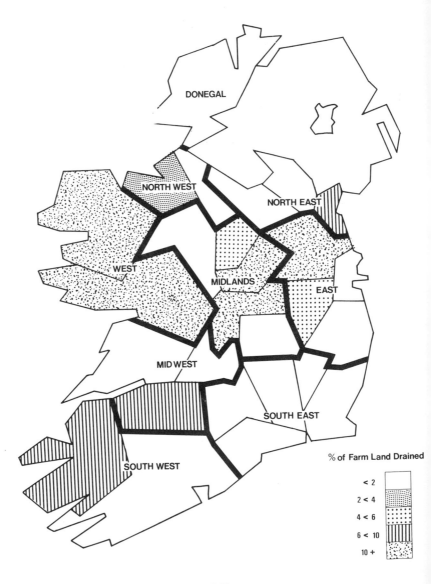

DONEGAL

NORTH WEST

NORTH EAST

WEST

MIDLANDS

EAST

MID WEST

SOUTH EAST

SOUTH WEST

% of Farm Land Drained

< 2

2 < 4

4 < 6

6 < 10

10 +

and Mayo being especially favoured. The state has spent £238 million (adjusted to 1980£) on the construction of arterial drainage schemes since the first post-War project was started in 1948. It is difficult to calculate the financial returns on this investment. Formal project appraisal was initiated by the Office of Public Works in 1970 but these analyses apply only to schemes initiated during the past decade, and returns are estimated using assumed productivities, outputs and prices which have not been validated on the basis of *ex post* analysis. It seems likely that the drainage schemes undertaken first – beginning with the River Brosna in 1948 – have yielded a substantial net financial return, but that diminishing returns have now set in. Some current and prospective arterial drainage projects will probably not generate sufficient additional net farm-income to cover the survey, construction and maintenance costs.

Arterial drainage affects water supply, fisheries, wildlife and amenities, and has aesthetic implications. With regard to water supply, the most serious problems arise when single purpose arterial drainage schemes utilise natural lakes to alleviate flooding. These can significantly reduce the amount of water available to augment low river flows and to support increased abstractions.

With regard to fisheries, while in some instances, e.g. the Bunree River, recovery after drainage is excellent, in others, e.g. the Blackwater tributaries, re-establishement fails to take place. The balance of experience with regard to sustained recovery of native fishery stocks is negative, partly because the channels have to be scoured periodically to maintain the effectiveness of the drainage, and this can impede recovery of the fishery.

Ireland is important for wildfowl for which it is a relatively temperate wintering area at the end of migratory flyways from Greenland, Iceland, Scotland, Scandinavia, Central Europe and Western Russia. The reduction in wetland areas is concentrating the wildfowl into increasingly fewer areas, where they are coming under pressure both from hunters and shortage of food.

Rivers in their natural state are aesthetically superior to the canal-like symmetry and reduced vegetation level associated with arterial drainage channels. Conversely, the appearance and vitality of well-drained land which enjoys high standards of husbandry is also pleasing; it is argued that it boosts the morale of a community to see such land being 'created'.

Turf development

Up to 1973, Bord na Móna peat production had to be subvented in the form of a price subsidy from the ESB; electricity generated from peat was significantly more expensive than that provided by burning oil. Bristow and Fell (1971) estimated that the subsidy from electricity customers for peat-fired electricity in the financial year 1968/69 came to £2.976 million, or £14.27 million in 1981£. There were substantial social benefits provided in exchange for this subsidy including the provision of employment in the relatively economically deprived Midlands, balance of payments savings, and a buffer against the adverse price effects of the post 1974 energy situation. Since 1974, peat-fired electricity has been more than competitive with oil-fired. Peat briquettes and sod peat (machine) are supplied by Bord na Móna to the wholesale and retail fuel markets. The price is controlled by the government at such a level that non-price rationing must be resorted to in allocating supplies. This new price and energy supply situation has led to the authorisation of a major peat development programme involving the exploitation of peat deposits which had previously been too costly to develop.

It is clear that peat development confers substantial net benefits: it provides energy at a price which is competitive with imports; it provides employment and generates income in economically deprived areas; it helps the balance of payments and is of some national strategic value.

Large scale state peat development has been concentrated on the raised bogs of the Midlands. As this work has proceeded, the number of remaining 'virgin' bogs has diminished, as has the extent of undisturbed wetland generally. For naturalists, it is as important to preserve representative examples of our natural endowment as it is for archaeologists to protect for posterity manifestations of past human intervention. Such protection provides a medium for the study of ecosystem processes, maintains our reservoir of germ plasm, to which we can turn in order to introduce new genetic strains into cultivated plants, and preserves 'living' examples of benchmarks in the evolution of the Irish landscape.

Milled peat development can also result in the release into water courses of very fine particles of peat 'dust', which inhibits the feeding and spawning of fish.

Once the surface layer of peat has been removed, the mineral soil underneath can be used to grow grass, vegetables and trees, so that peat extraction in a sense is creating a new resource.

Energy development

In late 1973 the Marathon company discovered natural gas off Kinsale Head. The potential rent – the difference between the maximum consumers would be willing to pay and the costs of extraction and transport – has been conservatively estimated to amount to £90 million annually (Convery, 1981). The offtake is at present allocated to the ESB (60%), NET (35%), and others (5%). An eighteen inch pipeline is being constructed from Cork to Dublin so that domestic, institutional and industrial customers in Dublin and along the pipeline route can have access to the gas. Pipeline connections with Belfast, Waterford and Limerick may also be made. In terms of impact on the physical environment, natural gas is a benign fuel, having virtually no adverse effect on the quality of either air or water.

The rapid expansion in electricity generating capacity which has taken place since 1957 has increased substantially the volume of emissions to the atmosphere of sulphur and particulate matter (smoke) from power stations. There is no time series of such emissions

Table 2   Electricity generating capacity

	1957/8 Capacity (MW)	1957/8 % of Total	1981/2 Capacity (MW)	1981/2 % of Total	1987/8 Capacity (MW)	1987/8 % of Total
Oil	44.5	7	1668	51	1884[a]	41
Coal – Imported	245[b]	38	—		900	20
Native	—	—	15	—	60	1
Natural Gas	—	—	645	20	730	16
Peat	145	22	447.5	14	527.5	11
Hydro	215	33	511	16	511	11
Total	649.5	100	3286.5	101	4612.5	100

[a] Some of the oil-fired capacity will be converted to natural gas if this is made available in sufficient quantity.

[b] The coal-burning plant also uses oil.

available, but we know that in 1974 electricity generation delivered 89,000 tons of sulphur into the atmosphere (McManus, 1975). When the 900 MWs of coal-fired capacity at Moneypoint, Co. Clare, comes on stream in 1985/86, it will add to these emissions. Conversely, the natural gas-fired capacity will have no emissions. Existing and prospective capacity is presented in Table 2.

Private sector activity and environmental quality
I will discuss elements of four sectors within this group, agriculture, industry, minerals and urban development.

Agriculture
Twenty five years ago, Ireland had an extensive, low, non-labour input/low output form of agricultural production. Fertilisers, pesticides and insecticides were applied sparingly, large concentrated housing units for stock hardly existed and on-farm silage-making was unknown. Fields and hedgerows remained unaltered. With such a farming system the natural assimilative capacities of soils could absorb waste loads; pollution problems were minor and localized.

Since 1957, there has been a steady increase in the intensity with which inputs are used: this is exemplified by the level of applications of Nitrogen (N), Phosphorus (P) and Potassium (K) in 1958 and 1980:

Table 3   Fertiliser use

	Quantity (000s Tonnes) Fertiliser Year – July to June		
	N	P	K
1957/58	18.0	27.0	43.5
1979/80	247.5	68.0	157.0

Some areas have had particular problems: in parts of Cavan, Longford, Westmeath and Monaghan, intensive pig rearing gives rise to the problem of disposing of a substantial volume of animal waste. This is commonly spread on adjacent land. Unfortunately, much of the soil in this area is non-porous, and cannot absorb large amounts of animal waste. During heavy rain, the slurry can be washed into adjacent rivers and lakes, thereby causing a serious pollution problem. The odour can also be extremely unpleasant.

252

Leakage from silage units into water also constitutes a major pollution hazard. Silage effluent is 200 times more potent than domestic sewage. Silage-making is particularly a feature of intensive dairy and cattle farms in the south and east, and the number of pollution incidents appears to be increasing.

Fertiliser run-off, which increases algae and plant growth in lakes ¦to the detriment of preferred fish species, is becoming a problem in some areas.

If the manufacturers' instructions for the application of herbicides and pesticides are followed there will usually be no pollution. However, if the instructions on either timing or the volume of application are not followed or if the chemicals are simply dumped into rivers, the effects on aquatic life can be devastating.

Since 1957, there has been a substantial increase in the acreage of fields drained under various government assistance programmes. The total area involved is 2.8 million acres,* and government grants total £310 million (1980£) over the twenty-five year period. In contrast to arterial drainage, field drainage has been concentrated in the South and East (Map 3). The evidence indicates that there has been a good return on investment in most projects, but that for a significant minority, returns didn't cover total costs. Furthermore, net farm income could have been increased in many cases, if a portion of the money spent on drainage had instead been used to purchase other inputs – fertilizer, improved stock, buildings and equipment – to be applied to already drained land (Bruton and Convery 1982). This does not imply that farmers behave irrationally: the much higher rate of grant support for drainage, vis-à-vis other inputs, encourages such behaviour.

It is difficult to assess the impacts of field drainage on the physical environment. The adverse effect on wildlife and fisheries of draining a single farm will be negligible, but when drainage occurs simultaneously on large numbers of contiguous holdings, the ability of wetland wildlife to find adjacent habitats is inhibited. However, very little is known about the thresholds which exist. Field drainage is often associated with field improvement, which can involve the removal of trees, hedgerows and stones. This can be very destructive for wildlife, but again the seriousness depends partly on the extent to which large numbers of adjacent landowners take such action. Field 'improvement' can also result in damage to and destruction of items of historical and

*2.3 million acres have been drained since 1957.

253

Map 3 FIELD DRAINAGE

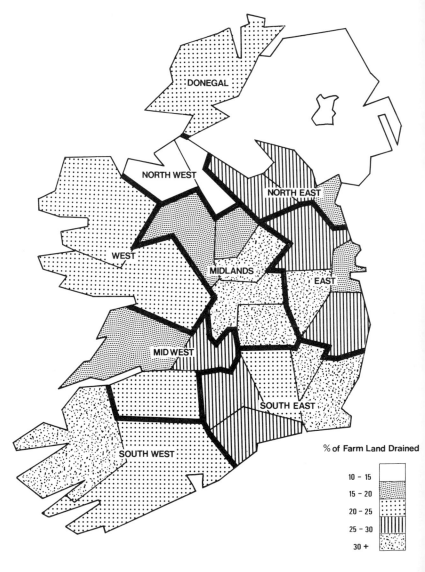

% of Farm Land Drained

10 – 15	
15 – 20	
20 – 25	
25 – 30	
30 +	

archaeological interest.

Industry

Since 1957, industrial production has increased dramatically: the index climbed from 102.5 in 1957 to 370 in 1980 (Base 1953 = 100). The first law of thermodynamics – the law of the conservation of matter and energy – states that matter (energy) can neither be created nor destroyed. Material can be transformed into solids, liquids or gases, but the world possesses only fixed amounts of these substances. An increase in industrial output on the scale experienced here in Ireland should increase the volume of 'waste' to be disposed of. However, Ireland's new industrial base has a high 'throughput' content: raw and semi-processed materials are imported, processed, and exported. Furthermore, much of the new industrial capacity established since 1957 has been in the 'clean' industries of light engineering, health care, consumer products, and electronics. There has also been a substantial investment in the pharmaceutical and chemical industries, and these can have a significant environmental impact including, especially in the case of the latter, the disposal of toxic wastes.

The only published studies of this area found that the 'traditional' industrial base – food processing, drink, pulp and paper, fertiliser and cement – was responsible for almost all of the emissions to the environment (McManus 1975). With only one point estimate available of emissions by source, it is impossible to get a sense of trends in this respect. However, it appears that, while the traditional sectors may be effecting some reduction in emissions of organic wastes, there is an increasing volume of pharmaceutical and chemical wastes.

Minerals and mining

In 1961, a major lead-zinc-silver ore-body was discovered at Tynagh, Co. Galway, and this was followed in 1963-64 by discoveries of a commercial deposit of zinc and lead-ore at Silvermines, Co. Tipperary and of barytes nearby at Ballynoe. The copper mine in Avoca, Co. Wicklow was reactivated with state help, and in late 1970 the largest zinc-lead deposit in Europe was discovered near Navan, Co. Meath. Thus, in the 1960-75 period, Ireland had somewhat unexpectedly become a substantial force on the European metals scene. Unfortunately, there have been no commercial discoveries since 1970, and the mines at both Tynagh and Silvermines are now closed. Labour problems, low metal prices and the highly leveraged nature of the investment have combined to keep the Navan mine in a difficult financial position. State subsidy is necessary to keep the Avoca mines operating. The processing of dolomite into a magnesia refractory in Dungarvan, Co. Waterford has been terminated. Thus the industry has gone from a boom in the late 1960s and early 1970s to contraction. The mining of aggregate minerals – stone, sand, gravel, limestone etc. – is cyclical, being dependent primarily on activity in the building and construction sector.

Minerals exploitation can be highly disruptive to the environment by generating large volumes of dust and considerable noise. Surface mines scar the landscape and in the case of very large surface mines, a lunar-type landscape, often with a large 'lake', can be left when the deposit is worked out. In the case of metals mining, emissions of metal and metal compounds into the water and the atmosphere, can constitute health hazards to plant and animal (including human) life if not carefully managed.

The smelting process can have equally bad effects, but neither zinc nor copper are smelted in Ireland and there only is some smelting of lead.

Urban development
Perhaps the most dramatic and significant changes in the physical environment during the past twenty-five years are those associated with urban areas, particularly in the Dublin region where the population has been expanding at such a rate that it is known as 'the fastest growing urban area in Europe'. This growth has been accommodated mainly by expansions to the West, with satellite communities in Tallaght and Blanchardstown, but all areas on the city periphery have expanded rapidly where space and services allowed. The industrial base in the inner city has atrophied as difficulties of access and parking have increased, and the potential area available for expansion has diminished; as the value of the industrial sites for alternative uses – office and commercial – has grown; and as the labour force has moved to the suburbs. While the industrial base has declined, there has been a boom in office developments since the 1960s. Central government and public agencies have provided a steady demand for 50 per cent of available office space. These developments have been heavily concentrated in particular zones on the south side of the city. In the past decade, there has also been a growth in construction of apartments on the south side and in the more

fashionable suburban areas. The trend towards enclosed shopping centres, both within the city and in the suburbs, has been a feature of most of the large urban areas. Thus in the past twenty-five years there has been expansion and vitality at the urban fringe, and decline and decay alternating with single-use zones of some prosperity in the centre.

The expansion in the number of residential, industrial and commercial buildings has resulted in an expansion of the construction and associated industries. However, as this sector has traditionally fulfilled the role of a charge tank in the economy, declining sharply during economic recession, and expanding with economic growth, prosperity is cyclical. Because of the rapid expansion at the urban fringe, and the changing use patterns within the inner city, some landowners have made large 'windfall' gains, substantially in excess of the minimum price necessary to accomplish the change in land-use. The most extreme instance of this is found on the south side of Dublin: Jennings (1981) estimated that the median price paid per acre of land for private residential development in the south in 1979 amounted to £76,000*, which is thirty times the price of agricultural land, and over three times the price paid for land purchased for private residential developments on the north side of the city.

The environmental impacts of urban development are various: developments require water and sewage disposal; the way in which sewage disposal is handled will have significant implications for water quality. The manner of development also has major interdependent aesthetic, economic and social consquences. 'Strip' development is more wasteful of both infrastructural investment (electricity, phones, water etc.) and publicly provided services (post, police, school transport, social services etc.) than 'cluster' development, and is less safe. Clusters of development which have a distinctly cultural and community character, separated by undeveloped open space are generally regarded as being visually more pleasant than an undifferentiated running-together of neighbourhoods.

In Dublin, the area of the city which is most attractive for office development has the greatest number of Georgian buildings in reasonable structural repair. When the bare site is worth several times the value of these buildings, the incentive to get rid of them is great, regardless of the beauty and historical architectural or cultural significance of the original buildings.

*Assuming 8 units per acre.

Much of Dublin has fallen to these and other pressures. Although some buildings of distinction have been built, there is widespread feeling that the overall aesthetic quality of Dublin has been sadly diminished in the 1957-82 period. This is not true of some other locations: urban areas such as Kilkenny, Kinsale and Waterford have had considerable success in conserving and in some cases restoring their old buildings and structures.

With regard to social impact, it is now generally recognized that diversity enhances stability. Thus a variety of uses in close proximity provide security, atmosphere, intensity of use, community spirit etc., all of which are absent from large blocks of homogeneous land-use. It is also clear that some building schemes and structural designs encourage a positive community atmosphere, are safer in terms of traffic hazard and reduce the likelihood of crime, while others do the converse. Likewise, the homogeneity in terms of income class, the lack of services in the recent developments outside Dublin are targets of criticism, as are the uniformity and lack of flair of most private residential developments.

However, there have been a few examples of aesthetic, functional and social excellence in project design and execution and there has been generous provision for open space in major new public developments, although there is doubt as to the effectiveness with which such space is used.

Environmental policies

It is clear that a substantial portion of environmental impact is a consequence of direct state action at national and local levels. Explicit environmental control policies, however, are directed almost exclusively at the private sector. Environmental policy directed at government action is modest, and is of three types: departments are required in certain instances to 'consult' with a minister, e.g. the Minister for Fisheries and Forestry, concerning proposed actions; departments and agencies have been told that they are responsible for the environmental impacts of their own actions; governmental units are directed legislatively or administratively to take responsibility for the environmental dimension of their activities, e.g. the ESB has statutory responsibilities concerning the salmon fisheries on the Shannon River.

With regard to environmental policies directed at the private sector,

258

it is convenient to distinguish between statutory provisions and administrative procedures.

Statutory provisions
The Local Government (Planning and Development) Act 1963 is the legal cornerstone of government efforts to shape private sector behaviour vis-à-vis the environment. Modifications were included in the Local Government (Planning and Development) Act 1976. The provisions of these Acts are administered by eighty-seven local government bodies, comprising county councils, county boroughs, borough corporations and urban district councils. Under the Acts, the local authorities have two primary functions. The first of these is to prepare development plans for their areas of jurisdiction, wherein future land use, transporation patterns, redevelopment areas, sanitary services, amenity areas etc. are identified so as to meet future demands while protecting natural and cultural amenities. This function is the responsibility of the elected representatives, and is where – subject to national policies, legal constraints and availability of finance – policy to guide development should be laid out. In practice, when the plan is being revised, the re-zoning of areas for development often becomes the only means whereby legislators are involved directly in plan preparation.

The second function is to grant, refuse, or grant conditionally, planning permission for all except exempted developments. The granting of planning permission is an executive function, carried out by (in the case of counties) the county manager, usually on the advice of the county planning staff, and subject to compliance with the provisions of the development plan. Exempted developments include most work relating to agriculture and forestry, work undertaken by local authorities themselves, work carried out under the provisions of the Land Reclamation Act 1949, and minor developments such as house extensions below a certain size, or interior changes in a building where the original interior is not listed in the development plan.

The applicant can appeal a refusal, or some or all of the conditions imposed with an approval, to An Bord Pleanála. Appeals against planning permission decisions by a local authority can be appealed to An Bord Pleanála by any third party.

Under section 4 of the City and County Management Act 1955, a council is authorised to direct the manager to take a specific action. In some cases this authority is used by the council to change a manager's decision on a planning application.

In some areas where planning permission is refused, the local authority may be liable to pay compensation. If the proposed development is judged to be 'premature', in terms of services available, would constitute a traffic hazard, or is in an area of particular beauty, then refusal is not compensatable. However, refusal to allow development of open space, e.g. sportsgrounds, in an urban, serviced area may leave the local authority liable to pay compensation.

Under the Local Government (Planning and Development) Bill 1982, the five year limitation imposed on planning permissions would be relaxed, penalties for offenses under the Planning Acts would be increased, and the introduction of charges for planning applications and appeals would be permitted.

A major limitation of the Planning Acts is that they only apply to developments initiated since the passage of the planning legislation; some of the most serious polluters of both water and air were in operation before this time. The Local Government (Water Pollution) Act 1977 has been enacted to help deal with this problem as it applies to water: all discharges (except by local authorities) from point sources into sewers, inland and tidal waters, and the sea must be licensed. As in the case of planning permission, the licensing authority may refuse permission, grant it, or grant it with conditions. Officers of the Central Fisheries Board can institute legal proceedings against polluters under this Act and the Fisheries Acts and have been active in this regard in recent years.

The Alkali, etc. Works Regulation Act 1906 remains the primary statutory vehicle for managing air quality. Firms which manufacture products such as sulphuric acid, fertilisers, nitric acid and cement are registered and subject to inspection. It is a condition of first registration that the 'best practicable means' of preventing the discharge into the atmosphere of noxious and offensive gases and for rendering them harmless and inoffensive be employed. Many processes which are not registerable should be included, while the transportation, power generation and domestic sectors – the latter is a major cause of the deterioration in Dublin's air quality since 1978 – are not eligible for inclusion.

The Wildlife Act 1977 is the primary legislation for protecting wildlife and natural areas. It provides the Minister for Fisheries and Forestry with substantial enabling powers to list species for protection and to designate and acquire wildlife and natural areas for protection and management. The National Monuments Acts 1930 and 1954 have been the main means of directly protecting structures and sites of archaeological, historical and cultural interest. However, intervention by the Office of Public Works has been confined to a very small number of sites in relation to the number under threat. The National Heritage Bill 1982 would, if enacted, establish a National Heritage Council which would be empowered to play a much more active and comprehensive role than has been possible heretofore.

Administrative procedures
The most significant administrative procedure is the environmental assessment of prospective grant-aided industrial projects. This is commissioned by the Industrial Development Authority (IDA). The aspects related to water quality are reviewed by the Water Resources Division of An Foras Forbartha and the Environmental Technology Department of the Institute of Industrial Research and Standards. The latter also provides additional information and reports on air pollution control, hazardous waste disposal, fire and safety, and industrial hygiene and noise. The information and recommendations are sent to the IDA. The planning authority makes compliance with the recommendations a condition for receiving planning permission. Since grants are usually paid in instalments over a number of years, the Agency can exercise considerable leverage over an extended period. The only published analysis with which to analyse system performances was undertaken in 1974, only 4 years after the I.D.A. had initiated environmental assessment (McManus, 1975). None of the industrial operations found to be causing water pollution and/or air pollution had gone through the environmental assessment process. Thus the limited evidence available indicates that the assessment system is effective, although in terms of the 1974 analysis, it could be argued that the newness of the assessed projects and the inherently 'clean' nature of most of the industrial processes in question assured a modest environmental impact at that stage.

Conclusions
It is difficult to judge the overall trends in environmental quality vis-à-vis water, air, wildlife, wetlands, our structural endowment and natural areas. This partly reflects difficulties inherent in measurement, but it also reflects the absence of a systematic data gathering and publishing capability, although there are a number of agencies

261

involved in some aspects: An Foras Forbartha is now collecting and publishing data on water quality, a number of agencies have gathered data on some dimensions of Dublin's air quality, and the Forest and Wildlife Service provides some fragmentary information on progress in species and habitat conservation.

An impressive body of law in planning, water pollution control and wildlife has been enacted during the past twenty-five years, and the IDA has implemented an environmental assessment process. These legal and administrative provisions have been most effective when:

1. A government agency has been given, or has adopted, an explicit and relatively straight-forward assignment in direct action vis-à-vis conservation. The parks of Dublin county council, the forest parks of the Forest and Wildlife Service and the structural restoration work of the Office of Public Works are of this *genre*.

2. There is an automatic link between compliance with environmental regulations and the self interest of the individual(s) involved. Examples include the requirement of Building Societies that a structure has planning permission before they will advance funds for its purchase, and the IDA's environmental assessment scheme, whereby payment of the grant is contingent upon appropriate performance.

The system is weak in the following respects:

1. While government departments and agencies have been exhorted to accept responsibility for the environmental impacts of their actions, little attempt has been made to encourage and assist them in developing this responsibility, which would require that they employ appropriately trained staff, adopt the necessary decision-making procedures and, in some cases, be given statutory recognition in this regard.

2. Both at national and local level, there has been a failure to articulate what steps should be taken to achieve the desired end. At national level, EEC standards – which in the nature of the Community decision-making process are the lowest common denominator of the ten member countries – tend to be adopted as goals; at the local level, the development plan has often failed to serve its purpose of articulating what the community wanted to achieve.

3. The planning and environment management system depends heavily on the threat of legal sanctions to encourage compliance with regulations. This is the achilles heel of the Irish environmental

management system. Our post-colonial cultural and social traditions and attitudes mean that the enforcement process is not seen to have the legitimacy and popular social sanction which such a system enjoys in most other Northern European countries. This has an adverse effect on the thoroughness and enthusiasm applied by enforcers to their task, and diminishes the degree of social opprobrium with which breaking the law is associated.

This difficulty is accentuated by the fact that concern for the well-being of the natural and built environment is felt by some to be an elitist avocation of the leisured and enlightened (former) landlord class, and not something to concern the 'common man'. While the significance of this ascendancy complex is diminishing, it still has sufficient adherents to diminish the legitimacy of enforcement of environmental standards as a mainstream political concern.

4. The planning and environmental management system tends to be negative rather than positive. Some environmentally deleterious actions are discouraged by the threat of court action, but, except in the case of IDA's capital grants scheme, whereby a portion of the cost of pollution abatement equipment is eligible for grant, no positive incentives are provided to encourage environmentally benign behaviour.

Rather than depend exclusively on legal sanctions, assessing charges per unit of emission, penalising derelict sites with a schedule of charges, and rewarding conservation of, for example, natural areas and buildings of distinction, would result in a more efficient use of resources, better enforcement, and an improved environment. I feel strongly that the environmental management system in Ireland will be seriously deficient so long as there is not an automatic and persistent cost associated with environmentally deleterious action, and there is no financial support available for selected actions which enhance environmental quality. Both of these features characterise environmental management in a number of European countries, including West Germany, France, the Netherlands and Hungary.

The charge should be applied equally to the public and the private sectors. It is very important that managers in the public services be given 'signals' – which the assessment of charges provides *par excellence* – concerning the adequacy of their environmental management performance. To argue – as is sometimes done – that it makes no sense for local authorities to charge themselves misses the entire point of this approach: Its *raison d'etre* is not to raise funds *per se* (although this is a not insignificant side-benefit) but to provide managers and the public with indicators of performance and incentives for managers to maintain or improve performance.

5. There are substantial gaps in the system, most notably in the domains of farming and air quality. With regard to the former, the large numbers involved, the fact that in many cases the pollution isn't emitted at a single point, and the current recession in agriculture all combine to produce an intractable enforcement problem in farming. The most promising opportunities in this respect would appear to lie in following something akin to the IDA model, whereby grants for piggeries etc. would be phased over a period, and continuance of the grant, and possible eligibility for future grants for a specified period, would be contingent upon following appropriate management practice.

Air quality management has some parallel to agriculture, in that there are a large number of emitters, namely households and drivers of vehicles; it can be difficult to admister an environmental management scheme cost effectively. This limitation is of practical significance, because most of the deterioration in Dublin's air quality is due to the sharp increase in the domestic burning of solid fuels, which occurred after the price rises in oil and gas after 1973 and the supply interruptions which characterised the former.

It is clear that, over the past twenty-five years, the physical environment of Ireland has been transformed, in many cases for the better. However there has also been deterioration, particularly in urban areas, but also in rural parts. A relatively pristine environment is a cornerstone of our faltering tourist industry, and it is no doubt one element which is influential in convincing some overseas investors and managers that Ireland provides an attractive ambience in which to work and invest. It also enriches the lives of the residents by providing better health, a varied and high-quality range of outdoor recreation experiences, and a sense of identity with the past.

We have undertaken substantial legislative efforts to protect environmental values in the past two decades. These need to be complemented by vigorous political and administrative leadership at national and local levels, and by the use of self-enforcing environmental management schemes such as pricing.

References
Bristow, J. A. and Fell, A. C. (1971), *Bord na Móna: A Cost-Benefit*

264

Study. Institute of Public Administration, Research Series 5.

Bruton, Richard and Convery, Frank J. (1982), *Land Drainage Policy in Ireland*. Policy Series Research Report No. 4, Economic and Social Research Institute, Dublin.

Convery, Frank J. (1979), *Irish Forestry Policy*. Report No. 46 (Part 2). National Economic and Social Council, Dublin.

Convery, F.J. (1981), 'Natural resource development and public policy'. *The Irish Economy and Society in the 1980s*. Economic and Social Research Institute, Dublin.

Environment Council (1980), *A Policy for the Environment*, Government Publications, Dublin.

Jennings, R. (1981). 'Recent developments in housing land in Dublin'. *Mimeo*, An Foras Forbartha, Dublin, quoted in *Business and Finance*, 8 October, 1981, p. 26.

McManus, T. (Ed) (1975). *National Survey of Air and Water Pollution, 1974*. Institute of Industrial Research and Standards, Dublin.

Impacts of Drainage in Ireland, (1980), National Board of Science and Technology, Dublin.

266

Law and The Legal System 1957–82

JAMES P. CASEY

Irish society has changed so much in the last twenty-five years that it would be extraordinary not to find some reflection of this in the law and the legal system. Change here has been extensive if not as radical as some might wish. The developments come under five heads: the legal system, constitutional law, administrative law, labour law, family law.

The legal system

The most obvious change might be called 'the litigation explosion'. This phenomenon is due to factors such as increases in traffic, industrialisation and crime and is simply demonstrated by the growth of the High Court. In 1957 this consisted of a President and six judges (only one more than in 1924); in 1982 it comprises the President and fourteen judges. The size of the District and Circuit Courts has also increased, though less dramatically.[1] This reflects in part the failure to decentralise justice effectively by extending the jurisdiction of those courts in line with economic and social factors such as inflation. Although the Courts Act 1971 had brought in some extensions – implementing recommendations made in 1966[2] – these were already out of date. The Courts Act 1981 attempts to redress the balance by increasing considerably the financial ceilings on the lower courts' jurisdictions, and by devolving a range of family law matters to them. Implementation of the latter changes is causing difficulties and the possibility of a constitutional challenge has been mooted.

The size of the practising legal profession has also increased, to such an extent that it has been found necessary to expand the Law Library. From 1982, both branches of the legal profession will be restricting entry, a development which has caused controversy. Unfortunately, this increase in the number of judges and practising lawyers has not

267

ended delays in litigation. These delays could have been reduced if the proposals on the jurisdiction of the Master of the High Court which were put forward in 1972 by the Committee on Court Practice and Procedure had been implemented. That committee has also deplored the failure to provide proper court accommodation in many places.

For many years there was little literature on Irish law, but publishers now find that there *is* a market for Irish law books and in the last few years works of high quality on most core legal subjects have appeared. The position in regard to the raw material of the legal system is much less satisfactory. The reporting of judicial decisions has been tardy and uncomprehensive, and there have been serious delays in producing volumes of statutes and statutory instruments.

Since 1957 there has been a steady increase in the use of specialised tribunals outside the regular court system. Under the Local Government Planning and Development Act 1976, appeals in planning matters now go to the independent Bord Pleanála, instead of to the Minister for the Environment. The Labour Court has taken on ajudicatory functions under the Anti-Discrimination (Pay) Act 1974 and the Employment Equality Act 1977, while disputes over alleged unfair dismissals fall within the remit of the Employment Appeals Tribunal. The Criminal Injuries Compensation Tribunal rules on applications under the Criminal Injuries Compensation Scheme.

Another major development has been state provision for legal aid, which was introduced in 1962 on a statutory basis for criminal cases and was made available in 1979 for civil cases by executive action. system by the state's adhesion to the European Convention on Human Rights and acceptance of the right of individual recourse to the EEC Commission and Court.[4] For the legal system the consequences of joining the EEC are that EEC regulations enter directly into the Irish legal order which is further shaped by the requirements of EEC directives. And several cases have already been referred to the European Court in Luxembourg for preliminary rulings under Article 177 of the Treaty.[5]

The tragic events in Northern Ireland have also made an impact on the legal system. In May 1972 the government issued a proclamation bringing into effect Part V of the Offences against the State Act 1939 and a Special Criminal Court of the type envisaged by Part V was subsequently established. The court has been composed of professional judges only, in contrast with earlier periods when it was manned by military officers under a provision in the 1939 Act.[6] The Offences against the State (Amendment) Act 1972 amended the Acts of 1939 and 1940 in various ways, including making the belief of a senior Garda officer as to an accused's membership of an illegal organisation admissible as evidence. It should perhaps be stressed that such belief is rendered admissible only; it is in no sense conclusive. The Criminal Justice (Verdicts) Act 1976 increased the powers of the Special Criminal Court by giving it the same authority as other courts to bring in alternative verdicts.

Like its UK counterpart, the Criminal Law (Jurisdiction) Act 1976 was passed principally to overcome difficulties about extradition of political offenders from the Republic to Northern Ireland. It provides that certain acts done in Northern Ireland are criminal offences in the Republic, and it established machinery under which evidence can be taken here for a trial in Northern Ireland and *vice versa*.

The Criminal Justice Act 1964 abolished the death penalty for all offences except treason and capital murder, as defined in section 1(1)(b). This category includes murder of a member of the Garda Síochána acting in the course of his duty. However, though several persons have been convicted of this offence, the capital sentences passed on them were commuted under Article 13.6 of the Constitution. The 1981-2 coalition government introduced a bill to abolish capital punishment entirely, but this lapsed with the fall of that government and is not to be revived by its successor.

A focus of attention in civil matters has been the jury. The Courts Act 1971 abolished civil jury trial in the Circuit Court (where it was rarely availed of). It remains available in the High Court where it is the norm, particularly in personal injuries and fatal accidents cases – much to the chagrin of insurers, who blame juries for inflated damages awards and hence, higher premiums. But the 1982 jury is more likely to be a cross-section of the public than its 1957 counterpart, since the Juries Act 1976 has greatly widened eligibility to serve. Women and non-ratepayers are now liable for jury service, and the qualifying age has been lowered to eighteen.

It remains to note two institutional developments. The new and independent office of Director of Public Prosecutions was created by the Prosecution of Offences Act 1974, which transferred to the holder all the prosecuting powers and responsibilities of the Attorney General. The Law Reform Commission Act 1975 established the Commission to discharge the tasks of keeping the law under review and making proposals for reform.

Constitutional law

It would be hard to overstate the significance of the developments in constitutional law since 1957. The merits and defects of the Constitution have been a constant subject of public discussion. It has been amended five times, and at the time of writing a referendum on another amendment – to outlaw abortion – has been promised. No action, however, has been taken on the two most controversial issues – the contents of Articles 2 and 3 and the ban imposed by Article 41.3.2 on the introduction of divorce.

In 1976-7 a group of Deputies and Senators carried out a general review of the Constitution. Their Report stated their finding that there was no demand or need for a departure from the Constitution's main principles but they recommended certain subsidiary changes, including the modification of Articles 2 and 3. Nothing has come of this. In 1981 Dr FitzGerald's coalition government instituted a review by a legal committee chaired by the Attorney General, but the government fell long before that review could be completed, and the committee has since been disbanded.

In the period under review, the first attempt to amend the Constitution was in the direction of abolishing proportional representation. This proposal was defeated in a referendum in 1959, and even more heavily in another in 1968.[7] Other attempts at amendment have had more success. The Fourth Amendment of the Constitution Act 1972 amended Article 16 by lowering the voting age to eighteen while Article 44 was modified by deleting a portion, including the celebrated reference to 'the special position' of the Roman Catholic Church.[8] The Sixth Amendment of the Constitution Act 1979 added a new section to Article 37 to protect adoption orders, and the provisions of Article 18 on university represenation in Seanad Éireann were altered, partly in anticipation of the statutory dissolution of the National University of Ireland.[9]

These amendments were uncontroversial and had all-party support. This was not the case with the amendment necessitated by joining the EEC but this was approved by an overwhelming majority in the 1972 referendum. The resulting Third Amendment of the Constitution Act 1972 did not amend individual provisions in detail, but its economical and continental-style[10] drafting effectively ensures that any constitutional barriers to community membership are lifted.

The Presidency – normally an office of low political profile – gave rise to discussion and some controversy. President Childers had indicated a desire for a more active role than his predecessors, but his short tenure hardly allowed time for any such development.[11] His successor, Cearbhall Ó Dálaigh, found himself in the forefront of controversy when his use of Article 26 was criticised by the Minister for Defence, Mr. Donegan. Mr. Ó Dálaigh's resignation fuelled the fire and gave rise to discussion of the President's liability to, or immunity from, criticism.[12] Though he too has used Article 26, Dr. Hillery has had a more tranquil time. When the coalition government fell earlier this year, his constitutional power to refuse a dissolution might have come into play. In the event the Taoiseach was granted a dissolution, and there has been no public criticism of the President's decision.

Northern events have also had their impact in the constitutional area. The wording of Articles 2 and 3 of the Constitution have been criticised. The legal issues involved in the suggested extradition of political offenders to Northern Ireland provoked sharply contrasting views from the members of the Irish/UK Law Enforcement Commission. The Irish members held that Article 29.3 ('Ireland accepts the generally recognised principles of international law as its rule of conduct in its relations with other states') would invalidate any statute permitting extradition for political offences, since it was a generally recognised principle of international law that there should be no extradition for political offences. The UK members denied the existence of any such principle and argued that Article 29.3 did not operate to restrict the legislative competence of the Oireachtas.[13] It should also be noted that the constitutionality of the Sunningdale Agreement under which the Law Enforcement Commission was established was challenged in 1974 in *Boland* v. *An Taoiseach.* The Supreme Court rejected the claim, holding in effect that making international agreements was an executive function with which the courts could not interfere.

The outstanding development in constitutional law, however, is the burgeoning of judicial review. The courts have been called upon with increasing frequency to consider the validity of statutes, and many other issues concerning the impact of the Constitution. The availability of judicial review has proved a boon for those with a legitimate grievance who have failed in their attempts to secure redress elsewhere. Thus, the Juries Act 1976 was passed when the Supreme Court held in 1975 in *de Burca and Anderson* v *Attorney General* that the earlier Act violated the Constitution. The Court's decision in 1974 in *McGee* v *Attorney General* ended the ban on the importation of contraceptives by married couples, while that in *Murphy* v *Attorney General* invalidated the legislation under which working married couples faced heavier tax bills than they would have had they simply lived together. Clearly, some interest groups, aware of the Constitution's possibilities, have adopted a test-case strategy to assist in securing their objectives.

The courts have given the Constitution an expansive interpretation in the sphere of individual rights.[14] In particular, it has been established that the rights guaranteed are not confined to those specifically enumerated. Thus there has emerged a right to basic fairness of procedures in decision-making,[15] a right to travel,[16] a right of access to the courts,[17] and a right to work.[18] Article 38.1's requirement of a criminal trial 'in due course of law' has had life breathed into it; an accused must be *told* about the availability of legal aid[19]; and statutes creating criminal offences must identify with reasonable precision the conduct which is forbidden.[20] The guarantee of personal liberty (Article 40.4.1) has been implemented by judicial emphasis on the right to seek *habeas corpus;*[21] by coupling it with the common law presumption of innocence to hold that bail cannot be refused because of a belief that the accused will commit offences while on bail;[22] and by holding that evidence obtained in violation of constitutional rights (e.g. an unlawful detention) is inadmissible.[23] Here, however, it must be noted that there are signs of a different attitude to some of these issues in the present Supreme Court, as compared with that chaired by O Dálaigh CJ.[24]

There has been considerable litigation on the constitutional separation of powers, and it was emphasised in *City View Press Ltd* v *AnCO* (1980) that while Article 15.2.1 does not prevent the delegation of legislative powers to ministers, etc., there are limits to the delegation permissible. Many decisions have stressed the limits to the conferment of judicial power on bodies which are not courts,[25] and a good deal of case law has been generated by Article 38's distinction between minor offences (triable summarily) and 'non-minor' offences (triable only with a jury).[26] The prohibition of discrimination on religious grounds (Article 44.2.3°) has been invoked in several cases, most notably in *M.* v. *An Bord Uchtála* in 1975, where Pringle J. held that it invalidated section 12(2) of the Adoption Act 1952.[27]

On the debit side, recent Supreme Court decisions have made the reach of the private property guarantee even less certain than before. Two things seem clear: that the main protection of individual property rights is in Article 40.3; and that the present Supreme Court takes a stronger line on interference with such rights than its predecessors.[28] Beyond that, little is certain, since the ultimate test of whether a statute in this sphere is valid or not is whether five judges consider it an 'unjust attack' on individual property rights. This, in Professor J. M Kelly's words, is 'a notion which invites highly subjective interpretation.[29] One consequence will doubtless be to delay even further the recommendations of the Committee on the Price of Building Land (the Kenny Report) since the recent decisions cast some doubt on the reasoning offered in support of the constitutionality of those recommendations.

Two other issues have been handled unimpressively – the guarantee of equality before the law (Article 40.1) and the position of children *vis-à-vis* their parents. As regards Article 40, the Supreme Court has held that it prohibits 'invidious discrimination', but has given little indication as to how this is to be identified.[30] It found no such discrimination in the situation in which married couples who worked paid more tax than working cohabitees! The impression has grown that the courts view with apprehension the prospect of striking down statutes on this ground, and US experience indicates that this is a field where strong judicial nerves are required. With regard to the position of children, the courts have laid heavy stress on the constitutional rights of natural parents. In 1977, in *M.* v.*An Bord Uchtála* the Supreme Court seemed willing to see a child returned to its natural parents, following the annulment of an adoption order, despite the fact that they had married only after it was adopted and had had no contact with it for several years. Decisions like this reinforce the widely held view that the adoption of legitimate children is not possible under the Constitution (a point which still remains open for decision). But the 1980 case of *G.* v. *An Bord Uchtála* gives some ground for thinking that a judicial reconsideration of this whole issue may be under way.

Administrative law
This area has been transformed since 1957. The long-standing assumption that the state was not liable for the torts of its servants was shattered by the Supreme Court decision in *Byrne* v. *Ireland* in 1977. While the full implications of this remain to be worked out, the decision has enabled many people to bring actions (subsequently settled) where previously they would have had merely the hope of *ex gratia* compensation. Two later Supreme Court decisions destroyed the

cherished belief that the courts could do no more than rubber-stamp ministerial objections to production of evidence in departmental custody. Now it is for the courts to balance the competing public interests involved here.[31]

It is also clear that the exercise of administrative discretion can be subjected to judicial scrutiny. The Supreme Court has emphasised that discretionary power must be exercised fairly and impartially, and in accordance with the objects of the Act which confers it.[32] A ministerial order made under statute was invalidated for unreasonableness in 1978 in *Cassidy* v. *Minister for Industry and Commerce* and the High Court has held that the exercise of discretion in regard to prosecutions and passports is not immune from review.[33]

The old common law concept of natural justice has been revived and given constitutional status as a 'right to basic fairness of procedures in decision-making'. On this basis the Supreme Court invalidated the government's removal of the Garda Commissioner Garvey in 1979, indicating in so doing that any statute purporting to permit dismissal from a career office without a hearing would be unconstitutional. It has further held that the right to know the case one has to meet may require access to documents in the decision-maker's possession, even if statute does not provide for this.[34] At High Court level the right to be heard has been vindicated in a wide variety of situations.[35]

The courts have done much, and can do more to ensure administrative justice, but there is a limit to what they can undertake. Their role in protecting children needs to be supplemented by *establishing* the office of Ombudsman already created by statute. This officer could deal with cases which necessarily fall outside the judicial purview because they lack a *legal* foundation. He could also deal cheaply and expeditiously with problems for which, in terms of time and expense, a legal remedy would be impracticable.

Labour law

There have been many advances in this area, although by contrast with administrative law, they are chiefly the product of statute rather than judicial decisions. The Oireachtas has improved the position of workers in several different ways. It has fixed minimum periods of notice, established a redundancy payments scheme, and obliged employers to consult unions on prospective redundancies with a view to avoiding them or mitigating their effects.[36] The Anti-Discrimination (Pay) Act 1974 is designed to implement the principle of equal pay for equal work laid down in Article 119 of the EEC Treaty (this latter is directly effective in the legal systems of the member states). Other types of discrimination based on sex or marital status are prohibited by the Employment Equality Act 1977 which established the Employment Equality Agency with a broad remit to work towards equality of opportunity between men and women in relation to employment. (This aspect of equal treatment is required by EEC Directive 76/207.)

The Unfair Dismissals Act 1977 introduced the remedies of compensation, re-engagement or reinstatement for cases of unfair dismissal. This was an advance on the previous common law of *wrongful* dismissal, which applied only to dismissals which were in breach of contract. Now a dismissal is deemed to be unfair unless it can be justified on substantial grounds such as redundancy, misconduct or incompetence. It is plain from the Act that trade union membership can never be such a ground. While the Act does not expressly state that dismissal for refusing to join a union is unfair, it should probably be construed to have that effect. This is because the Supreme Court held in 1961 in *Educational Co.* v. *Fitzpatrick* that the constitutional right to associate (Article 40.6.1° iii) necessarily implies a right to disassociate. And long before the 1977 Act that court indicated that a dismissal inspired by the exercise of either right would sound in damages.[37]

The right of dissociation proclaimed in 1961 meant that picketing to compel union membership was henceforward unlawful and this gave rise to lengthy discussions between government and unions in regard to changing the law.[38] Nothing has come of these, and attention has now switched to other issues. Unions have been greatly agitated by the inadequacies of the Trade Disputes Act 1906, the main protection against tort liability in regard to strike action. The Act's narrow definitions mean that many workers – e.g. nurses and public servants – are not covered, so that picketing by them may be restrained by injunction.[39] Failure to amend the law led the union representatives to quit the Commission on Industrial Relations. Notwithstanding this depletion of its ranks, the Commission completed its inquiry and published a report. Whether its wide-ranging recommendations will be implemented remains to be seen.[40]

Family law
The period since 1957 has seen many changes in family law, with the

pace noticeably quickening in recent years. This undoubtedly reflects changes in attitudes and in society. The first break with tradition was the Married Women's Status Act 1957. Antedating similar change in the UK, this enabled spouses to sue each other in tort. The main practical effect is to permit a wife injured by her husband's negligent driving to sue him for damages. The Act also laid down that a husband and wife were to be treated as two separate persons for all purposes of acquisition of property. It also provided a *procedure* for determining matrimonial property disputes, but the *principles* applicable are to be found in judicial decisions. Though this branch of law is still developing,[41] some would wish to see it replaced by a statute under which all matrimonial property would be held in equal shares by the spouses.

The Succession Act 1965 and the Family Home Protection Act 1976 have given increased legal protection to wives and children. Under the former, if a testator leaves a spouse and no children, the spouse has a legal right to a half of the estate; if there are children the spouse has a legal right to a third of the estate and the courts can decree proper provision for the children out of the estate if the testator has failed in this regard. The 1976 Act – which has given rise to conveyancing problems – is designed to ensure that no spouse can dispose of the family home without the written consent of the other spouse.

Other changes in the law reflect the somewhat tardy acknowledgement of marital breakdown as a social problem. The Social Welfare Act 1970 introduced a 'deserted wife's allowance', thus accepting a state responsibility to provide assistance to the deserted wife and family. The Family Law (Maintenance of Spouses and Children) Act 1976 modernised the law on maintenance and introduced enforcement of maintenance orders via attachment of earnings. The same Act empowered the courts to make an order barring a spouse from the family home; the relevant procedures have been improved and the powers of the courts extended by the 1981 amending Act. Thus the legal protection of 'battered wives' is now considerably improved.

The increasing incidence of marital breakdown is indicated by the fact that, in the High Court alone, family law cases now occupy the full time of two judges each week. Many such cases are custody applications made under the Guardianship of Infants Act 1964. In some cases the parties may already have obtained an annulment from the matrimonial tribunals of the Roman Catholic Church, but since the canon law of annulment has developed beyond that of the state they may not be able to rid themselves of their civil law married status – with consequent problems, should they remarry, in the spheres of succession and legitimacy. (In fact, while remarriage in such circumstances constitutes bigamy, in practice, the DPP – the only person who can do so – does not prosecute.) The civil law on nullity was examined by the Attorney General in 1976, and a discussion paper and draft bill were published.[42] In 1977 the government formally referred the subject to the Law Reform Commission, which has not yet reported. Recently, however, there has been an increase in nullity petitions in the High Court, and this has given an opportunity for some judicial development of the law.

While the ban on divorce remains in the Constitution some movement has occurred in relation to the recognition of divorces granted abroad. This issue produced a conflict of judicial opinion in the famous *Mayo-Perrott* case of 1958, Maguire CJ taking the view – since repudiated – that a marriage dissolved abroad remained a subsisting valid marriage here. It is now clear that a divorce granted by a court of the state in which the parties were domiciled *will* be recognised in Ireland.[43]

The law on adoption has been a matter of great concern in recent years, and the original Adoption Act of 1952 has been amended several times.[44] Doubts about the constitutionality of orders made by An Bord Uchtála were set at rest by an amendment to Article 37, but problems remain. The law still provides only for the adoption of illegitimate children and orphans, on the theory, voiced by successive Ministers for Justice, that a statute allowing the adoption of legitimate children would be unconstitutional. (In 1978 the Minister resisted pressure for a constitutional amendment paving the way for such a statute, indicating that such adoptions would be opposed on social grounds.) If this theory is correct, a shadow hangs over section 2 of the Adoption Act 1964, which permits the adoption of *legitimated* children.[45] Doubts have also been expressed as to the validity of section 6 of the 1976 Adoption Act which provides that where an adoption order has been declared invalid by the court and the child concerned is in the custody of the 'adoptive parents', the question of the child's future custody shall be decided on the principle that its welfare is the first and paramount consideration. Thus it would, under that Act, be *lawful* for the court to leave the child where it is; but in light of the natural parents' rights under Articles 41 and 42, it is not clear that this would be *constitutional.*

Unequal Achievement

In a number of areas including intestate succession,[46] the law treats illegitimate children less favourably than legitimate ones. This has provoked discussion as to the desirability of expunging the distinction between legitimate and illegitimate from our law. The matter is currently under review by the Law Reform Commission, which is expected to report shortly.

Notes to Article

1 In 1957 the Circuit Court consisted of ten judges; since the Courts Act 1977 the number is twelve. The Act increased the size of the District Court to forty justices, five more than the maximum fixed by the 1961 Act.

2 In the Fifth Interim Report of the Committee on Court Practice and Procedure, Pr.8936.

3 This change was effected by the Local Government (Planning and Development) Act 1976. See Joseph K. Zimmerman 'An Bord Pleanála', *Administration* 28, 3 (1980), 329-344.

4 See generally Claire Carney 'Growth of Legal Aid in the Republic of Ireland' (1979) XIV Irish Jurist (n.s.) 61-82, 211-228.

5 At the time of writing there have been nine such references. They, and other cases, are surveyed in the forthcoming *European Law Review* article by Finbarr Murphy 'Community Law in Irish Courts 1973-1981'.

6 For a valuable survey of the court's operation in its first two years see Mary Robinson, *The Special Criminal Court* (1974) D.U. Press Ltd.

7 See my article 'The Development of Electoral Law in the Republic of Ireland' (1977) 28 *Northern Ireland Legal Quarterly* 357-381, at 366-367.

8 Fifth Amendment of the Constitution Act 1972.

9 Seventh Amendment of the Constitution Act 1979.

10 The second sentence of the new Article 29.4.3° is in the present tense ('No provision of this Constitution invalidates . . . or prevents . . .'). The original text, following the normal statute-drafting style, uses the future tense in such cases.

11 See Basil Chubb *The Constitution and Constitutional Change in Ireland* Institute of Public Adminstration, ch. 4.

12 See David Gwynn Morgan (1978) *The Emergency Powers Bill Reference - I* XIII *Irish Jurist* (n.s.) pp. 67-82.

13 Law Enforcement Commission Report Prl. 3832.

14 See generally R.F.V. Heuston 'Personal Rights under the Irish Constitution', (1976) XI *Irish Jurist* (n.s.) 205-222.

15 *Garvey* v. *Ireland* (1979) 113 I.L.T.R. 61

16 *State (M)* v. *Att. Gen.* (1979) I.R. 73.

17 *Macauley* v. *Minister for Post & Telegraphs* (1966) I.R. 345: *O'Brien* v. *Manufacturing Engineering Co. Ltd.* (1973) I.R. 334.

18 *Murtagh Properties Ltd.* v. *Cleary* (1972) I.R. 330: *Murphy* v. *Stewart* (1973) I.R. 97.

19 *State (Healy)* v. *Donoghue* (1976) I.R. 325.

20 *King* v. *DPP and Att. Gen.* (Sup.Ct.31 July 1980)

21 See Raymond Byrne, Gerard Hogan and Paul McDermot (1981) *Prisoners Rights* Co-op Books ch. 3.

22 *People (Att. Gen.)* v. *O'Callaghan* (1966) I.R. 501.

23 *People (DPP)* v. *Madden* (1977) I.R.

336: *People (DPP)* v. *O'Loughlin* (1979) I.R. 85: *People (DPP)* v. *Walsh* (1980) I.R. 294.

24 See particularly the judgement of Griffin J. (Henchy and Parke JJ. concurring) in *Shaw* v. *DPP* (Sup. Ct. 19 Feb. 1981). Also *Moynihan* v. *Greensmyth* (1977) I.R. 55 and *State (McDonagh)* v. *Frawley* (1978) I.R. 131.

25 See J. P. Casey 'The Judicial Power under Irish Constitutional Law' (1975) 24 *International Comparative Law Quarterly*, pp. 305-324.

26 E.g. *Conroy* v. *Att. Gen.* (1965) I.R. 411: *In re Haughey* (1971) I.R. 217: *Cullen* v. *Att. Gen* (1979) I.R. 394.

27 See section 4 of the Adoption Act 1974.

28 *Blake & Madigan* v. *Att. Gen.* (1981) I.L.R.M. 34: *In re Article 26 and the Housing (Private Rented Dwellings) Bill 1981* (Sup. Ct. 19 Feb. 1982.)

29 J. M. Kelly, *The Irish Constitution* (Dublin: Jurist Publishing Co. 1980) p. 519.

30 *State (Nicolaou)* v. *An Bord Uchtála* (1966) I.R. 567: *de Burca & Anderson* v. *Att. Gen.* (1976) I.R. 38.

31 *Murphy* v. *Dublin Corporation* (1972) I.R. 215: *Geraghty* v. *Minister for Local Govt.* (1975) I.R. 300.

32 *East Donegal Co-op. Ltd.* v. *Att. Gen.* (1970) I.R. 317: *Loftus* v. *Att. Gen.* (1979) I.R. 221.

33 *State (O'Callaghan)* v. *O'hUadaigh* (1977) I.R. 42: *State (M)* v. *Att. Gen.* (1979) I.R. 73. But there are limits on the review of prosecutorial discretion: *Savage & McOwen* v. *DPP* (Finlay P., 31 July 1980).

34 *Nolan* v. *Irish Land Commission* (1981) I.R. 23.

35 *Ingle* v. *O'Brien* (1975) 109 I.L.T.R. 7: *Moran* v. *Att. Gen.* (1976) I.R. 400: *State (Shannon Atlantic Fisheries)* v. *McPolin* (1978) I.R. 93: *O'Brien* v. *Bord na Mona* (Keane J. 18 March 1981): *Williams* v. *Army Pensions Board* (1981) I.L.R.M. 379: *Doupe* v. *Limerick Co. Council* (1981) I.L.R.M. 456.

36 Minimum Notice and Terms of Employment Act 1973: Redundancy Payments Act 1967 and 1971; Protection of Employment Act 1977.

37 *Meskell* v. *CIE* (1973) I.R. 121.

38 See the Report of the Committee on the Constitution (Pr. 9817) pp.41-43.

39 See J. P. Casey (1969) 'The Injunction in Labour Disputes in Eire' 18 *Int. & Comp. L.Q.* 347-359.

40 For criticism of the Report, see Charles McCarthy and F. von Prondzynski 'The Reform of Industrial Relations' *Administration 29,* 3 (1982) 220-259.

41 See Alan Shatter, *Family Law in the Republic of Ireland* (1981) 2nd ed., Wolfhound Press, ch. 15 and Appendix E.

42 *The Law of Nullity in Ireland,* Office of the Attorney General, August 1976.

43 Adoption Acts 1964, 1974 and 1976. See Shatter, *op. cit.,* ch. 12.

44 See 'Children's Rights under the Constitution' (1977), Irish Council for Civil Liberties Report No. 2 p. 5.

45 *Ibid.,* p. 7.

46 *O'B.* v. *S.* (High Court, D'Arcy J. 5 March 1982).

THE ECONOMIC AND SOCIAL RESEARCH INSTITUTE

RECENT PUBLICATIONS

Book Series:

No. 29   *The Economic and Social State of the* J. F. Meenan
Nation A Series of Public Lectures to M. P. Fogarty
mark the twenty-first anniversary of Bishop J. Kavanagh
ESRI (May, 1982) (£4.00) W. J. L. Ryan

No. 30   *The Irish Economy: Policy and* P. Bacon
Performance 1972–1981 J. Durkan
(July, 1982) (£7.50) J. O'Leary

General Research Series:

No. 106 *Financing of Third Level Education* A. C. Barlow
(£5.50)

No. 107 *An Input-Output Analysis of New* E. W. Henry
Industry in Ireland in 1976 (£3.50)

No. 108 *Social Insurance and Absence from* J. G. Hughes
Work in Ireland (£4.50)

No. 109 *The Distribution of Income in the* D. B. Rottman
Republic of Ireland: A Study in Social D. F. Hannan
Class and Family-Cycle Inequalities
(£5.50)

Quarterly Economic Commentary, J. Durkan
August 1982 (£5.00) P. Bacon
  S. Scott

FORTHCOMING PUBLICATIONS

General Research Series:

No. 110 *The Economic and Social* B. J. Whelan
Circumstances of the Elderly in Ireland R. N. Vaughan

Quarterly Economic Commentary, J. Durkan
November 1982 P. Bacon
  S. Scott

A full list of ESRI publications is available.
(Special rate for students: half price).
Publications may be obtained from the Institute, 4 Burlington Road,
Dublin 4, Telephone 760115.

Politics and the Arts in Ireland
– the Dáil Debates

BRUCE ARNOLD

On 20 July 1949, John A. Costello, who was then Taoiseach of the first Coalition Government, spoke in the Dáil on the estimates for his own Department. It was a long speech and only in the last three paragraphs did he refer to the question of art. He announced to the Dáil that the government had 'engaged the services' of Dr Thomas Bodkin 'to advise us on certain aspects of our art, the application of art to industry and the development of the crafts generally, in connection with art development in Ireland'.[1] He gave the terms of reference under which Dr Bodkin was to work, and concluded his speech with references to the spiritual and material benefits that would follow, clearly indicating that the work was to consider both the cultural and the industrial application of skills in the arts.

Thomas Bodkin worked rapidly on his report, which was submitted to the Government in September 1949, and subsequently published. It has become, deservedly, a key document about the arts in Ireland, and may be said to have shaped arts legislation produced in its wake, namely the Arts Act, 1951, which was introduced for its second stage reading in the Dáil on April 24, 1951. Committee stage was taken in May and the Bill became law without controversy.

In 1966 the Act was amended by means of an Additional Function Order which allowed the Arts Council (set up by the 1951 Act) to establish and administer a fund from which annuities could be paid to creative workers, either ill or old, who had given outstanding service to the country. The fund was called Ciste Cholmcille.

In 1973 a new Arts Bill was brought in by Liam Cosgrave, Taoiseach of a new Coalition administration, the main purpose of which was to reconstitute the Arts Council established by the 1951 Act. It was debated at considerable length but was politically

281

controversial only in one area – the Taoiseach's right to appoint all sixteen members of the Council. This led to a division, which was carried by the government, fifty-nine votes to fifty.

Effectively, as regards the input of politicians into the arts, the two pieces of legislation of 1951 and 1973 are crucial, as are the debates, in what they reveal of political attitudes to the arts. They are not the whole story by any means. They do not embrace the effectiveness or otherwise of the administration of the arts, which is an enormously difficult area involving a wide range of different judgments. But they are crucial in the sense that a philosophic starting point is necessary, from the point of view of the politician, whenever there is a question of state funding and state management. Since this involvement is widespread throughout the arts at a variety of different levels involving quite substantial sums of money, it is not unreasonable to expect clear thinking and precise legislative direction from those responsible.

These elected representatives, some of them living, some dead, have shaped the administration of the arts, or failed to shape that administration, for more than a quarter of a century and must be answerable. This, therefore, is the point of departure.

In the short paragraphs with which John A. Costello announced the appointment of Thomas Bodkin, he managed three times to link together the fostering of art with the application of art to industry. This gave 'both a spiritual and a material aspect' to the inquiry which the Government were seeking from Bodkin. His terms were six-fold. He was asked to report on the following matters.

1. The constitution and working of institutions concerned with the arts in Ireland, in particular the National Museum and the National Gallery.
2. The facilities available in Ireland for education in the arts both from the historical and from the practical aspects, at elementary to professional levels, with particular reference to the teaching of art and art history in the schools, universities, the National College of Art and the provincial art schools.
3. The existing relations between the arts and industry in Ireland, including such activities as technical training in craftsmanship, the provision of industrial designs and of appropriate advertisements for tourist development, and the steps that might be taken to arouse the public interest and the interest of manufacturing industries in the

importance of design in industry.

4. The advisability of establishing an organisation or organisations for the purpose of encouraging and spreading a knowledge of the arts in Ireland and of Irish culture in foreign countries.

5. The advisability of establishing an organisation or organisations concerned with the preservation and acquisition by the state of sites and buildings of national importance and with the maintenance of aesthetic amenities in future building projects.

6. The advisability or otherwise of extending such services as those referred to above and of co-ordinating their administration.

A general comment is necessary about Thomas Bodkin. When he was being introduced to the Irish people by Costello, in July 1949 in the Dáil, Costello said:

We have engaged the services of an Irishman who has won fame and distinction for himself and brought credit to his country, by his work in England as Professor of Fine Art in the Barber Institute in Birmingham . . . and I would ask any people who have any contribution to make towards a solution of his problems and the advancement of his labours to co-operate with him and assist him in every way they can.[2]

The reality behind this tribute was that Bodkin's eminence had been achieved in England because of the extent to which his abilities and ambitions within Ireland had been frustrated, leading to his resignation as Director of the National Gallery of Ireland in 1935, in a storm of his own making. He was highly critical of the gallery's administration; this is outlined in his letter of resignation, which he insisted on having published in the annual report for that year. Secondly, his experience dated well back before the founding of the state. He had been a member of the gallery's board from 1917, until his appointment as director ten years later, and before that he had been a close associate of Hugh Lane, working at the centre of the arts in Dublin during what had been a heady period of activity and controversy. Thirdly, his experience from the time of his resignation until his secondment by the Barber Institute had been almost wholly in England.

It is difficult to define the state of his mind when he was called back. He had got on well with the W.T. Cosgrave administration until he was faced with obstructions, mainly because of financial difficulties, and he had then become outspoken. Like most Irishmen who go abroad and make reputations for themselves, he was in a position of some eminence. But the standards he respected were English standards, and the ones he was critical of were those which, to an extent, had driven him out. Furthermore, his sense of culture was aesthetic and academic. The arts, whether in the spiritual or in the material sense, were to be 'rescued' from administrative frustrations, and to this may be related the emergence from his report of a single 'solution' – the Arts Council. It was not his first choice. While he did not come down in favour of a Ministry of the Arts, Bodkin did favour a sub-department of the civil service for the arts. Then, anticipating difficulties and rightly so given the times, he thought that 'a less ambitious approach' would be to create a small autonomous body. This 'small autonomous body' became the Arts Council of the 1951 Act.

The distinction is important and suggests that Bodkin recognised that the problem he had been asked to advise on should be tackled from within the administrative machine. And if one looks back at the terms of reference it is obvious that the requirements of only one paragraph are satisfied.

Better one than none, one might say. And, given the dusty outcome recorded on so many official reports and the substantial contribution made by the Arts Council at different times, this is a justified response. But it is not necessarily the right response. If one considers all that was set aside in picking out the single solution of an Arts Council, and the subsequent fate of the National Museum, National Library, National College of Art, even the National Gallery for a further fifteen years, and many other institutions, it can be equally strongly argued that a wrong decision was made. It can also be argued that a fundamental point about culture was missed by Bodkin, and by the politicians who, then and later expressed interest in the arts, and commitment to their furtherance. To paraphrase Rilke, all things serious are difficult; and everything is serious. Bodkin may be excused for the attitude he adopted. After all, the word culture appears only once in the recommendations put to him, and is used in an imprecise way. His concern was with the arts, the institutions which preserve, promote and teach them. But the same kind of excuse does not apply to the politicians. They were responsible to the nation for the broad culture of the nation, which is really the expression of the life of the nation. They should have recognised the hopeless inadequacy of the 1951 Arts

284

Bill as presented to them, and even its potentially damaging effects on the very areas they wished to put right.

Hardly surprisingly, they did nothing of the sort. Even Eamon de Valera, who contributed to the debate, discerned no problem in what was being done nor the problems which might derive from it. In the debate a general political stance was established: art is good and the more we can have of it and the more money we can spare for it, the better. Viewed thus, art must be detached from culture. It becomes a separate thing, an extrusion, synthetically promoted and therefore falsely expressive of the culture on which it depends. That culture, which Bodkin only in part recognised, depends on myriad means of self-expression and feeds on multitudes of different sources only the most obvious of which – the galleries, museums, libraries, schools, colleges – can be covered, either in the kind of report which Bodkin submitted or in the kind of legislation which the politicians might contemplate. Of course we had remarkably little such legislation. The setting up of the Arts Council was seen as a kind of absolution for the politicians. With the exception of the Act dealing with the National College of Art, to which reference will be made later, the only other important Act was the 1973 Arts Act, which once again confined itself to the Arts Council. All the anticipated good, sought for by John A. Costello from Thomas Bodkin in 1949, referred to again in 1951 when he brought in his Bill, and gone over in detail twelve years later, was to be derived from the Arts Council.

To be fair to Costello, the expectations were extremely modest. In his second stage speech on 24 April 1951, he said: 'The Bill which I now submit to the Dáil is a modest, not to say a meagre, contribution to the practical giving effect of the intention and desires of the Government.'[3] It was 'only a beginning', but, he thought, a good beginning. He went on to say that 'since the State was established, successive Governments have been so fully preoccupied with other matters that they have had little opportunity of adopting any kind of policy in regard to the arts. Indeed, it is difficult to avoid coming to the conclusion that there was something in the nature of a deliberate policy to obstruct anybody who evinced any desire or inclination to do anything for the furtherance of art in Ireland or for the furtherance of the application of art to industry in Ireland.'

The rest of the speech is a polite example of political breast-beating about our artistic treasures and traditions and how they need to be matched by the politicians and the administration which they direct.

The old argument about the ending of private patronage is trundled out with no attempt to explain what has replaced it and why there is less need for its replacement anyway. This in turn is linked with a gracious genuflection towards Sir Alfred Chester Beatty for his gift to Ireland; but this, in turn, is followed by the almost slavish:

I feel that if we show in the future more interest in art, more interest in the visual arts and in the applied arts generally, it may be that people like him will feel that we are deserving of encouragement and support, and that we may get more voluntary gifts of that kind further to enrich our artistic heritage here in Ireland.[4]

Broadly, the Taoiseach said it was the duty of the state, as far as art and the art institutions were concerned, 'to step in and give the necessary encouragement and financial support.'[5] Yet at the same time, the Bill he was proposing signally failed to do just that. It dealt with one tiny aspect and in such a way as to lead to the possibility of subsequent abuse. This is best illustrated by taking Thomas Bodkin's intentions for the Arts Council, which were related to his own experiences, and seeing how they were changed in the conception of the Bill.

Bodkin's scheme, according to Costello, who was fair enough to put it on the record of the Dáil, and according to the 1949 Report, was that the proposed arts commission or council 'should be empowered to plan a scheme for the application of the arts in all the various directions covered by his report'. In other words, and taken in conjunction with his original view that the whole operation arising out of his report should be a 'sub-ministry', and therefore working from within the civil service, he was suggesting real power directed at real and finite targets: the National Gallery, the National Museum, the National Library, art galleries generally, the National Art College, and art education generally, and including ancient monuments, the preservation of Georgian Dublin and an input into architecture, industrial design and design generally. This would have been power indeed.

It would have been a direct attack, backed by the Taoiseach and answerable directly to the Government, on the neglect of the arts since the foundation of the state. Bodkin recognised, based on his experiences in England, that the institutions he had been commissioned to study were still coasting along in 1949 on a leftover British administrative practice. In the organic living sense, they had not been taken over. And this, whether he realised it or not, was recognised by Costello in his speech although it was not recognised in his proposed legislation. The Bill watered down the objective just as the decision to put the Arts Council outside the civil service reduced its powers. Costello said that:

The scheme of this Bill departs slightly from his recommendation. The object is to set up a small body which will be as far as possible autonomous, which will be entitled to work on its own, free from the trammels of Civil Service procedure. It is envisaged in the Bill that it will be subject merely to the Government. It is not intended that it should be under the authority of any particular Minister, except to the extent that it reports through the Taoiseach to the Government . . . We wish now to have this body working in such a way that every Department of State which requires its advice will be able to go to it and get from it advice and assistance and direction.[6]

Was there ever such a silly approach to legislation? Was there ever so absurd a use of the word 'merely'? Was it any surprise that Thomas Bodkin fled back to England and stayed there? When the niceties are set aside, the real implications of his report were ignored and in their place was substituted a quite different idea. The substituted idea failed subsequently to live up to the vague expectations which are quoted above. No practice developed of the Departments of State going to the Arts Council for advice, assistance or direction. Being subject to the Government was, indeed, 'mere'. And the Arts Council's input where it was needed, and where it would have mattered, was structured in such a way as to block the fulfilment of the need.

Without real power, direct ministerial responsibility, direct involvement within the civil service, a proper vote with political decisions about the spending of money, the Arts Council from its inception was set adrift on a course that left it to the mercies of its members and, more importantly, its director. This fact is implicit in the woolly aspirations of Mr Costello in his opening speech.

This body, in addition to encouraging art and the application of art to industry, might deal also with matters such as ancient monuments, design in advertisements in furtherance of the tourist traffic, official publications, State buildings, coins, medals, postage stamps, State ceremonies, art exhibitions, and might play an effective part in

carrying on the fight for the recovery of the Lane pictures.[7]
And, indeed, anything else as well. Administratively, it is an approach
which borders on the absurd. All the matters listed, together with all
the more substantial matters covered by Bodkin, were unlikely then to
be responsive to such advice except in a marginal way. And the more
substantial the problem, the less likely its resolution, as was to be the
case for many years after 1951 with art education, the National
Museum, the National Gallery and the National College of Art. What
was proposed is not the way things are done; it is the way in which
action is channelled and reduced to a mere trickle. The extent to
which John A. Costello or those advising him were fully aware of this
is shrouded in mystery. But it is a central point in the whole argument
about politics and the arts and how the administrative chasm between
them is correctly bridged.

There were interesting speeches and points made in the debate
which followed. Some touched implicitly on the heart of the matter,
for example, Thomas Derrig's questioning of the Taoiseach about
overcrowding in the National Library, similar problems in the
National Museum, and the government's intentions, if any, about a
new complex to cater for both. He expressed hopes that a new and
larger building could be made available for the National College of
Art. But the debate avoided the real issue: that Bodkin's report had
been adroitly side-stepped in all but one of its proposals. Many of
these proposals have been side-stepped ever since and those which
have been tackled, like the National College of Art, are still
administratively in something of a swamp, and even the central subject
matter of the Arts Act both then and in 1973 is far from being what
was then intended. This sounds like several issues rather than one; but
in reality it is one: the failure of politicians to address themselves
properly to the arts.

When one comes to the Arts Act of 1973, by way of very little
legislation indeed on the arts (I shall be dealing with one piece of
legislation later), the situation is infinitely depressing. After 22 years,
the substance of the Bill presented to the Dáil by the Taoiseach, Liam
Cosgrave, on 17 October, provided for the reconstituting of the Arts
Council. It transferred to the Taoiseach the power to appoint all the
members of the Council; previously, there had been provision for co-
option. It made the chairman part-time, and it provided for a full-time
director (previously, the two jobs had been part-time). A new
provision, described by Cosgrave as 'important', allowed for the

collaboration of local authorities with the Arts Council in organising exhibitions or other events. Those were the only legislative changes. Administratively, all funds for the arts would be channelled through the Council.

As in the previous debate, the other politicians taking part did not stray away from the polite tone of encouragement and support. The first Fianna Fáil speaker was John Wilson, then spokesman for Education, who looked for a substantial increase in money for the arts. He generally approved of the aim and set the tone for the debate, just as Thomas Derrig had done twenty-two years before. It was followed by other speakers; three of them deserve comment.

The first, John Kelly, then Parliamentary Secretary to the Taoiseach with the constraints this implied, addressed himself to the wider problems of the two Arts Acts. The advisory role of the Arts Council to Ministers or Departments, envisaged in the 1951 Act, had not been fulfilled, he said. This role had become increasingly important because of planning and the destruction of old and fine buildings; it should be more widely used, if necessary under public or political pressure. He also saw a North-South dimension, if the Arts Council could bring itself to be more adventurous.

Padraig Faulkner's speech dealt with an anomaly: that the Fine Gael Party, when dealing with the National College of Art Act, which he had put through the Dáil and Senate a couple of years earlier, had strenuously objected to the provision giving to the Minister the right to appoint all members of the Board of the College, whereas now they were supporting exactly the same provision in respect of the Taoiseach appointing all members of the Arts Council. It was a good and important point, and it projected the correct view of Faulkner in retaining political control, and being responsible for that control. He did not pursue the issue then. He was already extensively on record on the point of principle. But he was one of the few speakers who touched on reality and took issue, in a limited fashion, on a point avoided in all these exchanges by everyone else.

Charles Haughey, who succeeded him, made the longest speech in the debate. He criticised the fact that the Bill contained no extension of activity (in fact, it did). He called for a comprehensive policy for the arts and he pleaded lack of Opposition resources for the fact that he could not offer his own proposals. He was in fact quite uncertain about specifics, even to the point where he wondered whether there should be three Arts Councils, rather than one. The Arts Council

289

should be under the Department of Finance rather than under the Taoiseach, he thought, but then suggested that, leaving it thus, responsibility for promotion and development should be given to a minister.

It was curiously evasive, given that it was a major speech in a debate on the arts, from an experienced politician with a strong commitment to helping artists. Haughey dismissed the six functions given to the 1951 Arts Council as inadequate but put nothing in their place.

. . . it does not require any great attention to see ways in which they could be expanded. I think they could be made a lot more precise and a lot more clearly defined as well as being expanded in scope. In so far as there is nothing of that nature in this Bill I find it very disappointing.[8]

As a preamble to this judgment, Haughey had enumerated the six objectives covered by the 1951 Act as a charge to the then new Arts Council: to stimulate public interest; promote knowledge, appreciation and practice; to assist in improving standards; to organise exhibitions; to advise government; to co-operate and assist others in the arts. Of course it can be argued, and is so argued in Haughey's speech, that more things could be added to this list, and things in it changed; but without detail it is comparable to promising Northern Unionists that once they are 'round the table' all will be possible. Neither politics, nor administration, nor even the arts work quite like that.

On committee stage, Haughey said that he would have preferred the 1951 Act repealed and completely replaced, rather than amended by the 1973 Act. It was a curious approach since the grounds were so limited anyway and were not given in the relevant contribution (23 October 1973).

Both speeches, in the sense I describe, were negative but important for the implicit needs they express which have not been tackled in any speech on either piece of legislation. To be dissatisfied with what one has, to call for more money and better services and facilities, more comprehensive legislation, better advice flowing from experts to government, is criticism. Not to back up the criticism with proposed changes is failure on the part of the politicians, since they are the people responsible for changing the administration of the arts by legislation if they think it is defective. Beyond that, they are in the hands of the administrators; and with the exception of a few organisations, such as the Arts Council, this still means (as in 1951 and 1973) the civil service. Most of the problem areas outlined by Bodkin in his 1949 Report and covered by the six broad objectives of the Arts Council remain within the civil service structure, or in some way are affected by its reaction or lack of reaction. The will of the politician, therefore, and his determination to intrude, backed up by careful thought as to what is needed, leading in turn to detailed legislative proposals, is a necessary prerequisite to improvement. In none of the debates mentioned is there evidence of any serious application at all to this overall problem. Instead, a small, isolated, poorly-controlled, ill-defined task-force – the Arts Council – was set up with general blessing, modified twenty years later, and permitted to ramble on in the controversial minefield of fashion, taste, trend, subjective judgment, elitism, snobbery, under the peculiar arrangement of a membership wholly in the hands of the Taoiseach of the day.

On the lighter side, the debates threw up some pleasing images. The writer, John McCann, at that time a Fianna Fáil deputy, referred to the danger of creating more and more poseurs, 'blasé people smoking long cigarettes and passing remarks from strange angles.'[9] And Sean Moylan, in the same debate, had referred to himself as a 'rough-neck', all too ready to visualise 'a bareheaded young man with a beard and a young lady in slacks breathless in their appreciation of Picasso, particularly if the picture is hung upside down.'[10] We are content to laugh at this, remembering the very different circumstances. And when it came to his reply, John A. Costello, with James Dillon sitting beside him, referred particularly to poseurs and snobs, and long cigarette holders, to which Dillon replied: 'I hope the Taoiseach does not think that my cigarette holder is an indication of either of these personalities – snobbishness or poseur.'[11] It was, of course, a profound rather than a superficial point; the outward semblance is not the indication in art, no more than anything else, of falseness and the slacks and cigarette holders of 1951 are symbolised now by quite different and perhaps less obvious signs. But they are no less there. They were not germane to the 1951 situation in the same way as they were in 1973, when twenty two years of the first Act had revealed many faults of omission which permitted the Arts Council, among other things, to become a body engaged mainly in patronage of a narrow field of visual arts. There was controversy about the imbalance between the different arts and about the narrowness. To some extent

Cosgrave's government was responsive to this. And since 1973 there have been changes and shifts leading to an improved situation. But these were not something directly emerging from the legislation. New people, responding to old controversies, made new judgments; more money oiled the wheels of those judgments as they manifested themselves in decisions. And, using the loose language of politicians when they talk about the arts, it was more and it was better, and therefore it was good.

While it is not the overall answer, a check on all the legislation from 1951 until today reveals less than half a dozen measures which deal with the arts, including the National Film Studios Act, Censorship Acts, Coinage Amendment Act and the National Gallery of Ireland Act. And the more one looks, the more one has to accept that the idea of legislating for the arts is somehow ludicrous; it is legislating for an expression of the human spirit, an expression of part of the overall culture of the nation. It is like legislating for prayer or for leisure. These would evoke the same sort of response from politicians: that they are good, and that there should be more prayer and more leisure, even that they should be promoted. This is not what legislation is about, nor is it what the administration should be doing. Legislation is about the institutions which collectively form the culture out of which art arises.

The National Gallery of Ireland Act of 1963 was legitimate in providing for the building's extension which made better a vital source of inspiration for hundreds of thousands of people, not just painters but writers and dreamers and children and the like. The National College of Art and Design Act of 1971 was similarly concerned with an institution which, far more realistically than either of the Arts Acts, was concerned with many if not all of the objectives covered by Thomas Bodkin, but in a far more sensible, natural and evolutionary way. Its limitations, and the subsequent funding of the college, were administrative blocks to fulfilment; but in essence the motivation was politically rational, and however much one may argue about the rights and wrongs of it being only partially autonomous, it remained a manageable element in the institutional structure of art education, able to be deployed to meet human need on a sensible and logical basis. Because of this, and because of the environment in which it came into being, it was politically controversial. But this was good rather than bad and its development over the last decade, subject to many reservations, has been a natural evolution. And in the collective sense, year on year, it has probably been immeasurably more important to the development of the arts than either of the Arts Acts. If the NCAD Act could have been duplicated for the National Library and the National Museum, for monuments, for protection of buildings, for the expansion of art departments in schools and colleges, and for the many other objectives identified by Thomas Bodkin, with the politicians retaining, within the administration, the necessary control and surveillance, a totally different picture might have emerged.

Even then, the central reality of the National College of Art and Design Act of 1971 is that the force which led to the real progress of the last two years, during which the College has moved to a site more in keeping with its role in the twentieth century, was achieved for reasons which had nothing at all to do with art. It was the self-interest of politicians, seeking to get hold of the Kildare Street premises in order to expand the accommodation for members of the Oireachtas and their secretaries, which led to the purchase of the old Powers' Distillery in Thomas Street and the injection of large sums of money to turn it into an art college. The process is not yet complete and out of it an arguably much better college is emerging, slowly and awkwardly; with luck, it might lead to better training of art students and the wider expression of art within our society. Moreover, even the legislation which Faulkner put through the Dáil in 1971, which theoretically gives power to a board appointed by the Minister for Education, in practice has led to quite different arrangements of power, involving the Higher Education Authority, something which did not exist when the College Act was passed. Politically, legally, administratively, the National College of Art, like so many other cultural and artistic institutions is a mess. Its control and management is not as laid down in the Act. It *seems* to be; but it is not. And I speak from experience.

In judging the relationship between politicians and the arts or politics and the arts, over the past quarter century, there is the inherent difficulty of making any kind of judgment about the actual quality and range of art or of being able to compare it with what existed all those years ago. Yet if my general principle about the politicians' view is accepted: that art is good, and the more we have of it and the more we can spend on it, the better; then only by making some kind of qualitative judgment can the value of the relationship be measured.

We are on firmer ground when it comes to objectives and their realisation. When Bodkin under general, all-party approval set out to provide the politicians, parliament and the administrative machine with a set of proposals he did so in the not unreasonable belief that they meant what they said. He reported accordingly. The legislation that followed addressed itself to only one requirement. It did so loosely, and the subsequent body came in time to fulfil a rather different role from the one envisaged, and there was little political or government control over this. Furthermore, many of the additional tasks which it was expected to fulfil did not materialise, not always because of the council itself, but often because these additional tasks depended not on legislative requirement, but on a vague and ill-defined willingness to consult or seek help or advice.

One of the most elementary lessons of the legislative and the administrative process is that the legislator does not leave open to doubt the purpose of laws and the means by which such purpose is put into effect. The work of politicians, in framing such legislation – and it is a major part of their parliamentary duty – is to that end, and times without number during the past ten years I have witnessed, often with considerable admiration, the basic political principle being put into practice. Yet, as I have shown, it did not really arise on either of the major pieces of legislation designed for the arts and if it had done so, the approach would have been governed by the flaccid consensus demonstrable in almost all possible quotations of the relevant debates, as well as being inevitable by virtue of the extreme narrowness of legislative controls in those Acts designed to guide the administrators. The general intent (in my view a wrong one) was to free the vaguely defined operation of the Arts Council from the trammels of civil service procedure. This would only have been a valid approach if the initial intent – that the council should be a small advisory body to the government – had been sustained. If that had happened, then the advice would have provoked a whole range of further, and much more explicit legislation, designed to use the civil service to implement the much larger objectives outlined by Thomas Bodkin, agreed by the government of the day and endorsed by innumerable politicians since then.

In reality the Arts Council has pursued its autonomous course over the past twenty-odd years, changing and adapting itself on its own initiative, being changed marginally by a second Arts Act and increasingly becoming divorced from the civil service with which it should have been working closely. During the same period, the objectives which required alternative legislation and money to back it have been largely neglected. This has adversely affected such vital institutions as the National Library and National Museum, the National Gallery of Ireland, provincial and municipal museums and art galleries, art education, the design input in industry, in tourism, in road signs, stamp design, urban and rural planning, architecture, heritage protection, and so on. And all of these are arguably more central and more important in terms of our self-definition as a culture.

National institutions are the nation's responsibility. For better or worse, they represent the heart of our culture, and much more so than defined objectives in the arts which are under the control of an autonomous body such as the Arts Council, whose judgments can be, and have been, arbitrary and whose membership can be changed, thereby opening up the possibility of change in policy, simply because the policy is so ill-defined by the legislation.

I began with a report. I shall end with one. In 1976 the Arts Council and the Gulbenkian Foundation jointly published a report by J.M. Richards, *Provision for the arts*. Neither he nor the director of the inquiry on which the report was based were Irish, nor had they connection with the arts in this country. This was deliberate in order to preserve detachment. There was a consultative committee of Irish men noted in the arts.

The report is not directly comparable with that of Thomas Bodkin seventeen years earlier but it was vaguely hoped that it would be useful to the government in considering future policy. But its recommendations lack the precision of target and means offered by Bodkin and are offered in a spirit of vague hopefulness about things that might be done. It calls for larger funds, firm leads, more development, greater autonomy, better liaison, adequate endowments, special funds, special efforts and all sorts of other high-sounding action across a wide range of different aspects of the arts in Ireland. Most specifically of all, the report recommended, at paragraph 23.2.

The Arts Council should be officially regarded as the body responsible to the Irish nation for the welfare of all the arts and the Government should make a statement confirming that this is its view of the Council's role.

That is the summary recommendation. In its more extended form in the body of the Report it reads,

295

The Arts Council should be regarded as the body responsible to the nation for the welfare of all the arts, and it should be in a position to take action accordingly. It would be useful if the Government were to make a statement confirming that this is its own view of the Arts Council's role. This would clarify the Council's working relationship with other bodies and help build up its confidence in taking the many new initiatives needed. It would also put the Council under an obligation to prepare, and submit to the Government, a comprehensive programme for the development of the arts in consultation with other national bodies.

The two views, on pages 93 and 101, are in conflict with each other. More seriously, the extended view of the relevant paragraph is such a mish-mash of nonsense as to be almost meaningless. For the Council to be so regarded – as 'the body responsible to the nation' – would require substantial legislation. A mere government statement would not achieve this or clarify the Council's working relationship with other bodies, affect its confidence or put it under any obligations whatever. It would achieve nothing at all beyond giving to a body which has indulged for two decades in the twentieth century's equivalent of Medici-like patronage a further push forward on the same kind of course. Thankfully, the worst expression of this – the purchasing of works of art, mainly paintings – has been stopped. But the general trends in the operation of the Arts Council, more outwardly austere, are still similar in kind.

Personally, I object even to that narrow working of the Arts Council. Professionally, it is my judgment that the real value of the Arts Council, which was the subject of Bodkin's proposal and of pious aspirations in the 1951 debate, was abandoned early on in favour of the easier path of becoming a distributor of the state's largesse. This situation was not changed by the 1973 legislation. It is not likely to be changed at any time in the future. The politicians have engaged during the past twenty-five years in a well-meaning, collective conspiracy about the arts which has left us no better off, in real terms, than we were then. And the principal reason for this is the view that the arts are 'different'. No one is quite prepared to say what they are different from, because no one quite knows. The reality is, in political and administrative terms, in terms of the institutions which shape and develop the arts, in terms of making available public funds to organisations and individuals, that the same principles apply as apply to the control and management of public houses, dance halls, swimming pools, public land: the making of laws and the distribution of the taxpayer's money should be under the direct and answerable responsibility of the Dáil and of the state's administrative machine, the civil service. If advice is needed, by all means set up councils for that. But for anyone who values in the overall sense the idea of the nation's culture, the more democratic control there is over that culture, the better. It may be rougher; it will certainly be more honest.

Notes to Article

1 Dáil Report, 20 July 1949; Column 1371.

2 Dáil Report, 20 July 1949; Column 1371.

3 Dáil Report, 24 April 1951; Column 1284.

4 Dáil Report, 24 April 1951; Column 1288.

5 Dáil Report, 24 April 1951; Column 1289.

6 Dáil Report, 24 April 1951; Column 1293.

7 Dáil Report, 24 April 1951; Column 1293.

8 Dáil Report, 17 October 1973; Column 61.

9 Dáil Report, 24 April 1951; Column 1334.

10 Dáil Report, 24 April 1951; Column 1316.

11 Dáil Report, 24 April 1951; Column 1346.

Index

HELEN LITTON

abortion 32-3, 270
ACOT 143
administrative law 273-4
adoption 272-3, 277
Adoption Acts 277
Aer Lingus 170, 194
Aer Rianta 166
Agency for Personal Service Overseas
(APSO) 235
Agricultural Credit Corporation (ACC) 167
agriculture 26, 48, 50-1, 64, 65-7, 76, 81, 84,
93; labour force 22, 47, 69-72; and the
environment 140, 252-5, 266; farmers
10, 27, 28
Agriculture, Department of 131, 135, 169,
230, 233
Aiken, Frank 226, 228, 234
aireacht system 101, 124, 154, 156
An Comhairle Oiliúna (AnCO) 122, 272
Anglo-Irish relations 63, 67, 79, 93, 204,
226, 230-1, 235-8, 271; Free Trade
Agreement 49, 229, 230
Anti-Discrimination (Pay) Act (1974) 49-50,
268, 274
archaeology 94, 145-6, 250, 255, 261
archives 3-4
army *see* defence forces
arterial drainage 243, 247-9, 253; A. D. Act
(1945) 243, 247
arts and the Dáil 281-97
Arts Acts: *1951* 281, 284-5, 288, 289, 290;
1973 281-2, 285, 288-92, 294
Arts Council 281, 284, 285, 287, 289-91,
294, 295-7
Attorney-General, the 269, 270, 271-2

B+I Shipping Line 166
Beatty, Sir Alfred Chester 286
Blaney, Neil T. 133, 135

Bodkin, Dr Thomas 281, 282, 283-7, 288,
291, 292, 293-4, 295, 296
Boland, Kevin 271
Bord na gCon 13
Bord na nGaeilge 13
Bord na Móna 166, 169, 170, 180, 250
Bord Pleanála, An 259, 268
Bord Uchtála, An 272, 273, 277
Britain *see* United Kingdom
Bruton, John 199
Buchanan Report (1968) 80, 135-6
Building Land, Price of (Kenny Report) 273

Capital Investment Advisory Committee 92,
101
capital punishment 268, 269
Carter, Sir Charles 101
Catholic Church 2, 23, 30-1, 147, 270, 276-
7; and social change 11-13, 31-2, 37-8,
104, 203-4
Cavan 252
Ceimici Teoranta 167, 169, 170
Censorship Acts 292
central administration *see* public service
Central Data Processing Services 129
Central Fisheries Board 260
child care *see* family law
Childers, Erskine 270-1
Chubb, Basil 25, 28, 30, 33
Chubb Report (IPA) 142
City & County Management Act (1955) 133,
259
civil service: archives 3-4; growth in 98-9;
labour force 101, 115, 117-8, 121;
and state-sponsored bodies 116-17, 122-
3, 125; *see also* public administration;
public sector
Civil Service Commissioners Act (1956) 115
Civil Service Regulation Act (1956) 115
Clann na Talmhan 37

298

Clare 3, 252
class structure 68-85
Coalition governments 138, 142, 190, 270, 281
Coinage Amendment Act 292
Comhairle na nOspidéal 149
Common Agricultural Policy (CAP) 10, 233, 237
Conference on Security and Co-operation in Europe (CSCE) 234
Constitution, the 116, 269, 270-3, 275, 277
constitutional law 2, 270-3
Construction Industry Federation (CIF) 76
contraception 12, 32, 77-8, 271-2
Coras Iompair Eireann (CIE) 167, 168, 169, 170, 173, 177, 180, 187, 194
Coras Trachtála (CTT) 93
Cork 134, 149, 155, 162, 251, 258
corporatism 38, 106
Cosgrave, Liam 226, 281, 288-9, 292
Cosgrave, W.T. 283-4
Costello, John A. 92, 281, 282, 285-7, 291
Costello Report (Whiddy Island) 100
councils see local government
County and City Managers Association 143
County Councils, General Council of
County Management Acts 153
courts see legal system
Courts Acts 267, 269
crime 27, 258, 268, 269
Criminal Injuries Compensation Scheme 268
Criminal Justice Acts 269
Criminal Law (Jurisdiction) Act (1976) 269
cultural identity 13, 22-3, 284-5
Cumann na nGael 36

Dáil Eireann 25-6, 28, 30; and the arts 281-97; and the law 267-9, 273-4; role of 25, 98, 101-2, 109, 122-3, 125-6, 129, 148; TDs 27-30, role of 24-7, 33, Independents 28, 34, 36; and the Senate 29 (table)
decentralisation 100, 106
decolonisation (UN) 227, 234
defence forces 121, 122
de Gaulle, General C. 229, 231
Denmark 106-7, 233
Derrig, Thomas 288, 289
de Valera, Eamon 133, 230-1, 285
development co-operation (UN) 234-5
Devlin, Liam St. J. 101
Devlin Report see Public Services Organisation Review Group
Dillon, James 291
divorce 32, 270, 277

doctors 151, 156, 160, 161
Donegan, Patrick 271
Dublin 35-6, 80, 177, 247, 264; growth of 136-7, 204, 256-8; local government in 134, 138, 149, 155, 162; planning for 80, 94, 135, 141-3, 144, 251, 286; Wood Quay 94, 145-6
Dublin Housing Action Committee 204
Dun Laoghaire Borough Council 142, 151

Eastern Health Board 149, 150-1, 155
Economic Development (Whitaker) 1, 2, 4, 23, 51-2, 65, 68, 91-2, 128, 135
Economic Expansion: First Programme 43-4, 52, 65, 68, 91, 99, 128, 133, 135; Second Programme 53, 66, 72-3, 99, 101, 129, 135, 136, 171; Third Programme 53, 66, 95, 97, 99, 100, 129, 135
Economic Planning and Development, Department of 100, 127, 131, 136
Economic and Social Research Institute (ESRI) 3, 33, 68, 97, 138, 140, 187, 212, 221
economy, the: budgeting 56, 92, 99, 127, 172, 185, 196; economic development 5-6, 11, 22, 43-8, 56-7, 82, 91-3, 100-1, 127, 171, 195-9; economic planning 51-4, 64-8, 90, 91-3, 99-100, 127 see also Economic Development, Economic Expansion; GNP 43-5, 46, 47-8, 65, 82, 184-8, 189 (table), 190, 192, 193; GDPCF 185, 186; see also Public Capital Programme, public expenditure
education system 3-4, 12, 23, 28-9, 72-5, 82, 95-122; expenditure on 187, 194, 209-11, 216; and local government 134, 143; teachers 104, 211; vocational education 134, 143
Education, Department of 6, 12, 95-6, 134, 293
electoral commission 24
electoral system 34-6 see also proportional representation
Electricity Supply Act (1927) 174
Electricity Supply Board 167, 168, 169, 174, 177, 180, 243, 250, 251, 258
emigration 1-2, 11, 43, 64, 71, 76, 78-9
employer organisations 76
employment see labour force
Employment Equality Act (1977) 50, 268, 274
energy development 90, 91, 251-2
Energy, Department of 131, 180
environment 243-64; land re-zoning 144; and private sector 252-8, 259-61; and public sector 243-52
Environment, Department of 24, 137, 268

Europe, Council of 228, 233
European Convention on Human Rights 268
European Economic Community: and Ireland 5, 26, 49, 76, 91, 102, 118, 226, 228, 229, 231-9; and Irish agriculture 10, 50-1, 233, 237; and Irish law 268, 275
European Free Trade Agreement (EFTA) 229
European Local Authorities, Irish Council of 143, 144
European Municipalities, Irish Council of 143
European Political Co-operation (EPC) 234, 238, 239
External Affairs, Department of (later Foreign Affairs) 226, 228, 229

Family Home Protection Act (1976) 276
family law 275-8
Family Law (Maintenance of Spouses & Children) Act (1976) 276
family planning see contraception
farmers 10, 27, 28
Faulkner, Padraig 289, 293
Federated Union of Employers (FUE) 76
feminism see women
fertility rate 77
Fianna Fáil party 24, 27-30, 32, 34, 35-6, 38, 138, 139; in government 190, 228, 236-7
Finance, Department of 1, 4, 100, 123, 126, 130, 138, 143, 146, 197, 230, 233, 290; and economic planning 65, 91, 92, 127, 128, 131, 228; and Department of Public Service 130, 131, 132; and state-sponsored bodies 171, 172
Fine Gael party 24, 27-8, 29-30, 33, 34, 36, 289; in government 138, 142, 190, 236-7, 270, 281
Fiscal Crisis of the State (O'Connor) 218
fisheries 249, 260
Fisheries and Forestry, Department of 131, 258, 260
Fitzgerald Council (Hospital Services) 148, 162
FitzGerald, Garret 168, 232-3, 237, 270
Foras Forbartha, An 3, 6, 135, 261, 262
Foras Talúntais, An 68
Foras Tionscal, An 66
foreign affairs 26, 225-39; see also Anglo-Irish relation; European Economic Community; United Nations
Foreign Affairs, Department of 4, 98, 233, 234, 236 see also Department of External Affairs

foreign borrowing 46-7, 54, 56, 106
foreign investment 51, 52-3, 56, 64, 66-7
Forest and Wildlife Service 245, 247, 262
Forestry Act (1945) 243
forests 243-7
France 7-8, 229, 231, 233, 263

Galway 155, 162, 247, 255
Garda Síochána 121, 122
Garvey, E.P. (Garda Commissioner) 274
Gas Board 169, 174, 180
General Agreement on Tariffs and Trade (GATT) 229
General Hospital Services, Council on (Fitzgerald Council) 148, 162
General Medical Services (Payments) Board 160, 161, 162
Gould, Frank 188-91, 205
government: and the church 12; and the economy 43-57, 65-8; and the environment 243-52, 258-61; and planning 80-2, 93-5; and political change 23-34; role of 15, 16, 21-2, 37-9, 82-4, 89-110; and social change 23, 64, 95-7; and social policy 103-7, 203-21 see also Dáil Éireann, local government, public service, Seanad Éireann
government departments see under individual departments
grants: agriculture 140; education 211, 217, 221; health 147, 157, 211; housing 211, 216, 220; industry 51, 66-7, 80, 185, 253, 261, 263, 264; local government 139; state-sponsored bodies 165, 168-9, 170, 173, 175, 180, 194
Great Famine, the 14, 136
Griffith, Arthur 23
Gross National Product see economy
Guardianship of Infants Act (1964) 276

Haughey, C.J. 12, 237, 289-90
Hayes, Senator Michael 34
Health Acts: 1953 147; 1970 96, 130, 134, 148, 149, 150-2, 158-9
Health Authorities Act (1960) 134, 149
health boards 147, 150-4, 211
Health (Corporate Bodies) Act (1961) 129, 149
Health Education Bureau 149, 163
Health, Department of 96, 124, 134, 148-50, 154, 155, 156, 159
health services 82, 95, 122, 130, 147-64, 209-11; labour force 151, 156, 160, 161; expenditure on 154-5, 157-60, 187, 194; and local government 134, 144, 149-54 see also health boards

Health Services (Financial Provisions) Act (1947) 147
Higher Education Authority 75, 293
Higher Education, Commission on 129
Hillery, Dr. Patrick 271
Hobbes, Thomas 105, 183, 192, 195, 197
hospital services 150, 162-3
Hospitals Sweepstakes 158
Household Budget Survey 1973 211
housing 82, 94, 96, 204, 212; expenditure on 210-11, 216-17, 220; and local government 136, 216-17
Housing Act (1966) 136, 144
Humanae Vitae 77

income distribution 44-5, 55, 71, 84, 96, 119, 176-7, 187, 190-1, 204
income tax 83
incomes policy 55-6, 95
independent TDs 28, 34, 36
Industrial Credit Corporation 66, 167
Industrial Development Authority 56, 66, 80-1, 93, 229, 261, 262, 263, 264
Industrial Relations, Commission on 275
Industrial Research and Standards, Institute of 261
industry 47-8, 51, 65-6, 80-1, 255; growth of 66-7; labour force 22, 69-72; and private sector 53, 252-8 *see also* foreign investment
Industry and Commerce, Department of 1, 129, 230; *later* Industry, Commerce and Energy 131; Industry and Energy 132
inflation 44, 47, 90, 137, 139
Investment in Education 5, 73, 79, 95, 129, 204
Irish language 13, 25
Irish National Petroleum Corporation (INPC) 166, 169, 170, 180, 194
Irish Republican Army (IRA) 225, 230
Irish Shipping 166
Irish Steel Holdings 166, 169, 170, 194
Irish Sugar Company 166, 169, 170

Juries Act (1976) 269, 271
Justice, Department of 277

Keane Report *(Stardust)* 100, 144, 145
Kelly, Prof. J.M. 273, 289
Kenny Report *(Building Land)* 273
Kerry 155, 247
Keynesianism 92, 183, 184, 203, 206
Kilkenny 96, 258

Labour, Department of 95, 122, 129, 132, 236-7, 270
labour force 38, 43, 45-9, 53, 63, 64, 67, 69, 105, 120, 175

Labour Force Survey (1979) 69
labour law 95, 274-5
Labour Party 24, 28, 29-30, 36, 37, 142; in government 138, 142, 190, 270, 281
Land Acts 10
Land Reclamation Act (1949) 259
land re-zoning 144, 257, 259
Lands, Department of 131
law: administrative law 273-4; constitutional law 2, 270-3; labour law 95, 274-5; family law 275-8 *see also* legal system
law cases: *Byrne v. Ireland* 273; *Cassidy v. Minister for Industry and Commerce* 274; *City View Press Ltd. v. AnCO* 272; *de Burca and Anderson v. Attorney General* 271; *Educational Co. v. Fitzpatrick* 275; *G. v. An Bord Uchtala* 273; *M. v. An Bord Uchtala* 272, 273; *Mayo-Perrott* 277; *McGee v. Attorney General* 271-2; *Murphy v. Attorney General* 272
Law Enforcement Commission 271
Law Reform Commission Act (1975) 269, 278
Leaving Certificate 13, 74
legal aid 268
legal system 267-69
legislature *see* Dáil Éireann; Seanad Éireann
Lemass, Seán 1, 9, 10, 37, 107, 133, 167-8, 229, 230-1, 234
Leydon, John 92
Lichfield, Nathaniel 135
Limerick 134, 135, 149, 251
living standards 43-5, 47, 63
Local Appointments Commission 141
Local Finance and Taxation (White Paper) 138, 140
local government 103, 115, 122, 125, 128, 133-46; county councils 134, 135, 137, 139, 140, 141, 142-3, 144, 259; and education 134, 216; and environment 259-61, 263-4; expenditure 137-40, 144; and health 134, 144, 147, 149-55, 157-60; and housing 136, 216-17; reorganisation of 141-2, 145-6; and state-sponsored bodies 170, 177; urban councils 135, 137, 138, 141, 142-3, 145-6
Local Government Acts 133-4, 136, 139, 140-1, 143-5, 260; Planning and Development Acts: *1963* 94, 135, 136, 144, 259; *1976* 144, 259, 268; *Bill 1982* 260
Local Government, Department of 133-4, 135, 138, 142, 143, 144
Longford 252
Lynch, Jack 231
Lynch, Prof. Patrick 4, 6, 92, 95, 108

301

McCann, John 291
Maguire, Justice 277
marriage rate 77, 79
Married Women's Status Act (1957) 276
Maudling, Reginald 228, 229
Mayo 249
Meath 151, 255
Medico-Social Research Board 149
mental handicap 148
minerals 255-6
Minerals Act (1945) 243
ministers *see* Dáil Eireann
Minister and Secretaries Act: *1924* 102, 115, 116, 118, 122; *1973* 131-2
Monaghan 252
More Local Government (Chubb) 142
Moylan, Sean 291
Municipal Authorities, Association of 143

National Board for Science and Technology (NBST) 3, 6
National College of Art and Design 282, 284, 286, 288, 289; Act (1971) 285, 292-3
National Drugs Advisory Board 149
National Economic and Social Council (NESC) 3, 8-9, 68, 97, 103; Reports 47, 144-5, 212, 219 (table), 220, 221; *see also* National Industrial and Economic Council
National Film Studios Act 292
National Gallery of Ireland 282, 283-6, 288, 292, 295; Act (1963) 292
National Health Council 149
National Heritage Bill (1982) 247, 261
National Income and Expenditure Tables 187
National Industrial and Economic Council (*later* National Economic and Social Council) 3, 68, 97, 101, 103
nationalism 33-4, 38
National Library of Ireland 284, 286, 288, 295
National Manpower Service 122
National Monuments Acts 261
National Museum 247, 282, 284, 286, 288, 295
National Understandings 55, 119, 131
National University of Ireland 270
National Wage Agreements 55, 84, 119
natural gas 251
neutrality 226-7, 229, 231, 234, 237
Nitrigin Eireann Teo 166, 169, 170, 173, 194, 251
North Atlantic Treaty Organisation (NATO) 226, 228
Northern Ireland 14, 26, 27, 33-4, 38, 90, 91, 103, 130, 157, 235-8, 239, 268-9, 271, 290; Belfast 251; and United Kingdom 231, 235-8, 271
nuclear disarmament 227, 234

O'Briain, Colm 5
O'Dálaigh, Cearbhaill 271, 272
Offences Against the State Acts 268-9
Office of Public Works 98, 247, 249, 261, 262
O'Hagan, John 187, 190-1, 193
oil crisis 46, 118-19, 127
Oireachtas, Houses of *see* Dáil Eireann; Seanad Eireann
O'Malley, Donogh 95, 134
Ombudsman Act (1980) 105-6, 274
O'Neill, Capt. Terence 230
One Million Poor (Kennedy) 212 (table)
O'Regan, Brendan 93
Organisation of Economic and Cultural Development (OECD) 5, 7, 22, 99, 204
Organisation for European Economic Co-operation (OEEC) 65, 228, 229

parliamentary questions 25-6 (table)
peacekeeping (UN) 227-8, 234
Planning-Programme-Budgeting-Systems (PPBS) 119, 130, 172, 196
planning law *see* environment
political attitudes 30-1, 34-7
political parties 2, 16, 24, *see also* Fianna Fáil; Fine Gael; Labour
political system 16, 21-39
politics, local 27, 33, 34, 38
pollution 251-3, 255, 256, 260, 263, 264
population structure 44, 48-9, 64, 76-80, 84-5, 136
Posts and Telegraphs, Department of 100, 117, 121, 131, 187, 195
poverty 9, 96, 211-12; Kilkenny Conference 96
Pringle, Justice 272
private sector: and economic planning 53, 82; and environment 259-61; expenditure 125, 187; and industry 53, 252-8; investment 185; and public sector 118-19
proportional representation 24, 270
Prosecution of Offences Act (1974) 269
protectionism 52, 65, 66, 92
Provision for the Arts (Richards) 295
psychiatric services 148, 149, 162; Commission on Mental Illness 148
public administration 38-9. 89, 90-103, 108-10, 115-16; *see also* civil service; public sector; state-sponsored bodies

Public Administration, Institute of (IPA) 68, 96, 107, 143, 212, 217, 235
public expenditure 53, 54, 56, 90, 92, 99, 127-8, 183-99; education 187, 194, 209-11, 216; health 154-5, 157-60, 187, 194; housing 210-11, 216-17, 220; local government 137-40, 144; state-sponsored bodies 170, 177, 194
publications, scholarly 2-3
Public Capital Programme 56-7, 91, 92, 99, 171, 188
Public Prosecutions, Director of 268, 271
public service, the: and the economy 43-8; labour force 49, 53, 67, 121, 127, 186-8, 221; and environment 243-52, 258, 262; foreign affairs 228-31, 232-4, 236-7, 238-9; reform of 122-8, 148-57; role of 15, 82-4, 89-110, 115-32, 194-5; Report on Higher Remuneration in Public Service 9, 13; see also civil service; public administration; public expenditure; state-sponsored bodies
Public Service, Department of 98, 101, 123, 126, 130, 131, 132
Public Service Advisory Council (PSAC) 7, 198-9
Public Services Organisation Review Group (Devlin Report) 100, 101-2, 116, 117-18, 123-4, 125, 126, 127, 130, 148-9, 154, 233
Radio Telefís Éireann (RTE) 8, 13, 187, 194, 197
rates 137-8, 144, 147, 157, 159
Reagan, Ronald 183
recession 124, 183, 190
Regional Development Organisations 136
regional planning 80-1, 85, 93-5, 106, 135
Revenue Commissioners 98, 100, 129
Richards, J.M. 295
Road Traffic Act (1961) 136
roads 95, 136
Rome, Treaties of 93, 225
Roscommon 151
Ross, Michael 187
Ryan, James 91
Ryan, Fr. Liam 11

Seanad Éireann 28-9, 102, 267-78, 281-97
see also Dáil Éireann
Shannon Free Airport Development Company (SFADCO) 93
Sinn Féin 38
Smith, Paddy 140
social development 4-5, 22-3, 32-3, 63-85, 95-7; and the Church 11-13, 31-2, 37-8, 104, 203-4; regional pattern 80-2; social responsibility 103-7

social policy 203-21
Social Welfare Acts 203, 276
Social Welfare, Catholic Council for 96
Social Welfare, Department of 100, 122, 164, 206, 209
social welfare services 15, 72, 82, 96-7, 99, 205-11, 217-21; expenditure 206-9
Stardust disaster 100, 144, 145
State Lands (Workhouses) Act (1962) 149
state sector see public sector
state-sponsored bodies 98, 101, 115, 116, 121, 165-80; labour force 105, 121; expenditure 170, 177, 194; Joint Committee on 102, 172-3, 180, 181, 196; role of 122-3, 125, 178-9, 194
Statistical and Social Enquiry Society of Ireland 92
Succession Act (1965) 276
Sunningdale Agreement 236, 237, 271
Supplementary Welfare Allowances 157
Sweden 92, 158, 227
Sweetman, Gerard 91

Taoiseach, Department of 98, 233, 236, 290
taxation system 51, 52, 67, 82, 83, 99, 106, 198, 220-1, 272
teachers 104, 211
Teachtaí Dála (TDs) see Dáil Éireann
technology 5-7, 120, 125
telecommunications 94, 95, 117; Dargan report 100
television 4-5, 11, 13, 23, 197, 204
Thatcher, Mrs. M. 183, 237
Thornley, Dr. David 2
Tipperary 255
town planning 93-5
Trade, Commerce and Tourism, Department of 132
Trade Disputes Act (1906) 275
trade unions 10, 75-6, 105, 119, 175, 275
Transport, Department of 131, 180
Transport and Power, Department of 100, 124, 128, 131
travelling people 145
turf development 243, 250-1; Act (1945) 243
Tussing, Prof. Dale 2-4, 104, 216, 221

unemployment 43, 49, 67, 90, 127-8, 185
Unfair Dismissals Act 275
United Kingdom 53, 56, 73, 77, 124, 141, 197, 269, 276, 283; economy of 44, 47, 193, 217, 218; and the EEC 228, 229, 233; and Ireland 49, 63, 67, 79, 93, 204, 226, 229, 230-1, 235-8, 271
United Nations 96, 204, 225, 226-8, 234
United States of America 8, 9, 130, 158, 198, 204, 217, 226, 236, 273

303

urbanisation 23, 80, 81, 136-7, 145, 256-8;
    Urban Development Areas Bill 137

Vatican II 2, 11, 23
Voluntary Health Insurance Board 147, 159
voluntary organisation 211

wages see income distribution
Wagner's Law 190
Waterford 134, 149, 251, 256, 258
Westmeath 252
Whiddy Island disaster 100
Whitaker, T.K. 1, 2, 4, 23, 51-2, 65, 68, 91-

2, 108, 128, 135, 228, 230
Whitegate refinery 166, 180
Whyte, John 203-4
Wicklow 255
Wildlife Act (1977) 247, 260
Williams, T. Desmond 3
Wilson, John 289
women, position of 10, 34, 48, 49-50
Wood Quay 94, 145-6
Workers' Party
Workers' Party 36
World Bank 44, 48
Wright, Myles 135

Advertisers Index

Aer Rianta 41
Aspect 242
Blood Transfusion 20
Bord Bainne 61
Bord Failte 42
Bord na Mona 19
Byrne & McCrea 240
CIE 62
Cork Co. Co. 241
Dept. of the Public Service 88
ESB inside front cover

ESRI 280
Iona Print 202
Irish Biscuits 223
Irish Gas Board 182
Irish Glass Bottle 201
Irish Sugar Co. 224
Meath Co. Co. 132
NCEA 113
Osborne King & Megran 266
RTE 114
Sun Alliance 112